A Freewheelin' Time

A Freewheelin' Time

A MEMOIR OF
GREENWICH VILLAGE
IN THE SIXTIES

.:.

SUZE ROTOLO

.:.

BROADWAY BOOKS   NEW YORK

Published by Broadway Books
Copyright © 2008 by Suze Rotolo

www.broadwaybooks.com
BROADWAY BOOKS and its logo, a letter B bisected on the diagonal,
are trademarks of Random House, Inc.

Grateful acknowledgment is made to the following for permission
to quote from copyrighted material:

"The Times They Are A-Changin'." Copyright © 1963; renewed 1991
Special Rider Music. All rights reserved. International copyright secured.
Reprinted by permission.

"What Was It You Wanted?" Copyright © 1989 Special Rider Music. All
rights reserved. International copyright secured. Reprinted by permission.

"Go Away You Bomb." Copyright © 2007 Special Rider Music. All rights
reserved. International copyright secured. Reprinted by permission.

Interior book design by Terry Karydes
Illustration credits appear on page 371

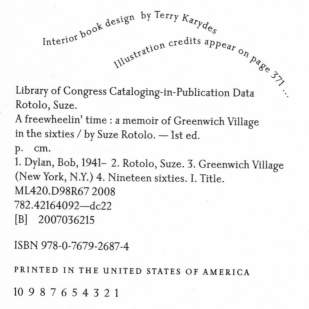

Library of Congress Cataloging-in-Publication Data
Rotolo, Suze.
A freewheelin' time : a memoir of Greenwich Village
in the sixties / by Suze Rotolo. — 1st ed.
    p.   cm.
1. Dylan, Bob, 1941– 2. Rotolo, Suze. 3. Greenwich Village
(New York, N.Y.) 4. Nineteen sixties. I. Title.
ML420.D98R67 2008
782.42164092—dc22
[B]   2007036215

ISBN 978-0-7679-2687-4

PRINTED IN THE UNITED STATES OF AMERICA

10 9 8 7 6 5 4 3 2 1

First Edition

Table of Contents

For Luca
so he will know
and Enzo
who always did

"Who are we,
if not a combination of
experiences, information,
books we have read,
things imagined?
Each life is
an encyclopedia, a library,
an inventory of objects,
a series of styles, and
everything
can be constantly
reshuffled and reordered
in every
conceivable
way."

ITALO CALVINO,

Six Memos for the Next Millennium

1 GERDE'S FOLK CITY

N.E. CORNER OF W.4TH & MERCER

2 GASLIGHT

118 MACDOUGAL BETWEEN W.3RD & BLEECKER, EAST SIDE OF STREET

3 KETTLE OF FISH

118 MACDOUGAL BETWEEN W.3RD & BLEECKER, EAST SIDE OF STREET

4 THE BITTER END

BLEECKER, BETWEEN LAGUARDIA & THOMPSON, NORTH SIDE OF STREET

5 WHITE HORSE

567 HUDSON AT 11TH STREET

6 LIMELIGHT

SEVENTH AVENUE SOUTH, BETWEEN BARROW & BLEECKER, EAST SIDE OF STREET

7 RIVIERA

SHERIDAN SQUARE, SEVENTH AVENUE SOUTH, AT W.4TH, N.W. CORNER

8 THE BAGEL

W.4TH, WEST OF SIXTH AVENUE, SOUTH SIDE OF STREET

9 THEATRE DE LYS

121 CHRISTOPHER AT BEDFORD

10 SHERIDAN SQUARE PLAYHOUSE

SEVENTH AVENUE SOUTH BETWEEN GROVE & BARROW, EAST SIDE OF STREET

a 185 EAST 3RD STREET

BAILEYS' APARTMENT, BETWEEN AVENUES A & B

b 190 WAVERLY PLACE

VAN RONK'S APARTMENT, BETWEEN W.10TH & CHARLES

c WAVERLY PLACE APARTMENT

BETWEEN MACDOUGAL & SIXTH AVENUE

d 129 PERRY STREET

BETWEEN GREENWICH & WASHINGTON

e ONE SHERIDAN SQUARE

AT APEX OF BARROW, W.4TH, & WASHINGTON PLACE

f 161 WEST 4TH STREET

BETWEEN CORNELIA & JONES

g 106 AVENUE B

CORNER OF 7TH STREET ON AVENUE B

h 309 EAST HOUSTON

BETWEEN CLINTON AND ATTORNEY, SOUTH SIDE OF STREET

i 344 WEST 12TH STREET

BETWEEN GREENWICH & WASHINGTON

j 196 WEST 10TH STREET

BETWEEN W.4TH & BLEECKER

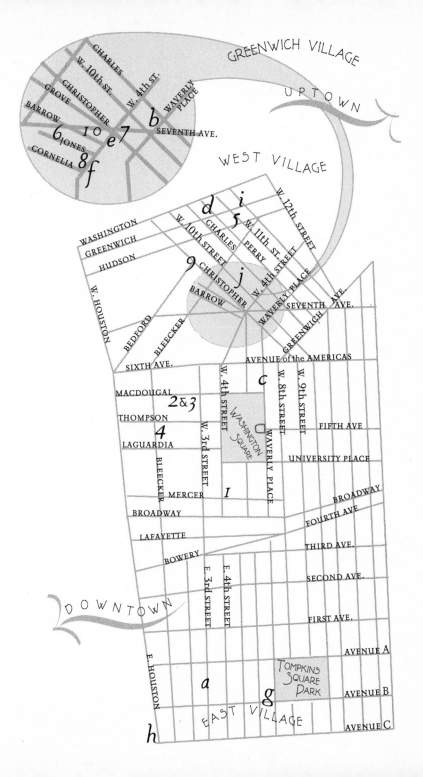

GREENWICH VILLAGE

UPTOWN

CHARLES
W. 10th St.
W. 4th St.
CHRISTOPHER
GROVE
BARROW
WAVERLY PLACE
6 10 e 7 b
JONES SEVENTH AVE.
CORNELIA 8 f

WEST VILLAGE

WASHINGTON
GREENWICH
HUDSON
W. HOUSTON
d i
CHARLES W. 11th ST. PERRY
W. 10th STREET
W. 12th street
5
9 CHRISTOPHER
j
BARROW W. 4th STREET
WAVERLY PLACE
BEDFORD
BLEECKER
SEVENTH AVE.
GREENWICH AVE.
SIXTH AVE.
AVENUE of the AMERICAS

MACDOUGAL
THOMPSON
2 & 3
4
LAGUARDIA
BLEECKER
MERCER
BROADWAY
LAFAYETTE
BOWERY
W. 4th STREET
W. 3rd STREET
WASHINGTON SQUARE
c
W. 8th STREET
W. 9th STREET
WAVERLY PLACE
FIFTH AVE
UNIVERSITY PLACE
1
BROADWAY
FOURTH AVE.
THIRD AVE.

E. 3rd STREET
E. 4th STREET

SECOND AVE.

DOWNTOWN

FIRST AVE.

E. HOUSTON
a
g
AVENUE A
TOMPKINS SQUARE PARK
AVENUE B
h
EAST VILLAGE
AVENUE C

I MET BOB DYLAN in 1961 when I was seventeen years old and he was twenty. This book is a memoir of my life as it intertwined with his during the formative years of the 1960s.

I've always had trouble talking or reminiscing about the 1960s because of my place close to Dylan, the mover and shaper of the culture of that era. The kind of adulation and scrutiny he received made that conversation awkward for me. He became an elephant in the room of my life. I am private by nature, and my instinct was to protect my privacy, and consequently his.

I was writing a bit before we met—poems, little stories, observations—and I kept at it while I was with him. The writings served the same purpose as the sketchbooks I kept—except that these were verbal drawings:

M e m o r y
> It isn't you baby, it's me and my ghost
> and your holy ghost.
> There is a saying about one's past catching up
> with them
> mine not only did that, it overran the present.
> So tomorrow when the future takes hold
> I'll be sitting in the background with the Surrealists.

Though I no longer remember what triggered those thoughts, recorded in January 1963, reading them in the present gives me an eerie feeling of prescience. In so many ways my past with Bob Dylan has always been a presence, a parallel life alongside my own, no matter where I am, who I'm with, or what I am doing.

Dylan's public, his fans and followers, create him in their own image. They expect him to be who they interpret him to be. The very mention of his name invokes his myth and unleashes an insurmountable amount of minutiae about the meaning of every word he ever uttered, wrote, or sang.

As Bob Dylan's fame grew so far out of bounds, I felt I had secrets to keep. Though I kept my silence, I didn't relish being the custodian of such things. Time passes and the weight of secrets dissipates. Articles are written and biographies are churned out that trigger memories only because they are often far from the reality I knew. They tend to be lackluster yet fascinating in their fantasy. I acknowledge that memory is a fickle beast. Fragments of stories stride in and out; some leave traces, while others do not.

Secrets remain. Their traces go deep, and with all due respect I keep them with my own. The only claim I make for writing a memoir of that time is that it may not be factual, but it is true.

In these times, seeing Bob Dylan's life and work and the people he was close to documented or fictionalized on film, on display in museum exhibits and other commemorations in all categories, only intensifies the feeling I have of possessing a parallel life. It is an odd sensation to see myself on the screen, under glass, and written about in books, forever enshrined and entombed alongside the Legend of Dylan.

When I look at the pictures and hear the songs I also see and hear the story behind them. A still photograph morphs into a home movie and a scrawl on a page evokes a scene in a room or on a street. I hear a laugh coming from somewhere off to the side . . .

It has taken me many years to allow my parallel lives to converge. But there will always be a space between the image and the reality because ghosts live there and they cannot be contained under glass. Over time I have learned to be more at ease with the holy fascination people have with Bob Dylan. A song, a poem, a book, a film, an exhibit are simply representations of a period, a place, a person. And because memory is the joker in the deck I try not to take the representations of the past too seriously. Life goes on for those who live it in the present. Nostalgia, cheap or otherwise, is always costly.

I see history as a reliquary—a container where relics are kept and displayed for contemplation. So much has been written about the sixties that the more distant those years become, the more mythic the tales and the time seem to be. Facts and statistics are pliable. Truth and accuracy are truly Rashomon-like. Each story is true from the teller's perspective; the weight shifts. My decision to add my relics was not an easy one. Hindsight meddles with memory, after all, so the best I can do in writing about those long-ago years is to try to make them recognizable.

The stories I tell are about my place within that time and about the early years that made me who I was when I migrated from Queens, New York, to Greenwich Village. The backstory has to be considered: where my family came from, who they were, and all the other bits and pieces that make a person whole. I reminisce to the best of my ability.

Since I was born in one of the boroughs of New York City, the concept of coming to the city to find (or lose) oneself doesn't apply. But it was to Greenwich Village that people like me went—people who knew in their souls that they didn't belong where they came from. I was drawn to the Village with its history of bohemia—where the writers I was reading and the artists I was looking at had lived or passed through. Their spirits led the way, showed me the road, and named the place. I got on the subway.

The 1960s were an amazing time, an eventful time of protest and rebellion. An entire generation had permission to drink alcohol and die in a war at eighteen, but it had no voting voice until the age of twenty-one. Upheaval was inevitable. Talk made music, and music made talk. Action was in the civil rights marches, marches against the bomb, and marches against an escalating war in Vietnam. It was a march out of a time, too—out of the constricted and rigid morality of the 1950s. The Beats had already cracked the façade and we, the next generation, broke through it.

Traveling with the past within us, we were ready to roll into the future. It has now become a historical time made up of many personal stories, songs, and sidebars. There are many reliquaries from that era in American life. This is mine.

Part One

Preamble

Love:

Excitement anticipation
big joy big bang big
bliss big white-hot
sizzle in the gut.
A person in love
appears perfectly
normal within
his or her
own parameters of normal.
Nothing seems out of the ordinary other than a
noticeable shift to a lighter mood. But the inner
personality is ecstatic—jumping about
pumping the air with
unrestrained
happiness—shouting
big gusts
of glee.

A photo Bob gave me not long after we met

In the 1960s Bobby wore a black corduroy cap, with the snap on the brim undone, over his head of curly khaki-colored hair. His clothes were sloppy and didn't fit his body well. He wore shirts in drab colors, chinos and chunky boots, which later gave over to slimmer-fitting jeans and cowboy boots. I slit the bottom seams on his jeans and sewed in an inverted "U" from an older pair so they would slide over his boots. He is wearing them on the cover of the *Another Side of Bob Dylan* album. My solution was a precursor of the bell-bottoms that came on the market not too long afterward.

He had baby fat, and Dave Van Ronk, already a well-known folk musician dubbed the Mayor of MacDougal Street, loved to tease him about the way he looked. As a folksinger, he advised, Bob had to develop and present an image to the outside world, his future public. Such things might have been talked about in jest, but in truth they were taken quite seriously. Much time was spent in front of the mirror trying on one wrinkled article of clothing after another, until it all came together to look as if Bob had just gotten up and thrown something on. Image meant everything. Folk music was taking hold of a generation and it was important to get it right, including the look—be

authentic, be cool, and have something to say. That might seem naïve in comparison with the commercial sophistication and cynicism of today, but back then it was daring, underground, and revolutionary. We believed we could change perceptions and politics and the social order of things. We had something to say and believed that the times would definitely change.

*B*obby had an impish charm that older women found endearing, though my mother was immune. He was aware of it and used it when he could. But in general he was shy around people. He had a habit of pumping the air with his knees, a kind of marching in place, whether standing or sitting—all jumpy. Onstage he did it in time to the music. He looked good, despite his floppy clothes. He had a natural charisma, and people paid attention to him.

At the height of his Woody Guthrie phase, he talked through his teeth and when he laughed he would toss back his head and make a cracking *ha ha* sound or a small *ha*, with fingers covering his mouth. His walk was a lurch in slow motion. He had a touch of arrogance, a good dose of paranoia, and a wonderful sense of the absurd.

It was very important t him at that time t write as he spoke. Writin like speech an without havin any punctuation or t write out the word to.

We got on really well, though neither one of us had any skin growing over our nerve endings. We were both overly sensitive and needed shelter from the storm. But Bobby was also tough and focused, and he had a healthy ego. The additional ingredients protected the intense sensitivity. As an artist he had what it took to become a success.

We hadn't been together long when we went to Philadelphia with Dave Van Ronk and his wife, Terri Thal, for a gig she had booked for the two of them at a coffeehouse. When Bobby got up on the stage, he stood straight with his head slightly back and his eyes nowhere and began to sing "Dink's Song," a traditional ballad I had heard sung before by others. I watched him as he sang:

> If I had wings like Nora's dove
> I'd fly 'cross the river to the one I love
> Fare thee well oh honey,
> Fare thee well

He started slow, building the rhythm on his guitar. Something about him caught my full attention.

He pushed out the lyrics as he hit the strings with a steady, accelerating drumlike beat. The audience slowed their chattering; he stilled the room. It was as though I had never heard the song before. He stilled my room, for sure.

In those early years Bob Dylan was a painter searching for his palette. He had in mind the pictures he wanted to paint; he just needed to find the right color mix to get him there. He savored all that was put before him, dabbing his brush here and there, testing, testing, adding new layers and scraping old ones away until he got what he wanted. He would delve into ideas—latch on to them with incredible intensity and deliberate their validity. He had an uncanny ability to complicate the obvious and sanctify the banal— just like a poet. Some hated that about him because they felt he was putting them on, scrambling their brains, which he was. It was his way of examining and investigating what was on his mind. It worked for me, even when he made me nuts at times, because I liked to ponder other possibilities too, to find the bit that made a thing that was smooth suddenly produce a bump.

One evening we went to Emilio's on Sixth Avenue and Bleecker Street, a restaurant that was a fixture in what was then still an Italian neighborhood. It had a lovely outdoor garden in the back that compensated for the stereotypical food. Bobby was all fired up about the concept of freedom. What defined the essence of freedom?

Were birds really free? he asked. They are chained to the sky, he said, where they are compelled to fly.

So are they truly free?

Long ago, when New York City was affordable, people who felt they didn't fit into the mainstream could take a chance and head there from wherever they were. Bob Dylan came east from Minnesota in the winter of 1961 and made his way downtown to Greenwich Village. Like countless others before him, he came to shed the constricted definition of his birthplace and the confinement of his past.

I first saw Bob at Gerde's Folk City, the Italian bar and restaurant cum music venue on the corner of Mercer and West Fourth Streets, one block west of Broadway and a few blocks east of Washington Square Park. Bob was playing back-up harmonica for various musicians and as a duo with another folksinger, Mark Spoelstra, before he played sets by himself. Mark played the twelve string guitar and had a melodious singing voice.

Bob's raspy voice and harmonica added a little dimension to the act. Their repertoire consisted of traditional folk songs and the songs of Woody Guthrie. They weren't half bad. Bob was developing his image into his own version of a rambling troubadour, in the Guthrie mode.

A drawing I did of Pete Karman

Before I actually met Bob I was sitting with my friend Pete Karman at the bar one night at Gerde's watching Bobby and Mark Spoelstra play. Pete was a journalist at the *New York Mirror*. Back then there were seven dailies, as I recall, and the *Mirror* was right up there with the best of the tabloids.

Pete was a fellow red-diaper baby, as the offspring of Communists were called, who lived in Sunnyside, Queens, where I'd been born. He had gone through traumatic times, his parents having been jailed during the McCarthy era. His father was a Yugoslav seaman who had jumped ship as a young man. Left without papers, he also couldn't get any because he had been born in Austria-Hungary, a nation that went out of business after World War I.

Pete's parents were involved with other Yugoslavs in the American Communist Party when a woman they knew informed on them. They were jailed for about six months under threat of deportation, although there was no country that would take them. Shortly after their release, Pete's father died of a heart attack. Pete, a junior high school student, was home alone when two policemen rang his doorbell to give him the news. A few years later he met my older sister, Carla, and they became close friends. During those years he spent a lot of time at our Queens apartment talking politics with my mother and soon was part of the family. When I was living by myself at seventeen, house-sitting an apartment in the Village, my mother delegated Pete to be my surrogate guardian and asked him to keep an eye on me. I had been living pretty much without any parental supervision since my own father had died three years earlier, but since Pete took me into bars I saw no need to chafe at his guardianship. In those days the legal drinking age in New York was eighteen. Underage girls could get into bars without being carded as long as an older guy accompanied them: Pete was my passport to legality.

That night, Pete was going on about something, in his gregarious way, and commented on a woman with a good pair of legs. In response, I pointed to Mark Spoelstra up on the stage and said, That cute guy up there has a nice pair of shoulders. Pete turned it into a running joke, pointing to guys and asking me what I thought of their shoulders. Not as nice as Mark's, I'd reply. He has a real nice set.

When Bob and Mark left the stage Pete called out: Hey, Mark Shoulders, come meet Suze. She says you're cute.

I was embarrassed and Mark looked confused. A natural storyteller, Pete often told the tale for laughs, until eventually it ended up revised and expanded in several books about Bob Dylan.

In those years Little Italy extended into the streets of Greenwich Village below Washington Square Park and Gerde's was a hangout for local Italians, stray musicians, and Village types. Mike Porco owned it and ran the place with his brothers. Mike was a warm, generous man, and if his English wasn't perfect his instincts were. He knew a good thing when he saw it, whether it was a struggling musician or a business deal and he was always ready to give someone a chance. I'm sure Mike knew I was underage, yet when he found out I could draw he let me try my hand at making the fliers that advertised the performance schedule and I joined the ranks of his rotating stable of fledgling artists. One of his younger brothers who tended bar spoke very little English, but he had the vocabulary he felt went with his job. Looking at me meaningfully one night as he topped a drink with a maraschino cherry, he said, Girls gotta guard their cherries.

I learned about Gerde's history as a folk music club from the inimitable music man and raconteur, Dave Van Ronk. Dave always knew the story behind everything, and could tell it with the veracity and aplomb required to effectively eliminate other versions.

Sometime around 1959, Israel "Izzy" Young and a friend approached Mike Porco about making Gerde's into a club for folk music. They wanted to call it The Fifth Peg (as in the fifth peg on a banjo). Mike wasn't aware of the growing popularity of folk music, but he was game to try something that would improve business. He did have music in the bar now

Izzy Young (left) and
Albert Grossman at the
Folklore Center

and then, some jazz or blues musicians and the occasional accordion player. It never hurt, so he said sure.

The verbal agreement was simple: Izzy and his partner would charge an entry fee and out of that they would pay the performers and for publicity, while Mike would keep the profits from the sale of drinks and food. Mike couldn't lose, but it wasn't a winning deal for Izzy. Word spread that there was a bar in the Village that featured live folk music, and people started coming to listen. Soon Gerde's evolved into a destination.

The disastrous finances made it inevitable that others more savvy in the ways of running a club would ease Izzy out. The Fifth Peg reverted to its original name of Gerde's, to which Mike added Folk City, but most people just called it Gerde's. (The origin of the name Gerde's Bar and Restaurant goes back to the 1950s, when Mike bought what was then a hangout for local factory workers. He never changed the name.)

Since Izzy Young didn't specialize in hanging out, drinking, and smoking, he wasn't around much in the evenings. He was the sole proprietor and founder of the Folklore Center over on MacDougal Street, a store that took up most of his time. Izzy sold books, magazines, broadsides, records, guitar strings, and anything else related to folk music and folklore. The store thrived as a gathering place for professional musicians, aspiring musicians, and folk music aficionados, with Izzy as its up-to-the-minute historian and archivist. You didn't stop to talk to him unless you wanted to do a lot of listening. To engage with Izzy meant entering his universe, listening to his tales, and following his theories wherever they went. He never made much money at anything he did, even though he promoted many events in the world of folk music and folk dance. He was always full of information, ideas, and enthusiasms—his interests went way beyond the borders of the folk world— but he had no business acumen. No one would dispute that Izzy Young played a significant role in the rise of folk music in the 1960s.

Broadway was considered no-man's-land, dividing Greenwich Village from the Lower East Side (soon to be re-named the East Village). During the day, the area around Broadway and Mercer Street was bustling with small manufacturing businesses on every floor of the ornate loft buildings, but after five there

Gerdes **Folk City**

open every night

never a cover charge

· new york's center of folk music ·

· presents ·

april 10th ← → april 22nd

Ron Eliran

dynamic Israeli folk singer

and

sensational 12 string guitarist: **Mark Spoelstra**

april 24th ← → may 6th

Bob Dylan

"– bursting at the seams with talent"
· n.y. times ·

and

international songstress: **Varda Karni**

songs with → **Gil Turner** ← added nightly feature

every monday
hootenanny &
guest night

show begins 9:30
11 west 4 st.
· 1 blk west Brdwy ·
AL4-8449

every sunday
no cover -no minimum
- no admission charge
open house

open every nite
AL48449

~ gerdes
FOLK CITY

11 west 4 st.
near Broadway

• new york's center of folk music •

March 3-15 Popular Blues King : **Lonnie Johnson**

International folksinger : **Phyllis Lynd**

Deirdre O'Callaghan : from 2nd appearance on Ed Sullivan   **March 17-29**

Jimmy & Jake : new banjo-duo

March 31- April 12 Back from European Tour : **the Grandison Singers**

Singer of folksongs & ballads : **Murv Shiner**

John Winn : lyric Balladeer   **April 14-26**

Fleury Papadantonakis : International Vanguard Recording Artist

---

April 28 May 10 Bluegrass Specials : **the Greenbriar Boys**

Voice, charm & beauty : **Lynn Rosner**

Show at 9:30   **Hootenanny**   never a cover charge no admission charge

• every monday •

S. ROTOLO

was no activity anywhere except on West Fourth Street, at Gerde's. Most of the coffeehouses and other music clubs were farther west on MacDougal and Bleecker Streets.

The entrance to Gerde's opened onto a small vestibule with another door that led into the place proper. The bar was straight ahead. Just to the left of the door, past a dividing wall maybe four and a half feet high, was a small elevated stage against the back wall. Directly in front of the stage were the tables and chairs with waiter service. The dividing wall continued opposite the bar, and customers there could lean over it and watch the show, drinks in hand. Sitting on a bar stool afforded a view only of the top of a performer's head. Past the length of the bar was a door leading down a steep flight of stairs to the basement, where the food, booze, and performers were stored.

If there were more than three people onstage at the same time, it was a crowd. It was fun to watch the bluegrass musicians choreograph their moves. They had to angle their instruments—guitar, banjo, and mandolin—just so, to be able to come together at the one microphone and sing a chorus, then separate for solos, without a collision. The music spanned a variety of genres that included, besides bluegrass, traditional ballads, folk songs in many languages from many lands, blues, and gospel. Whoever came through the doors and signed up to play could perform at the Monday night hootenannies. Gerde's was on the bar circuit for jazz and blues artists of an earlier generation, from the forties and fifties, artists who'd encountered the legendary musicians of the twenties and thirties when they started out. Many who were playing gigs at Gerde's were legends in their own time and carried a long history of musical information for the younger players to learn from.

Bob Dylan played harmonica for many of the older musicians when they performed at Gerde's Folk City: Victoria Spivey, a blues and jazz singer and pianist, and blues man Lonnie Johnson, both of whom worked with Louis Armstrong in the twenties, and Big Joe Williams, born in 1903, who probably played with every musician over the years, all the way into the sixties in New York City.

I had a special weakness for the harmonica. I loved that bluesy wail and crying sound. When I was a child my parents played recordings of Sonny Terry and Brownie McGhee, and I was enchanted by Sonny Terry's harmonica playing. When Bob played harmonica for other musicians he was unobtrusive, standing at the back of the little stage, yielding to the main performer but really wailing and tearing into the harp. I liked to watch him go at it.

When he played with the veterans Bob called himself Blind Boy Grunt as a tribute to, and playful take on, the nicknames of the blues and jazz greats who preceded the young white pretenders. He had the eyeglasses for the role. After a gig at Café Lena's in Saratoga Springs, New York, we spent a week at the home of photographer Joe Alper and his family in Schenectady, New York. At a thrift shop in town Bob found a pair of wire-rimmed eyeglasses with opaque blue glass lenses in them.

At a certain point Mike Porco had asked Charlie Rothschild, who was not a musician but knew the ins and outs of the folk music world, to take over the job of booking musicians at Gerde's. Since it had been Izzy Young's idea to turn Gerde's into a folk club in the first place, his replacement by Charlie resulted in a bit of a dustup. Izzy put up a sign at the Folklore Center in essence proclaiming, "Charlie Rothschild: Wanted for Theft." Izzy was furious about the injustice; Charlie was grateful for the fifty bucks a week Mike Porco paid him to hire folksingers and to emcee, as well.

By the time I started going to Gerde's in the spring of 1961, the tiff was history. Mike himself was doing the hiring (with input from the club's regulars) and most of the emcee work was handled by the flamboyant Brother John Sellers and the folksinger Gil Turner.

In between sets some of the musicians would jam with each other in the basement or, in good weather, outside on the loading dock around the corner on Mercer Street. Eventually Mike Porco or Brother John Sellers or perhaps the musicians themselves would mix up the sets onstage so they could play together for the audience. It made for great music. On those nights at Gerde's, the cross-fertilization of different styles and musical eras forged important links in the chain of American musical history.

John Lee Hooker was one of the blues singers on the circuit. He used to sit quietly on a stool at the bar and smile at anyone who spoke to him. He stuttered when he talked, but not when he performed. When his name was announced to play a set one night, to me it was like hearing that someone as mythic as Woody Guthrie was in the room. I had no idea John Lee Hooker was alive, let alone performing in New York City.

Just a couple of years earlier, when I was still in high school, I'd headed to Harlem to work for the civil rights organizer Bayard Rustin, who was running Youth March for Integrated Schools. Before climbing the stairs to Youth March headquarters on 125th Street, I would stop by the record store next door, a small, narrow place full of albums in wooden bins where the owner always had a record playing. One day as I walked in, I heard music that stopped me in my tracks. It was as if the store were suddenly enveloped in an intense glow, and I lost a sense of where I was, aware only of the sound coming from the speakers. I was transfixed by the thumping guitar beat and the thick deep baritone of the singer. I had never heard anything like it and I don't think I moved an inch until the end of side 2, when I managed to ask, What was that?

The guy behind the counter showed me the album cover, with a drawing of a truck in the grass and the name John Lee Hooker written across it. I couldn't wait to take it home and play it for my sister. I bought it and ran up the stairs with my treasure.

When John Lee Hooker's name was announced at Gerde's no one else seemed to think it was a big deal, but I insisted to everyone around me that they had to listen to him. I don't remember what he played that night, but the room got quiet when he took the stage. When his set was over and he walked back to the bar and sat down, I overcame my shyness and went over to him, though it was a while before I managed to tell him how I first heard one of his albums and how much I loved it. Whenever John was around, I would talk with him. And when Bob and I were together, the friendship expanded. The Broadway Central Hotel, just a block or two away from Gerde's, was the place where traveling musicians stayed, including Hooker. It became another spot for musicians to hang out and jam together.

It took way too long for John Lee Hooker to become famous, but even though he was a shy and unassuming man, he was very smart and knew how to protect his interests.

Decades later, when a music writer friend, Tony Scherman, was doing an interview with Hooker, the old blues man began to reminisce about his early days in Greenwich Village with Bob and Suze. Tony told him he knew me and gave him an update. After a blues concert at the Beacon Theater in 1991 where John Lee Hooker was the headliner, his manager brought me backstage. When John saw me, he raised his hands in the air like the Healer, grinned, and said, Hey, Suze! The good old days!

Queens

I was born in Sunnyside, Queens, across the bridge from Manhattan. My actual birth took place in Brooklyn, though—in Brooklyn Jewish Hospital—where a sympathetic doctor took good care of young Communist women with little money who were starting families.

My parents had moved to Queens from an apartment on Horatio Street in Greenwich Village around 1940, shortly after they were married. Like several of their friends who had joined the American Communist Party in the 1930s and were now married with children on the way, they moved to a complex of apartments called Sunnyside Gardens specifically designed for working-class families by an architect who was the father of one of the couples. The apartments themselves were small but had back doors opening onto little gardens that were a nice draw for growing families. My parents and their friends who went to live there were on the left, but the residents in general were politically all over the map, a mix of new and old Americans of various ethnic backgrounds and religions.

Several of our family's friends moved away to modern homes they were building on a rural wooded lane in Rye, New York, in Westchester County. There they reestablished the left-wing community they'd had in Sunnyside, but in more luxurious homes and surroundings.

The Rotolo family never made it to suburbia. My father was an artist but couldn't support a family as a painter and instead found work at various factory jobs, joining the shop union or, if no union existed, organizing one. As a result, he was fired often and was on strike even more often. He felt very strongly about the importance of unions, for white- and blue-collar workers alike. Working conditions were terrible in the early half of the last century, and the fight to establish unions that could guarantee eight-hour days, eliminate child labor, and deliver a decent environment for the working man and woman was essential. So many benefits now taken for granted were fought for long and hard, and the story of this struggle has largely been ignored. It is a proud history that affected labor conditions worldwide for the better.

My father, Gioachino Pietro Rotolo, was born in Bagheria, Sicily, in 1912. In the 1970s I went to Bagheria, which by then had become a suburb of Palermo and was no longer the rock pile so many poor Italians had escaped from to find a livelihood in America and elsewhere. "Rock pile" is really a misnomer. Tony Buttitta, a writer I knew in Greenwich Village who was born in 1907 and died when he was well into his nineties, was also from Bagheria. He dispelled the notion of rock pile, telling me about the many poets, writers, and artists born there who gained national fame in Italy and abroad. Most had left for someplace else, I reminded him, but I understood what he meant to convey.

In Bagheria, the Rotolo family worked as either *bottai*, barrel makers for wine, or in *ferro battuto*, decorative ironwork. My grandfather Andrea Rotolo was in the latter trade and as a skilled iron maker found work fairly easily in the new country of America. He emigrated in the late 1890s and traveled back and forth to Sicily several times before finally settling in New York.

My father came to the United States in 1914, when he was two, with his mother, his older brother, Filippo, and his older sister, Francesca. They joined his father, who had already established a home for them in a brownstone at 321 Sackett Street in Brooklyn, a neighborhood where many other Italian immigrants had settled. Today the area is known as Carroll Gardens.

Gioachino, Joachim or Jack in English, chose to go by the name Pete, which was the translation of his middle name, Pietro. He grew up speaking Sicilian at home and English everywhere else. His mother, Marianna, acceded to her children's wishes that she use their American names and called her youngest son Jack. I still remember her at his funeral years later, standing at his graveside as the first shovelful of dirt hit his coffin, calling quietly, Jack, Jack . . .

A skilled dressmaker, my grandmother found work in the garment industry even though she didn't speak fluent English. She worked hard, as did the many other immigrants who came to America during the European immigration boom of the late nineteenth and early twentieth century. She was fortunate not to have worked in the sweatshops of lower Manhattan, where the disastrous conditions resulted in the notorious Triangle Shirtwaist Factory fire of 1911 in which so many young Italian and Jewish women died. Instead she worked in the Garment District, farther uptown, where the conditions and pay were better.

My grandparents did well. Their oldest son, Philip, became an engineer; Frances was an executive secretary (now her title would be executive assistant); and their youngest, Pete, my father, was an artist who won a scholarship to Pratt

Institute, unusual in those times for the son of an immigrant family.

My father always said that no job is worth doing if it is not worth doing well, and to never undervalue the importance of work. His dedication to these beliefs as a young man led him to the writings of John Reed. Sometime during the Depression he joined a John Reed Club, and there he found the Communist Party. His commitment to the importance of union organizing began then. When he met my mother, he proposed to her with the words "I think I need to set up a picket line around you."

He became a union organizer. That was his duty, his "Communist" work. He rarely painted, yet he did get a few

My parents, Pete and Mary Rotolo, 1940

editorial illustration jobs for the *New York Times* and other periodicals. After he died my mother told us that he had turned down an offer to teach art at a school in upstate New York but had let her know about it only after the opportunity had long passed.

My parents had been radicalized by the class differences they saw firsthand, but especially and irrevocably by the fate of Nicola Sacco and Bartolomeo Vanzetti, two Italian immigrants involved with the anarchist movement who were accused of a robbery and murder in South Braintree, Massachusetts, in 1920. After a tumultuous trial and worldwide attention to their case, they were put to death seven years later. Books, plays, movies, and songs have been written about the prejudices of the presiding judge, the unfairness of the trial, and the terrible anti-immigrant, antiradical climate of the time. Growing up, both my parents were influenced by the terrible prejudice against Italian immigrants, and the injustices surrounding the Sacco and Vanzetti story.

My mother was an editor and columnist for *L'Unità*, the American version of the Italian Communist paper of the same name. She was paid very little, if anything, and times were very hard for my parents, especially with two children. During our childhood, my sister and I were sent to live with my mother's relatives outside of Boston when times were especially difficult. We were separated; Carla would be placed with one set of relatives, and I'd go to another. I remember being frightened by these stays away from home. The relatives who took me in were loving and attentive, but because I was a very shy and overly sensitive child, I was not easily comforted.

One of my father's illustrations for
the New York Times

C HESS has gone democratic. Discarding their traditional aloofness, the masters are taking the innocents by the hand and are guiding the faltering footsteps from square to square. Milton Hanauer is a teacher in the New York public schools, and, like a good teacher, he does not talk beyond the range of the pupil's knowledge. In "Chess for You and Me" he begins at the very beginning and, with informal language and lots of very helpful diagrams, leads you as far as a small first book can go.

In his "Manual of the End-Game," J. Mieses (oldest of the living old masters) gives you what you must know, what he calls an "iron ration" of theoreti-

BOOK REVIEW, AUGUST 15, 1948.

We moved from Sunnyside when I was about three, to another working-class Queens neighborhood, Jackson Heights, populated predominantly by white families from different backgrounds, including Irish, Polish, Jewish, and Italian. My childhood recollections originate in this new neighborhood. The complex was called Garden Bay Manor, or, as my mother referred to it, Garbage Bay Manure in Jackson Frights. She frequently expressed her frustrations about living in Queens, which she felt was the outback.

The buildings were faux Tudor brick two-story attached apartments with basements. The long row of buildings faced each other from the back with a parklike space in between that was a haven for all the kids in the neighborhood. There were no back doors leading to it, and the grounds weren't landscaped like a park or a playground. Instead it was an open communal area with trees and grass and a scattering of benches in the center walkway. To get to the park you walked to the end of the long row of apartments and rounded the corner.

We lived on the ground floor somewhere in the middle. My father set up an electric saw in the basement of our building and made nearly every piece of furniture we had.

This was the 1950s, the height of the McCarthy era. I grew up watching my older sister trying hard to fit in where we so obviously did not belong. She attempted for a time to make herself over into the mode of the girls in the neighborhood and to fight against the way she grew up. She wasn't ashamed of how our family lived and what we believed; she was just at an age when it was important for kids to belong, to be like everyone else. We had bookshelves filled with books, a record player, and a collection of treasured 78s and $33\frac{1}{3}$ long-playing records. We listened to the radio; we didn't own a television. The other apartments were carpeted, had curtains on the windows, not Venetian blinds, and no bookshelves in the living rooms.

Most families in the neighborhood went to a church or a temple, to Sunday school or to Hebrew school. My sister and I were raised with no formal religion, but we were taught to accept the beliefs of others. We were brought up not to believe in the superiority of any culture or religion over another but rather to take people as they were, as individuals.

I tried my best. The Catholic girl next door attempted to save my heathen soul and teach me about God, telling me God was everywhere, saw everything, and knew everything. She said that it was important to bow your head with every utterance of the name Jesus. I would challenge this God who was everywhere to come out from behind the prickle bushes to shake hands, and I would cruelly repeat JesusJesusJesus until she got dizzy from nodding her head so much.

The Jewish kids were somewhat more accepting, but a few of their parents made a point of ignoring me. They would say hello to the other children and not acknowledge my presence at all, either because I was the only goy, or shiksa (as they called me), in the group or perhaps because they knew of my parents' politics and were wary of associating with Reds and their offspring.

Outsider status was inevitable. Culturally we were Catholic, but my parents had long ago left the church for the idealistic, as opposed to the hardcore Stalinist, wing of the American Communist Party. The only thing that passed for a religious education was sitting in my father's lap while he paged through a big book of Renaissance Italian paintings with many pictures of the Crucifixion. I know I must have asked why that man was nailed to the cross—and no doubt my father told me.

When my older sister was an infant our Sicilian grandparents managed to sneak off with her under false pretenses to their local church to have her baptized. After that, my parents never left me alone with them while I was a baby.

At the time I finished elementary school and Carla was starting high school, we moved several blocks away to the second floor of a small two-story attached row house owned by the Shills, fellow Communists, who were doing a good deed by charging us an affordable rent. This was a better situation overall. The Shills had two daughters younger than we were, a TV set, and a finished basement, in addition to a house full of books. It was a Commie kids' refuge of sorts. I put on plays in the basement, painting the scenery on large sheets of paper and taping them to the walls. I lip-synched a production of *Hans Christian Andersen,* using an album of the songs from the movie starring Danny Kaye. My father encouraged me, and when *West Side Story* opened in 1957 he took me to a matinee performance at the Winter Garden Theater on Broadway.

My memories of Queens reflect my general unhappiness as a child. I just never fit in and even if I'd tried, as my sister had, I would have failed; the other kids just thought I was weird. I found solace in books and poetry and in making storybooks for myself filled with characters I created from an invented world. The good memories come from the culture I lived within, being around interesting adults from different backgrounds, all kinds of music, and all those books. Though we were economically working class and money was always an issue, we had a rich cultural upbringing that I relished; maybe that is what sustained me, compensating for the bad stuff later on. The relative wretchedness that we go through as wee ones notwithstanding, it is as adults that the real horrors of life are fully realized.

I went to Bryant High School in Long Island City, Queens, a bus and subway ride from where I lived in Jackson Heights. When I graduated in 1960, at sixteen years old, my prospects were limited to an extended version of what had been my summer jobs. My father had died suddenly in 1958 and I missed two weeks of school. The first week was for obvious reasons, and the second was a gift of a trip to Puerto Rico.

My mother worked for Samuel Rosen, an ear doctor who had originated stapes mobilization, a surgical procedure that cured a certain kind of deafness. The singer Johnnie Ray was one of his patients, but Dr. Rosen wasn't able to do much for him. My self-educated mother knew French and Italian, and her job involved translating correspondence, some medical papers, and writings about his procedure.

After my father's sudden death, Sam and his wife, Helen, gently insisted that my distraught mother and I come with them, all expenses paid, to a medical conference in Puerto Rico. At fourteen years old I had never been in a hotel, but I knew this was an especially luxurious one, with a pool, a balcony, room service, and all. The Rosens were wonderful people.

When I returned to school I was even more distracted and withdrawn than usual, and I didn't do well. The only class I looked forward to was Drama Workshop, or maybe it was called Theater History. The teacher, Mr. Kaufman, did not give me a hard time about what I had missed. I was in the plays the class put on for the school, and he made sure I continued reading and doing scenes.

Other teachers were less sympathetic about my circumstances. The science teacher gave me a D, citing excessive absence. Others left out the written comment but gave similar grades. I distinctly remember one teacher who chose to tell me directly what a loser I was and that I had better shape up or I would never amount to anything. He was the same English teacher who in my sophomore year felt it was his duty to use me to illustrate to the class what the expression *lack of poise* meant. Justice was mine, however, because many years later, while I was waiting for a subway train, I spotted him walking along the platform mumbling to himself with a large wet stain on his crotch. I knew who he was despite the change in his demeanor, but he didn't recognize me.

With nine hundred kids in the graduating class, Bryant High School worked on shifts, and the classes were overcrowded. I was aware that the teachers were overworked and underpaid and didn't always know their students, but understanding that didn't help. My attitude changed. I stopped caring and didn't even attempt to keep up. I preferred the extracurricular activities the school offered. In addition to Drama Workshop, I did artwork and layout for the school newspaper and joined a current events discussion group. The result was a low average, which was not helped by the fact that I scored slightly above fool on my SATs. I didn't do well on tests. In any case, college material I was not.

Wrapped up in grief, my mother was in no condition to care. At forty-seven, she was widowed for a second time— her first husband had drowned in an accident when she was in her early twenties—but now she was left with two teenaged daughters. It was not comforting or comfortable to be around her. She spent a lot of time trying to find survival skills inside a bottle.

Life at home was thrown off the last vestiges of balance. It was the end of our world as we had known it, the end of childhood—the end of innocence and the beginning of a new kind of fear.

My father had suffered what was diagnosed as a mild heart attack two years earlier, shortly after President Eisenhower suffered a serious one. I don't know if Eisenhower smoked, but my father did. He was six feet tall and in no way overweight, but he had had tuberculosis as a child, making him unqualified for military service. I've heard it said that TB takes a toll on the body, even if one recovers from it. Cigarettes certainly took a toll, but smoking in his day was promoted as good for you.

My father worked at Mergenthaler, a linotype factory near the Brooklyn Navy Yard. He was a shop steward for the union and well liked by his coworkers, even though they were aware of his politics.

He had bought a car, which made the trip to Brooklyn from Queens a little easier. When he had the heart attack he was driving home from work. My mother was very anxious because he was unusually late. When he finally made it home, he could barely climb the stairs. Apparently he had stopped the car by the side of the road several times to wait for the pain to subside before continuing.

He took a medical leave from work and began to paint

and to cook. It was strange having someone at home when I returned from school. Painting with oils was difficult in a small apartment, so instead he used gouache or watercolors, and he did a lot of drawing. I would often pose for him when I got home but after he died, in the upheavals that ensued, somehow the drawings were lost.

His coworkers from the Mergenthaler factory visited him on weekends, and when the decision was made to leave his job for good, they took up a collection and bought us a television set. He planned to work as a freelance illustrator and take up painting again. Despite the fact that he had suffered a heart attack, he was noticeably happier. He sang as he worked on drawings at the kitchen table.

He continued to smoke, however, even though the doctor told him to quit. Both he and my mother smoked unfiltered Chesterfield cigarettes. By then so did my sister, but maybe she smoked something with a filter, newly on the market. Not too many years later, I took up the family tradition.

Just when he seemed to be getting stronger, my father was hit by some sort of ministroke that left half of his face paralyzed. I was embarrassed to have my friends see him with his face held together with medical tape, looking disfigured. Gradually the feeling in his face came back, but he did not look well. He was thin and drawn and looked much older than his years.

On top of this, my mother had been diagnosed with an overactive thyroid and an ulcer; it was a highly stressful time. I was in my junior year of high school, and Carla had started Hunter College.

Socialist realism for Christmas

We both traveled by bus and subway to our respective schools, but at different times, so our paths never crossed. On an unusually mild February day, considering there had been a snowstorm a few days before, my sister chose to go home right after her last class ended, and we caught the same bus at the Roosevelt Avenue subway station.

We thought that it was an odd thing for us to meet and

we laughed over the coincidence. On the three-block walk home from the bus, we were in a good mood. Just a few yards from the apartment, Selma Shill came running out, calling, Girls, girls, come here! She sounded frantic. She ushered us in to her house to block our view of our father's car, motor running loudly, with him slumped over the steering wheel.

Selma was saying over and over that something terrible had happened. And of course it had. Our father had been headed to meet his painter friend, Ralph Fasanella, who worked in a gas station for many years and wasn't discovered until the 1970s, to see the studio they were planning to rent together. Afterwards he was to pick up our mother at Dr. Rosen's office in Manhattan. My father had gone to the car, turned on the motor, and died. Selma said later that she kept hearing this strange sound, and when she looked out her window, she saw him in the car. Realizing what had happened she called an ambulance and then sat in wait for it and for us. At some point I saw from the window my father lying on the ground in front of the building, covered by a sheet. A crowd had gathered. People were standing nearby staring, and the neighborhood kids were dancing around and playing. They had no idea the sky had fallen. It was fortunate that my sister and I came home together that day.

The year my father died I was reading the poetry of Lord Byron and Edna St. Vincent Millay. I came across her poem "Lament," which begins:

Listen, children:
Your father is dead.

And concludes:

Life must go on,
And the dead be forgotten;
Life must go on,
Though good men die;
Anne, eat your breakfast;
Dan, take your medicine;
Life must go on;
I forget just why.

Its accuracy stunned me.

As I grew up and older and my life became what I made of it, I acquired a habit of taking special note of technological developments. I would think of a way my father, who died in 1958, might regard these new inventions. We had a telephone back then and a TV, and Dr. Rosen had given us a reel-to-reel tape recorder. So reasonably my father could have grasped the technological evolution to cassette tapes and portable music. Cell phones, CD players, DVDs, and videos—he could have handled all that. Computers were problematic, but once I walked him through the other stuff, he might grasp it.

It was a game, really. I didn't for one minute believe anyone could come back alive. It was a way to think about the world as it was and to inventory the changes I would normally take for granted.

A trauma creates a freeze frame, stopping time in a still series of snapshots that pop up in total recall if the day or subject is referenced in some way. The year 1958 became my yardstick.

But a thought struck me as the century ended and the new one began. It's not so much the technological advancements that show how different our world is: it is the change in people. The people of New York City in 1958 were predominantly white or black. Immigrants came from Europe, as my father had. To compare the faces on a subway train in 1958 with the faces in the twenty-first century becomes incomprehensible. I couldn't possibly walk someone through the immense cultural changes, both the visible and the invisible. So I let my father go. I no longer idly sift through the changes around me and attempt to define them. I let them accumulate and use what I need to live in the present.

McCarthyism reigned supreme during the 1950s, its influence—like a slowly retreating flood—permeated the decade, and the damage left in its wake was evident in the beginning of the next one. In the span of ten years Stalin had died and the Rosenbergs had been sent to the electric chair. General Dwight D. Eisenhower, a Republican, was elected president in 1952 and served two terms. A notable act he was responsible for, in addition to denying executive clemency to the Rosenbergs, was completely desegregating the armed forces.

Since we didn't own a television set until 1957, the radio and the phonograph held sway. The music we listened to included recordings of folk music from around the world, the Édith Piaf and Billie Holiday records my mother loved, opera arias my father sang along with, classical music, and Toscanini conducting the NBC Radio Orchestra. A program called *Make-Believe Ballroom* delivered mostly bland popular music until the day the DJ placed a single titled "Sh-Boom" on the turntable, inaugurating the arrival of rock and roll on mainstream radio.

Folk music had been sidelined as being for radicals, especially after the nationally known folk group the Weavers, with the Communist Party member Pete Seeger on banjo and vocals, had become victims of the blacklist, making it impossible for them to appear on TV or in concert halls and clubs. The Cold War had hit its stride.

My sister Carla was seventeen in 1958, in her first year at Hunter College. She had a group of friends whose families had a political background similar to ours. I was a with-drawn fourteen-year-old, and our mother might have asked her to take me under her wing. For whatever reason, she de-cided to bring me along to a party she was going to. She and a girlfriend put a few tissues in my bra, undid my ponytail, and gave me a cute skirt to wear so that I'd look less like a kid. I was still very awkward, but progress was being made. They schooled me in a few dance moves and made sure I knew the words to the Gene Vincent song "Be-Bop-A-Lula." I was happy. Usually my sister treated me like a bug she needed to swat away, but life had radically changed a few months previously with the death of our father, and now I was getting some friendly attention.

I had a great time at the party. There was no way to hide

With Carla and my mother, ca. 1959

in a corner with this group. Right away a few boys headed my way, to my amazement. In school I was another sort of bug, to be avoided by boys and even some of the girls. In contrast, this party was heaven. I felt less like an outsider with these people. We actually had things to talk about. One boy read the same poetry I did and told me he was learning to play classical guitar. The other boy liked opera; I didn't think anybody knew about opera but my family, some of our friends, and the man who played it on the radio. He invited me on a date (a date!!) to go to the Amato Opera House on the Bowery to see a performance of *La Bohème* the following week. The boy who read poetry looked a little miffed. I lied and said I was fifteen when he asked my age and for my phone number. He was sixteen, and I thought he was very intelligent.

After that life definitely improved. I was more confident and my circle of friends gradually grew over the next few years. Most of them lived farther out in Queens than I did or out on Long Island. Because we went to different high schools, we would arrange to meet in the Square (as Washington Square Park in Greenwich Village was called) to listen to the folk musicians who gathered there to play on Sundays. Folk music was the antiestablishment music, the music of the left. In addition to traditional folk songs there were songs about unions and fighting fascists, about brotherhood, equality, and peace.

Most of us were children of Communists or socialists, red-diaper babies raised on Woody Guthrie, Leadbelly, and Pete Seeger. We had listened to Oscar Brand's *Folksong Festival* on the radio while still in our cribs. The pop radio stations played ridiculous treacle, the worst of which was a song called "How Much Is That Doggie in the Window?" sung by Patti Page.

Late at night Carla and I would listen to WWVA, a country music radio station out of Wheeling, West Virginia. We heard Les Paul and Mary Ford, Hank Williams, Faron Young, the Everly Brothers, and others on a program called *Grand Ole Opry*. This was new and exciting for us; I adored the Everly Brothers and Hank Williams, especially.

The atmosphere in Washington Square Park was lively. Groups of musicians would play and sing anything from old folk songs to bluegrass. Old Italian men from the neighborhood played their folk music on mandolins. Everyone played around the fountain and people would wander from group to group, listening and maybe singing along. A banjo player gave me an ebony banjo peg and I wore it on a string around my neck for a long time. There were poets reading their poems and political types handing out fliers for Trotskyist, Communist, or anarchist meetings and hawking their newspapers. Children played in the playground while their mothers talked together on the benches. The occasional religious zealot held forth, waving a Bible, haranguing sinners about redemption. Everything overlapped nicely.

I looked forward to Sunday in the Square with my friends and to that particular atmosphere. On Friday or Saturday nights we would meet and go to folk concerts—hootenannies—at Town Hall, Carnegie Hall, and a concert hall that no longer exists and whose location I no longer remember,

Sunday in Washington Square, early sixties

the Pythian. Pete Seeger, who personified the power of folk song, was the draw, heading the roster of a list of performers that included his sister Peggy Seeger and her husband, Ewan MacColl, who sat on a chair on the stage with his hand cupped around his ear singing Scottish ballads and sea chanties a cappella.

The Clancy Brothers with Tommy Makem, four Irishmen wearing thickly knit white fisherman sweaters, always brought down the house with their energetic renditions of everything from bawdy drinking songs to heartrending ballads of the Irish struggles. A more formal concert might be a program of "Folk Songs from Many Lands," with Cynthia Gooding as headliner. Cynthia was over six feet tall and sang songs in several languages in a throaty alto. She stood on the stage in a flowing dress with her guitar high on her body, looking elegant as she rendered an old Italian folk tune in perfectly enunciated Italian. Though an incongruous combination of elements, the performance worked because of her sexy voice.

At one of these folk concerts I saw the singer John Jacob Niles, who looked like an ancient balladeer brought forth from the dead. With his spectral appearance and eerily high voice—which I later learned was a classic countertenor—he provoked thoughts of the castrati of bygone times. Watching him perform, reaching for a still higher high note, made me feel that he might lose control and dissolve into a puddle on the stage—or maybe disintegrate into a pile of bone and ash instead. He truly scared me.

Some years later, when I was living in the Village, I met a countertenor named John Winn whose voice did not sound unnatural at all; it was lovely and warm and it helped that he was young and not scary looking. John Winn's repertoire consisted of the songs of John Dowland, ballads, and folk songs, but he also sang old bawdy ballads. He would get Van Ronk, Dylan, and the bass-voiced Ed McCurdy up onstage with him to sing madrigals. The four of them were quite an unruly and truly funny sight—no formal attitude or attire—yet they never failed to bring patrons of the clubs and bars to their feet as they belted out the madrigals in four-part harmony, because they really sounded extraordinarily good.

The satiric songwriter and performer Tom Lehrer, who also taught mathematics at Harvard, was a big draw and my friends and I went to his concerts at Carnegie Hall or Town Hall. He wrote very funny songs satirizing the politically dangerous and socially strangled times we were living in, banging them out on a grand piano, singing at full volume with a deadpan delivery. One song exposed the dubious ethics of Wernher von Braun, who first developed rockets for the Nazis and later for the United States:

> Don't say that he's hypocritical,
> Say rather that he's apolitical.
> "Once the rockets are up, who cares where they
>   come down?
> That's not my department," says Wernher von Braun.

None of us had much money, and over time we developed a system to get into Carnegie Hall without a ticket. We pooled our resources and bought one or maybe two tickets. Then we'd charge the entrance door. When the usher asked for the ticket, we'd say that the person behind us had it and point in that direction. Far behind in the crowded line, the designated person would wave the ticket for a second, and we would pass through, repeating, he's got them, as we pointed vaguely off to the rear. Then we would race up the stairs to the top balcony and sit in any available empty seat or hide in the bathrooms until the concert began. We knew the ushers could not leave their posts to come after us. This technique worked well back in those more open and inno- cent times. We got so good at it that we stopped buying tickets altogether.

We also went to the Ethical Culture Society on West Sixty-fourth Street, just off Central Park, a humanistic reli- gious and educational organization that gave classes on a va- riety of subjects for all ages. In the big gymnasium they offered weekly folk dancing lessons. Though I went to a few of the political study classes with fellow red-diaper babies, I was never enthralled by theoretical political discussions of Marxism, socialism, or any other ism. Mostly we were there to socialize, like the other kids. I hated the folk dancing; I was young and curious, but not that curious.

My political beliefs were based on a dislike of injustice and a fear of the bomb. It is hard to comprehend this fear now, as it is only one of so many, but postwar culture was possessed by the threat of Communism and the hydrogen bomb. All throughout elementary school we were in- structed to duck and cover: duck under our desks, face away from the windows, and cover the backs of our heads. When the siren stopped, we took our seats again and the teacher resumed the lesson. In high school I was put on probation for soliciting signatures on a petition to ban the bomb dis- tributed by the Committee for a Sane Nuclear Policy, or

SANE, a worldwide organization for nuclear disarmament with Eleanor Roosevelt, Albert Schweitzer, and Bertrand Russell as prominent spokespersons.

Two of my close girlfriends and I volunteered to be ushers at a rally in Madison Square Garden for SANE in 1959. The three of us were taken backstage to meet Eleanor Roosevelt, the keynote speaker that evening. Overcome by adolescent shyness, we weren't able to recall what she said to us, but we have a clear memory of her smile as she came forward to shake our hands. It was thrilling for each of us to encounter this remarkable woman.

The 1950s were a very repressive and politically black-and-white time; there were no shades of gray. To conform was the ideal and to be different was to be suspect.

Joseph McCarthy, the anti-Communist Republican senator from Wisconsin, ruled the media, spinning horror tales about Reds hiding everywhere, ready to destroy the American way of life. Communists were lurking not only in the government but also in the classroom, taking over the unions, writing books and songs, and making movies. A Red could be your child's piano teacher.

The FBI was knocking on doors, tapping phones, visiting people's workplaces, and always leaving behind a sprinkle of doubt. The imprisonment and execution of the Rosenbergs as Russian spies left young children of Communists unable to comprehend what was really going on and fearful that their parents might be next. I know I was. I would stare at the newspaper pictures of the Rosenberg children and be paralyzed with worry for them and for myself.

There was a boy in the group of kids who went to political studies classes at the Ethical Culture Society who was serious, quiet, and nice-looking. He smelled of Old Spice. In the classes he could speak knowledgeably and intelligently about Marxism, socialism, capitalism, and politics in general. I was flattered by the attention he paid to me, but when the two of us were together, we were too shy to carry on much of a conversation.

If he said he was going to call me, I would frantically read the newspaper in order to have something to say. Many years later I learned that all during that time his father, the head of the American Communist Party, was in jail. No one ever said anything about his family. If you pretend everything is normal, maybe it will be. The fifties were repressive in more ways than one.

The summer of 1958, the summer after the party that drew me out of my shell, I went to Camp Kinderland as a counselor in training, or CIT. Kinderland was a socialist Jewish camp in upstate New York but was open to everyone, as is the socialist credo. To qualify as a CIT you had to be fifteen years old, as many of my new friends were. I was only fourteen, so all I had to do to be eligible was to lie about my age again.

At Camp Kinderland I made good friends and never, ever was referred to as a goy or as an Italian, with the inevitable snide remarks about the Mafia. I had a few good friends in Bryant High School, but I was always aware of being different. I had to work at being part of the culture in the school and convince myself to be interested in what interested

*Camp
Kinderland
— I'm in the
pointy hood
next to Sue
Zuckerman
(far right).*

other students, then work at introducing them to what interested me. With my other friends and with the kids at Kinderland, I could be more spontaneous since we knew we came
from the same left-wing background; that was our bond.

There was no reason to create subdivisions for religions
or ethnicity. We'd been brought up to unite, not separate.
We had in common an outsider status inflicted on us by the
Cold War and our parents' political beliefs. Other than our
seriousness about freedom, justice, equality for all, and
banning the bomb, we were still just a bunch of teenagers.

The big event of the Kinderland summer was a play for
the entire camp put on by the CIT group. The counselors
picked the musical *The Pajama Game*, a recent hit on Broadway, for its theme about a union in a pajama factory seeking

a pay raise and better working conditions for the employ-
ees, as well as for the central love story between Babe, the
head of the union grievance committee, and the plant's new
superintendent, Sid.

I was picked for the role of Babe, and Sid was to be
played by my boyfriend. Fun, except that I cannot carry a
tune. The counselors cum directors must have had second
thoughts about my voice after the first few song rehearsals,
but they did not act on them. I must have been god-awful,
yet everyone was enthusiastic and we had a great time doing
all the work that putting on a stage production entails. I forgot to be afraid of singing in front of people.

The Babe and Sid offstage romance didn't last the summer, however. I don't think it was because I couldn't sing
and he could and I massacred all our love duets—but that
might have contributed somewhat.

When the school year began again, so did the trips to Washington Square on Sundays. My friends and I would meet at Astor Place, then wander off to a coffee shop, a bookshop, or Nedicks, a nondescript hot dog place at Eighth Street and Sixth Avenue, where the painters and Beat writers of the forties and fifties had hung out, to carry on intense conversations about the world we were learning about and how we figured in it. And we made plans to see one another at the next folk concert.

I traveled back and forth on the subway from Queens to Manhattan and did a lot of reading if I was alone. One book that intrigued me was *The God That Failed*, a selection of essays by internationally known writers of the time, including Stephen Spender,

Washington Square Park with friends

André Gide, Ignazio Silone, and Richard Wright, explaining why they quit the Communist Party. The appeal of Communism was the search for a better, more equitable society, but the disillusionment each of these writers experienced was a long, agonizing journey. As an examination of the Cold War and Stalinism by these important thinkers, without the usual rhetoric, the book made an impact.

The fact that these respected intellectuals publicly repudiated their previous beliefs was a blow to the left. Because *The God That Failed* had been so touted and praised by anti-Communists, I felt I was betraying the elders by reading it. Hence I read in secret. In those terrible times of anti-Communist fervor, you were either on one side or the other; there could be no middle ground, at least publicly. Behind the scenes the book was read and discussed by the left, as well.

I was wary of dogma, of black-and-white opinions. In this climate, it wasn't easy for red-diaper babies to raise questions about the Soviet Union and Stalin, since we knew our parents were living within a siege mentality. When the writer Howard Fast left the Communist Party he was denounced by it as a traitor and an opportunist. His book *Spartacus*, about a Roman slave revolt, was made into a Hollywood movie starring Kirk Douglas. My pal George Auerbach, also a red-diaper baby, said that the condemnation of Fast, who had also written *Tony and the Wonderful Door*, a children's book I loved, was bogus. The implication that he was no longer a good writer because he no longer believed in Stalin seemed absurd. As in a comic book, a Big Question Mark suddenly appeared over my head. I began to doubt.

The forbidden had always had an allure for me. Growing up, I remember overhearing my parents whisper the name Carlo Tresca, together with the words *anarchist* and *anti-Communist*. I had no idea who Tresca was, but the fact that he was talked about sotto voce made me never forget his name. He was something illicit, an outlaw; and I was immediately curious. The secrecy surrounding Tresca made him infinitely attractive to me.

It was the same with comic books, which we weren't allowed to read. The babysitter was told never to bring any with her when she came to sit for us—so naturally I had to find out what they were about. Fortunately the other kids in the neighborhood had stacks of comic books in their rooms. Devouring them, I forgot all about Tresca.

I loved looking at *Archie, Superman,* and those mysterious "love comics" that were easy to find in the hidden stash belonging to an older sister of a friend. I would come home from reading comics at other people's apartments and spend hours making up characters and stories and drawing intricate maps of the towns they lived in. I came up with a complicated language, similar to hieroglyphics, for them to "speak." When I showed these to a like-minded playmate, we worked hard to develop the hieroglyphics into a sign language that we used with each other, to the delight of the adults, because we were oh so clever and absolutely quiet for hours.

I also made storybooks in which the main character was always sweet and sensitive yet tended to have some terrible fate befall him or her. My parents found these amusing and seemed to enjoy my developing sense of humor. When *Mad* magazine came out in the early 1950s, I was ready for it. Around that time, my parents' disillusionment with the Soviet Union's version of Communism was cresting. They had also forgotten about the comic book ban.

As for Carlo Tresca, this is what I found out:

Tresca was an Italian who became a well-known labor organizer in America and was an important man fighting for the soul of the Italian American community during the early years of the twentieth century. He published articles and newspapers in an attempt to educate Italian immigrants and all workers to fight for their right to better working conditions. Because he was an anarchist, an anti-Communist, and a foe of big business and the mob, he made many enemies. As a result, he also had few allies. He was murdered in broad daylight at Fifth Avenue and Fifteenth Street in 1943.

The crime was never solved. My parents probably felt they had to speak of him sotto voce because he was anathema to Communists. I like to think that they secretly admired Carlo Tresca and disagreed with the Communist Party line.

In the summer of 1958, the friends I'd met at Kinderland and I heard about plans for a march on Washington, D.C., that fall called Youth March for Integrated Schools. Following the Supreme Court's 1954 decision, *Brown v. Board of Education*, declaring segregation of schools unconstitutional, the question of integration in the South was coming to a head. Governor Orville Faubus of Arkansas and other Southern politicians were denouncing organizations, such

Youth March for Integrated Schools
312 West 125th Street • New York 27, N. Y.

Washington, D. C.
April 18

FREEDOM RIDE
CORE

SIT-IN
DON'T
GIVE IN

MARCH ON WASHINGTON
FOR
JOBS & FREEDOM
AUGUST 28, 1963

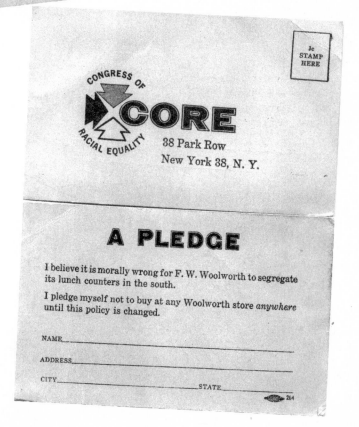

CONGRESS OF RACIAL EQUALITY

CORE

38 Park Row
New York 38, N. Y.

3c
STAMP
HERE

A PLEDGE

I believe it is morally wrong for F. W. Woolworth to segregate its lunch counters in the south.

I pledge myself not to buy at any Woolworth store *anywhere* until this policy is changed.

NAME_____

ADDRESS_____

CITY_____ STATE_____

264

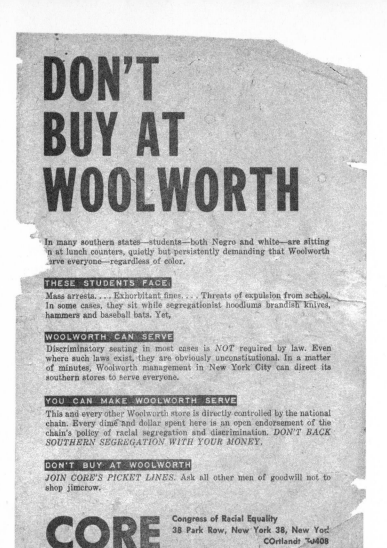

DON'T BUY AT WOOLWORTH

In many southern states—students—both Negro and white—are sitting in at lunch counters, quietly but persistently demanding that Woolworth serve everyone—regardless of color.

THESE STUDENTS FACE:

Mass arrests. . . . Exhorbitant fines. . . . Threats of expulsion from school. In some cases, they sit while segregationist hoodlums brandish knives, hammers and baseball bats. Yet,

WOOLWORTH CAN SERVE

Discriminatory seating in most cases is *NOT* required by law. Even where such laws exist, they are obviously unconstitutional. In a matter of minutes, Woolworth management in New York City can direct its southern stores to serve everyone.

YOU CAN MAKE WOOLWORTH SERVE

This and every other Woolworth store is directly controlled by the national chain. Every dime and dollar spent here is an open endorsement of the chain's policy of racial segregation and discrimination. *DON'T BACK SOUTHERN SEGREGATION WITH YOUR MONEY.*

DON'T BUY AT WOOLWORTH

JOIN CORE'S PICKET LINES. Ask all other men of goodwill not to shop jimcrow.

CORE   Congress of Racial Equality
38 Park Row, New York 38, New York
COrtlandt 7-0408

as the NAACP, that were fighting against segregation, insisting they were really Communist groups. The majority of Americans were in favor of integration of the public schools, however, and the defamation didn't stick. Leaders of various equal rights organizations banded together to announce there would be a demonstration by students in Washington on October 25, 1958. Young people nationwide would travel to the capital to demonstrate their support for the end of segregation in the schools. On Saturdays and sometimes after school during the week some friends and I started working as volunteers for the march.

Bayard Rustin, from the Congress of Racial Equality (CORE), was a coordinator of the march and ran the Harlem headquarters of the organization at 312 West 125th Street. To us, a young group of mainly white student volunteers from left-wing backgrounds, Rustin was an imposing and elegant figure, a taskmaster and an educator. Our jobs were to get signatures on a petition demanding an end to segregation and to help raise money for and spread the word about the upcoming march. At the Harlem headquarters I'd meet up with George Auerbach and the other kids, and we'd break up into groups and choose neighborhoods in which to go knocking on doors.

George and I and a few others decided to go to the theater district and wait at the stage door for Sidney Poitier, who was starring in Lorraine Hansberry's play *A Raisin in the Sun.* When he came out, we ran up to him rattling our cans and explaining our mission. He was gracious, but as he dropped coins in each of our cans, he told us: Oh, man, I have given so much already.

Students from all over the country came to this first youth march on Washington. It was thrilling to be one of ten thousand young people, black and white, who marched from the White House to the Lincoln Memorial. A small delegation led by Harry Belafonte attempted to deliver a petition to President Eisenhower, but they were not successful. The march itself was a success, if only because it inspired all of us who were part of it to continue to work for civil rights. We just knew that the next march would be even bigger and more successful. And the next one, in April 1959, was bigger, and soon there were the Freedom Rides and the sit-ins in the South. By the time the third and most recognized march on Washington was held in August of 1963, there were more than a hundred thousand people. This march, along with Martin Luther King's "I Have a Dream" speech, pushed the agenda of civil rights forever into the national consciousness.

As the civil rights movement gained momentum, my friends and I picketed the nationwide chain store Woolworth's, which had segregated lunch counters in the South. While we marched in front of stores around the city, we handed out information to passersby, informing them of the chain's policy down South and of the sit-ins that were taking place at the lunch counters. We would try to deter potential customers from going in to shop or to eat at any Woolworth's. One Saturday my aunt walked out of a store, mortified that she had crossed a picket line, albeit unwittingly since she had gone in before we showed up. She joined the line for a little while and I felt very proud.

At Bryant High School I eventually discovered a core group of kids who were politically involved with the world around them, and what I perceived as two different worlds suddenly had more in common with each other than I ever expected.

A boy I had known since elementary school was an outsider like me. He was well liked but known as a "fairy nice boy." He played the piano and sang wonderfully. He was smarter than anyone else and was a lot of fun to be with. We were soul mates and ended up going to the senior class prom together. Even though he was nearly a head shorter than me, and queer, we were a great couple.

I began to wear black most of the time and I had my ears pierced at an earring store on West Eighth Street in the Village. After my ears healed I removed the little gold hooks and made a pair of earrings out of copper wire and bits of leather. I cultivated a French accent and used it whenever anyone I didn't know spoke to me or if I was in a store buying something. One day when I was riding home on the bus a young man sat next to me and attempted to start a conversation. I knew he thought I was exotic. This was Queens in the late fifties, after all. Maybe he thought I was French. Maybe *he* was French. I didn't dare use my accent, in case he was. When he stood up to get off at his stop, he smiled at me and said, I could have sworn you were French.

My closest girlfriend outside of the red-diaper baby/Kinderland group was Genie Zeiger, who passed around petitions with me at school and came to picket Woolworth's on Saturdays and to Washington Square on Sundays now and then. She read poetry and listened to folk music, too. We spent a lot of time together at each other's apartments. Her mother was always very welcoming; it never made a difference to her parents what the Rotolo family believed or didn't believe. When my father died, they had a tree planted in Israel in his name.

It was hard for Genie to take a detour from the path of the more middle-of-the-road friends in her Hadassah club, but she was always attracted to the nonconformity of my family. She was intrigued that my mother didn't go to beauty parlors and that my father built our furniture and painted the walls in our apartment different colors. After high school she went away to college but then left to marry and have children. She came to the Village to see me on a school break when I was house-sitting an apartment on Waverly Place, but by then we didn't have much in common anymore. She was living the life of a college girl in upstate New York while I was on my own at the university of Greenwich Village. We found each other again, though, not too many years later.

During the summer of 1956, I had been a mother's helper, or nanny, for the family of the ear doctor my mother worked for. The Rosens lived in Katonah, New York, in a wonderful house with a pool that was constructed to look like a real pond, and filled with water from a nearby spring. Sam and Helen Rosen had dinner parties with many interesting people coming and going, the great Paul Robeson among them. Two years later, after my father's death, Helen invited my mother and me to Robeson's historic concert at Carnegie Hall. We went backstage afterwards and when the physically imposing and charismatic Paul Robeson smiled down at me and shook my hand, which disappeared in his huge one, I was awestruck.

My job that summer was to take care of the Rosens' two grandchildren, a boy and girl. A cook named Odette ran the household. Tall, wiry, probably in her forties, she was funny, warm, and also a bit of a scold. I spent a lot of time with her.

At meals I was expected to sit at the table with the fam-

[High school, 1959]

ily and the company, if there was any, while Odette ate in the kitchen. Her job was to serve each course to each person and clear away the empty plates. Having grown up working class, bohemian, and schooled by my Marxist parents in equality for all, I felt very uncomfortable being waited on. It was beyond my comprehension. To have Odette treat me formally embarrassed me. It wasn't the way things were between us the rest of the time. I would get up from the table in an attempt to help her clear plates and she would say, Sit down, and give me a look.

After dinner Odette and I would usually go for a walk along the quiet lane that circled the houses. I told her I wanted to eat in the kitchen with her since I was not at ease with being treated like a guest. She made fun of me, saying I didn't know my place as a white girl, and had a good laugh. She told me that I'd better make up my mind fast and figure out what color I was and where I belonged in the world.

During the summer of 1959 I had another nanny job, for family friends who had two young girls who were older than the Rosen grandchildren and quite a handful. This family was middle class, and the only hired help was me. There was always something to do, and I was the one to do it. I had no one to share "after hours" with, but at least by then I knew my place as a working white girl.

Leaving Home

During my last year of high school, theater class was my refuge. There was something wonderful about becoming someone else that eliminated my natural shyness. I also liked making scenery. A friend I had met in Kinderland, Sue Zuckerman, lived on Long Island but would cut school and come to the city to go on auditions for plays in Greenwich Village theaters. When she won a part in one, she was over the moon.

Her parents would not let her miss high school, and she had to turn down the part. It was terrible. We decided to do summer stock together the following summer, after high school graduation. We chose the Massapequa Children's Summer Theater, near where Sue lived. I went to live with her family for a month.

In a production of *Peter Pan* I was Tiger Lily, and in *Hansel and Gretel* she played the witch. After a great summer together, she went off to college in the fall, as did all of my close friends. I got a job at a convenience store while I thought about what a loser I was and how scary things were at home. My sister was rarely there and eventually went to live with someone in the Village. My mother was working part-time for Dr. Rosen, but she was drinking an awful lot. I had pretty much been without parental guidance since my father had died. This did not make me wild and carefree. On the contrary, I was always careful and fearful because I knew I had no one to depend on. Now and then in the evenings, my mother would talk about her life, about death, and about philosophical issues. These occasions frightened me profoundly. I felt she was speaking not to me but to my father—or maybe to no one at all.

I felt fragmented; I had no mirror to see myself in a context. It never dawned on me to say anything to anyone about what was going on. What could be said and to whom would I say it?

My mother had had a rough life: At forty-seven she had already been widowed twice and had survived breast cancer. My father had just died of a heart attack, and her first husband had drowned in a freak storm off Boston harbor after she had been married only six months. They had been together with a friend on a small sailboat when the storm struck. Only her husband, who couldn't swim, died.

She was a beautiful woman, with big brown eyes and straight dark hair dramatically pulled back in a bun at her neck. Her name was Maria Teresa, but she was always known as Mary. She was born in 1910 in Boston, the next to the youngest of four surviving children out of eight and the third child that her parents had named Mary. The first Mary had died of diphtheria and the second in a scalding accident. The family had temporarily moved back to Italy to live and the second Mary had died there.

When I was an adult with my own child, my mother lent me a small leather-bound diary her father had written after the death of the first Mary at the age of three. I read it, thinking I would translate it. Both the prose and the handwriting were florid and the content was heartbreaking as he described the devastating effect his daughter's death had had on him. He didn't mention anything about what his wife must have been feeling, however.

The largest emigration of Italians to America began in the late 1880s and continued nonstop into the early part of the twentieth century. The majority of immigrants were un-skilled and uneducated. Italy before Fascism was an agricul-tural society under a monarchy; for the peasant class conditions were little different from those under feudal-ism. Unless you came from a family that had a profession or were part of the aristocracy or royalty, life was hardscrab-ble. This was especially the case in southern Italy and Sicily. Some Italians who emigrated were skilled workers, as was my Sicilian grandfather, or had a profession, as did my ma-ternal grandfather, Sisto Pezzati, from Piacenza in the north of Italy, an area of family farms not far from Milan. He chose to come to America to check out this great new land of op-portunity where jobs were plentiful.

Cesarina and Sisto Pezzati left Italy right after they were married, living initially with his sister in Boston. Sisto was a well-educated man who had studied to be a land surveyor. I believe he worked as a salesman and clerk for his brother-in-law when he first arrived.

After my grandfather Sisto was diagnosed with tubercu-losis, everything changed. He could no longer work, and there were medical bills to pay. The family moved to a less expensive apartment in another neighborhood. And so it went until he died of the disease, when my mother was five. Peter, the oldest child, was thirteen, Josephine nine, and the youngest, Albert, three. Their mother, Cesarina, who unlike their father spoke little English, was left a widow with four children to raise alone.

My mother's stories about the years after her father's death are tales out of Charles Dickens. The family moved from one place to another, always with worse conditions. The sleeping drunks in apartment doorways, the smell of urine in the halls, the Irish kids in the neighborhood chasing down and beating up the Italians. My grandmother took in laundry and cleaned houses. The older boy became the head of the family at thirteen, leaving school and going to work.

My mother and her younger brother went out to the railroad tracks to pick up bits of coal to heat the apartment. They chased after the ice wagon for ice chips to keep the food cold in the icebox, a precursor of the refrigerator. The older sister made soup by boiling water and throwing in bits of vegetables. Polenta, the cornmeal today offered in restaurants as a refined dish, was what they lived on. My mother was never able to eat it later in life as a result.

The family went from relative respectability to grinding poverty in a time when Italians were lower in the pecking order than the Irish, who had suffered horribly when they first arrived as immigrants and were now finally able to take it out on somebody deemed even lower than they were. So it seems to go. Along with polenta, my mother had trouble digesting the Irish.

The older brother and sister were able to remember a better time. They could pass on their father's love of literature and the arts to their younger siblings—at least they had that. Their big brother taught them to recite Dante and Petrarch, to help them understand that they came from a great culture. That saved them all, even though they each took it in different directions and came to different conclusions. They were, and remained, a volatile bunch.

My mother and her younger brother, Albert, were very close their whole lives and eventually joined the American Communist Party to fight for the underdog. The oldest, Peter, in addition to gaining success as a portrait painter for the Boston upper classes—he was able to earn a living and support a family as a painter his entire life—believed in Mussolini and the Fascist idea of cultural supremacy. The other sister was a liberal and a practicing Catholic. Their mother, Cesarina, was calm and even-tempered. Despite a very difficult life, she always managed to maintain relative harmony at family gatherings. Fortunately all four siblings agreed on one thing—the love and respect and fierce loyalty they had for their mother. This was the unshakeable bond that united them, and in her presence they did their best to keep the peace.

Cesarina was the daughter of a peasant family, a delicate and beautiful girl. My mother said that Sisto's family did not approve of their marriage initially because he was educated and had "prospects" and therefore shouldn't marry a farm girl.

A young farmer who lived nearby named Ludovico Rossi had also courted her, but he lost her to the man with prospects, education, and what she said she admired most—his intelligence. Many lifetimes later, when Rossi found Cesarina in America, they were both widowed with children. He wanted to marry her, but she refused him; she had to *sistemare i figli*, wait until all her children were settled. It was a mentality left over from the old country: She was responsible for her children and had to see each one of them established with husbands, wives, professions, homes of their own, before she could think of doing something for herself. When she was sixty-five, she finally accepted his proposal and went to live with him on his dairy farm outside of Torrington, Connecticut. Pop Rossi was the only grandfather any of Cesarina's grandchildren knew, and we loved him dearly, as did all four of her children.

After my father's death, my mother saw no light at the end of the tunnel—the future held no prospects—not then anyway. I couldn't talk to her friends, sister, or brothers about her drinking and the stress I felt; they had their own lives, children, jobs, and troubles. I would not have told them in any case. And I never said a word to my friends, ever. We all complained about our mothers, but I didn't know how to complain about my situation—so alien from the typical bitching a teenager does.

The solution for an escape came about rather surprisingly. My mother's younger brother, to whom she was close, had left his wife for another woman. I went to live with my aunt Val, who was to become his ex-wife, and my cousin, who was a few years younger than me. They lived at 158th Street and Riverside Drive in Harlem. Val was originally from Seattle and had been a Rockette at Radio City Music Hall. She was a beautiful, willowy blonde, and sang in a full, clear soprano. She and my father, who had a baritone voice like Ezio Pinza's, would sing together at family gatherings in the days when things weren't so bad. They sang everything from show tunes to opera, as the other grown-ups argued

politics and the kids drank the wine left in the bottom of
the adults' glasses. That was a long time ago.

I found a job as a clerk at the Book-of-the-Month Club
way downtown on Hudson Street—my introduction to the
nine-to-five world. I worked in a big classroomlike space
with rows of women sitting at typewriters with earphones
on. All day long they typed letters dictated to them over a
machine called a Dictaphone. There was a supervisor who
sat at a big desk in the front, where the teacher in a classroom would be.

My job was to collect the finished letters with addressed envelopes and add whatever inserts were necessary.
These letters would be put in a big basket to be picked up by
the mail clerk. My desk was at the head of the classroom opposite the supervisor/teacher's desk. Next to me was a tall
gray metal closet filled with pamphlets and folders advertis-
ing the books offered by the club. I taped to the closet
doors, outside and in, Book-of-the-Month Club advertise-
ments that had reproductions of paintings or photographs I
liked.

The women typists, who were creeping up in age and
had been working at the company for years, thought I was
very daring and warned me that the higher-ups would disap-
prove. They wanted to help me learn the ropes and offered
to teach me to type. I was like a pet for them, and I relished
the attention. I would make drawings, and they would tape
them to their desks. The place was looking less austere.

One day the supervisor told me with some reluctance
that I had to take down the pictures, or at least the ones on

the outside of the closet, and then keep the doors closed. I agreed, but after a while I stopped closing the closet doors. Nothing more was ever said. One of the women told me to forget learning to type (I had never even considered it; filing was much easier) and go to art school instead.

It was a long commute to my job by subway from one end of Manhattan to the other, but it was easier than the tedious subway and bus trip from Queens. Weekends in the Village—which didn't involve coming home to my mother's rages or to her profound, low-voiced soliloquies—were also a lot more bearable. I think my mother was relieved to see me go. She needed to be by herself and sort things out.

Compared with my mother, Val was in great shape, and my cousin and I had fun together. Their apartment—with only one bedroom, where my cousin and I slept—was on a low floor in a large, ornate apartment building. The living room had a big, freestanding floor-to-ceiling bookcase that served as a wall to create a bedroom for Val. The place was fine, but it was overrun with cockroaches. When you turned on a light, the kitchen seemed to liquefy as the roaches scurried away en masse. They didn't mind the cold, either, living comfortably in the refrigerator.

My friend Pete Karman had a car and would often come pick me up in the evening. He was like an older brother at a time when I was very much in need of that kind of relationship. We would drive up and down the West Side Highway for hours on end talking about everything and anything and listening to the car radio, which picked up stations as far away as West Virginia late at night. Weekends we would

head for the Village and sometimes meet up with my sister
and go to parties or music clubs. As a newspaper reporter,
he read a lot, remembered everything, and liked to talk. He
was a big part of my schooling back then. I have always been
grateful to him.

My mother was doing better. We had a few normal telephone conversations, and although I don't remember any details, I am sure we saw each other at Christmas. She had been working on a plan to move to Italy and since I was still a minor she would take me with her. It seemed like an interesting idea. I wasn't planning on having a career as a clerk at the Book-of-the-Month Club, and all the people I used to hang around with were away at college. I applied for a passport and gave notice that I would be leaving my job around mid-March 1961. My mother had friends in Rome who would help us begin a new life. I hadn't lived with her in a while, but I wasn't overly worried because living in Rome would be a completely new situation. She seemed to be her old self again, and even though that wasn't necessarily reassuring, at least as her old self she was familiar.

She was still living in the Queens apartment and I said I would come and stay to sort through my things and pack away what I wanted to keep, which would be stored at the home of a relative on Long Island who had offered space in her basement. But when I got home, to my shock my mother had already gone through everything and had gotten rid of things I wasn't ready to part with. You just could not trust her, really. After she died one of her oldest friends said of her: Mary was a great friend to be with because she was entertaining and fun, but she wouldn't be there for you. You would be there for her. She was my good friend, but not a best friend.

My mother did not spare the rod, especially with my sister, who challenged her. I watched and learned that survival meant silence. I learned where to and how to hide myself for protection. Once when I objected to something or other, she said, No, don't you start. Not you, too.

I had nightmares about her in her red bathrobe, black hair flying about her face as she hurled her rage at us.

No one is ever just one thing, though. My mother had a magnetic personality, intelligence, beauty, and convictions. She was a great storyteller and had many friends who adored her. I always understood and forgave her. From early on, within the turmoil of our family, I had the temperament most similar to that of my quiet, thoughtful father. My mother and sister were more volatile and often entangled with each other. After his death I was heir to his role as peacemaker, although I was hardly up to the task. Still, it was better than succumbing to chaos. As the years went by, however, I began to feel more and more like the English Prime Minister Neville Chamberlain before the outbreak of World War II.

As we got closer to the date in April when we were to leave on a passenger ship bound for Italy, I had a dream that was very perfunctory: we could not get on the boat. Something was wrong and we weren't able to board.

Toward the end of March my mother and I drove to my grandparents' farm in Connecticut, where we stayed a few days before continuing on to Boston to say good-bye to the rest of the family. Everyone felt it was the right choice for my mother to live in Rome and an excellent opportunity for me. We had a nice sendoff. My mother was relaxed and in good spirits. After passing a tollbooth on our way back to New York City, I had a vision—there is no other way to put it. I saw in front of us the little gray Renault car we were riding in. I watched us in our car, clear as a bell, driving ahead of ourselves on the highway. The sight gave me a very unsettled feeling, because we looked so small and vulnerable. But after a minute it was gone, and the road in front of me returned to normal.

It was a long drive from Boston to New York. We had left early in the day in clear weather and now it was heading toward dusk, with a light rain falling. I must have dozed off, and when I woke up I heard a voice saying, Just cut her clothes off. Just cut them.

Through what seemed like dirty eyeglasses, I could make out someone wearing a mask, peering into my face. I remember thinking that I didn't really like the pants I was wearing, but I was sorry about the sweater. And then I thought of something my aunt Val had laughingly said to me when I showed her the red satin bra I had bought: You better think about where you are going when you wear that. If you're in an accident, someone might get the wrong idea. I wasn't wearing the bra that day.

We had been heading south on the Hutchinson River Parkway in a lot of traffic with low visibility. A woman driving a big white Cadillac had missed her exit and decided to back up and across four lanes of highway to return to it. She never saw us, in our little gray Renault, and my mother never saw her. Now we were in a hospital in the Bronx lucky to be alive since the Renault was crushed like an accordion. Back then, in 1961, there were no seat belts. My mother's kneecap had smashed into the steering wheel post and she needed an operation to have her kneecap removed. She had a small crescent-shaped cut on her forehead. I had crashed into the side window of the passenger seat and my right eyelid was lacerated. I couldn't move my left side and we both had broken ribs and concussions. I later learned that the young doctor in the emergency room that night had stitched the area around my eye together by matching eyebrow hairs.

I was ready to be sent home after three or four days wearing a neck brace and a bandage over an eye, which I later covered with a black patch. My mother was still in the hospital recovering from the knee operation and in a full leg cast. I went to stay with the Ehrenbergs, family friends who lived on the Upper West Side of Manhattan, and my mother eventually moved in with friends who lived a few blocks away.

Mike Ehrenberg and my mother had met as teenagers in Boston. He was the friend on the sailboat when her first husband drowned. Our families grew up close; their children and my sister and I were part of the red-diaper baby bond that originated in Sunnyside, Queens.

After many trips to specialists and neurologists, I was told I had suffered severe whiplash, but because I was asleep and my body relaxed at the moment of impact, my spinal cord hadn't been damaged. I was extremely lucky though I had to wear the neck brace and go to physical therapy. My eye was another matter: the cuts had severed nerves that might or might not grow back, and I could neither open nor close my eye all the way. The thirty stitches across my eyelid and eyebrow would leave a scar that would fade over time, but once again I had been lucky, because my vision was not affected. A half-lidded eye with a jagged scar made me look dangerous in a monster-movie way. And a black eye patch wasn't a bad accessory.

Annie, Mike's wife, was working at the Metropolitan Opera Guild and she could get free tickets. Deciding it was time I left the house, she gave me a ticket to see a matinee performance of Alban Berg's *Wozzeck*. She knew I was self-conscious about going out in a neck brace and eye patch, so she lent me a long, flowing chiffon scarf and helped me wrap it elegantly around the brace as she pushed me out the door. I will never forget *Wozzeck*. I was an Italian kid brought up on Puccini and Verdi. I never knew an opera could sound like that! To my ears, accustomed to the melodic drama of lyric opera, this music sounded like moaning; it was guttural and slightly menacing and it was thrilling beyond words.

Thanks to Annie, the ice was broken and I began venturing out beyond visits to the physical therapist and to my mother a few blocks away, miserable about being immobile in a full leg cast for six months. She told me that she never lost consciousness during the accident and would forever be haunted by the sight of me crumpled in the car with my face covered in blood. I know she didn't mean it that way, but I felt as if I had done it to her on purpose.

Fortunately Pete called and took me for more car rides and eventually, when I looked better, to Gerde's Folk City.

After Effects

The plan to move to Italy was put on a back burner and I soon forgot about it. My eye had improved, and I had graduated from a neck brace to a foam cervical collar that I wore to alleviate the pain from a pinched nerve. A lawsuit was in the works, but there was no way to know how long it would take to sort it out. A great deal depended on whether the insurance companies involved would settle or go to trial. The outcome seemed obvious, but the companies still had to duke it out.

My mother's lawyer came up with a strategy that he felt would benefit me, the passenger. He suggested I sue my mother (in actuality, her insurance company) in a separate suit. We'd go after the insurance company of the woman driving the white Cadillac in a separate legal action.

This scheme was legally possible because, although a minor, I was living on my own and was financially independent of my mother at the time of the accident. An innocent young passenger on the witness stand with a scarred eye and nearly broken neck would pull on the heartstrings of a jury, said the lawyer. And he insisted that my separate suit would not mean that my mother was at fault. This was a common tactic, he assured us, used in civil suits that involved insurance companies suing each other.

No one liked this notion, particularly my mother, who felt horribly guilty about the accident. But in the end she deferred to the professional. Didn't the lawyer handle things like this all the time? About a year or more later, the case went to civil trial. During the voir dire process,

each prospective juror was asked whether he or she objected to a daughter's suing her mother. It was not legally
permissible to say that it was really about suing her insurance company. My mother and I had to sit there and listen
to the majority of them respond with disgust. One man even
made an indignant What is this world coming to? speech for
the occasion.

Uh-oh. I was put on the witness stand to describe the
pain from the pinched nerve and the various effects of the
whiplash, which limited neck movement and sapped my
overall endurance and strength. The cross-examining
lawyer stunned me by saying that none of that seemed to
hamper my ability to participate in political protests in
Washington, D.C., and elsewhere, to work at places like
CORE and as a waitress carrying trays, to attend art classes
at the Art Students League and the School of Visual Arts,
and to live the life of a beatnik in Greenwich Village (hippies hadn't been invented yet). The cultural divide of the
1960s was already evident.

In the end I was to receive something like $7,000 and
my mother about half that, once the two lawyers had de-
ducted their fee of one-third from both of us. This provoked
a comment from my mother about the possibility of there
being some truth in the stereotype of lawyers as sharks. The
check arrived sometime in the fall of 1964, more than three
years after the accident.

Though my mother did not want to move back to Queens,
she changed her mind once she was out of the leg cast.

Many things needed doing. Eventually she planned to move into Manhattan and possibly share an apartment with her brother, Val's soon-to-be ex-husband. It was a scary time because she had no money except a small sum from a life insurance policy; she no longer worked full-time for Dr. Rosen. I have no idea how either of us got by. I was seventeen and overwhelmed by my life, so I did my best not to think about anything. My escape was to read books and to draw. But I needed to earn a living.

It was easy to find a job as a waitress or what was known as a girl Friday, which meant you were a girl and you could file, answer telephones, type, make coffee, and run errands for the male boss. Before I found the job at the Book-of-the-Month Club in the fall of 1960, I had searched the want ads for the most mindless jobs I could find. I remember getting work for two weeks in a dingy warehouse somewhere in Midtown counting coupons that people had mailed in for rebates. I knew I couldn't go that route again and still have a will to live.

After I left the apartment of my surrogate family, the Ehrenbergs, on West End Avenue, I stayed at my sister Carla's apartment on Perry Street. It was a small railroad flat that was fine for short stays. We had a tempestuous relationship at times, and neither of us wanted to hedge our bets and live together in a small space for an indefinite period. She could be bossy like an older sister, but she was generous and protective, too. I was welcome there until I found something of my own.

As it turned out, a couple my sister knew who had an apartment on Waverly Place just west of Washington Square

were going to England for a few months and wanted someone to house-sit. It was perfect. The Waverly Place apartment was within walking distance of every bookstore,
coffeehouse, and music club in the Village. Whatever job I
had during the day gave way to nights with good music and
good talk. I began to accumulate some possessions again.

I shopped along Fourth Avenue, at the many secondhand bookstores with great selections and great prices, and
in Midtown, at a record store somewhere in the Forties with
bins and bins of long-playing records in plain white card-

Artwork on a blank album

board covers with a hole punched in the upper corner. It was possible to find all kinds of music at unbelievable prices. I bought all of the Harry Smith recordings of American old-time folk music, one at a time. I would paint or draw my own cover art.

Now all I needed was to find a way to earn my living, something more solid than the odd freelance jobs I'd taken at strange places around the Village that never paid much or involved seedy characters doing shady things. Or maybe that was just my imagination.

I answered the telephone for a man who ran a mail order business and was a follower of Wilhelm Reich, the Austrian scientist and psychologist who believed that the cause of all sickness (physical and psychological) was failing to achieve true orgasm. Reich claimed to have discovered an energy called orgone that was the "basic life-stuff of the universe." He developed and marketed something called the orgone box that could cure all ills if you sat in it for a certain amount of time each day. The man I was working for had an orgone box somewhere in the back of his home office that he would go into on lunch breaks. One day he came out wearing only a towel and walked by me, letting it slip slowly to the floor as he passed. I was out the door in no time.

I found work making puppet body parts in a loft near Delancey Street for Peter Schumann, master puppet maker and artist, who'd just started his Bread and Puppet Theater. A very sincere and committed man, Schumann was a true visionary. At that time he was using a product called celastic to make the heads and hands for his oversized puppets. Similar to papier-mâché, celastic was mixed with an acetone solvent and layered in strips over a mold until it hardened. When it dried, it was lightweight and very durable—perfect for theatrical use. The smell was intoxicating and probably toxic.

We worked hard but happily. The pay was nothing much, but living in New York City in those years was very cheap and working with Peter and other artists was certainly worthwhile. Unfortunately the work ended when the puppets and props project was completed. Not long after, Peter moved the Bread and Puppet Theater to Vermont.

Sometime in the spring I began working at the New York City office of CORE. It was a markedly different time from two or three years earlier, when we were picketing the Woolworth stores around the city, protesting their policy of segregated lunch counters in the South, and collecting money and signatures door to door for the marches on Washington for Jobs and Freedom and the Integration of Schools.

It was 1961, the year of the first Freedom Rides and the expansion of sit-ins at segregated lunch counters. Pure, unadulterated white racism was soon to be splattered all over the media as the violence against civil rights workers escalated. White people were looking at themselves and what their history had wrought, like a domestic animal having its face shoved into its own urine.

Exposed for all to see was the ugly and misshapen reality of two societies, separate and unequal. Voices coming to the fore to speak out on these things were many and em-

anated from everywhere. Cases were being brought before
the Supreme Court that would change the laws of the land
and the culture of the country.

The New York CORE office was at 38 Park Row in downtown Manhattan, across from City Hall Park. Facing the
park from the opposite side on Broadway, always in view as
I crossed the park on my way to work, stood one of New
York City's architectural beauties, the Woolworth Building,
built in 1913.

My recollection of the office itself was of a not very big
main room at the end of a dark corridor with a few dusty
windows on the far wall that looked out on the narrow
street below. Desks and chairs were set up wherever there
was a need for them. I think there might have been only one
room with a door, which was used as a private space separate
from the main office.

Meetings and consultations took place spontaneously.
It was a heady time. It was necessary to keep track of the sit-
ins and the Freedom Rides in order to get information to
the news media. Staff made fund-raising calls and organized
fund-raising events. I worked with a few others sending out
mailings and cataloging the donations that were coming
in. Those cumbersome old black telephones rang off the
hook, lights flashing on the row of buttons below the round
rotary dial. CORE field-workers were calling in from all
over, reporting on the latest beating or the latest actions.
The violence in the South was terrifying; all of us working
in the New York office were in a constant state of tension.
The media weren't that interested initially in the random
acts of violence aimed at civil rights workers, but when the

Greyhound bus carrying the first group of black and white Freedom Riders was firebombed in Anniston, Alabama, a rest stop on the way to Birmingham, the press came to full attention.

Jim Peck, a committed pacifist who had worked since the 1940s with James Farmer, the founder of CORE, was on another Freedom Ride bus when it arrived in Birmingham, Alabama, on Sunday, May 14, 1961. Peck was a tall, thin, middle-aged white man. When he and the others sat down at the Trailways lunch counter in the bus station, all hell broke loose. A group of white men ripped them from their stools and savagely beat them with lead pipes as the crowd, spewing verbal abuse, egged the attackers on. There was no police presence at all. It was Mother's Day and the police were all visiting their mothers, was the explanation given by the local police chief.

With the scene captured on film, the story went around the world. Over many years we have become accustomed to seeing such things, but at that time it had a chilling effect. Whites were bound to pay attention now that a white man was in serious condition after being viciously beaten by a mob.

On Monday the CORE office was in a frenzy of activity. With everyone now frantic with concern over the condition of the Freedom Riders and the future of the rides, the climate at the office was altered. You just knew that the civil rights movement had gone to another level—at last attention would be paid. So it was, and the rest is history.

Civil rights was on everyone's mind. It was part of the conversation of our times, along with the fear of nuclear war and the recent revolution in Cuba. Hope lay with John F. Kennedy as the new president, the first one to be born in the twentieth century, who might really do something about the horrors happening in the South and bring a sense of vitality and hope to a country that seemed to be stagnating. There was a fascination with Fidel Castro and Che Guevara, who had made the revolution in Cuba and were challenging the monoliths of the Cold War, both the United States and the Soviet Union, with their dashing, rebellious thumb-in-your-eye-plague-on-both-your-houses behavior. Not to mention the contrasting philosophies of Martin Luther King's nonviolence and Malcolm X's militance. But nothing was ever publicly discussed about women, black or white, being at the bottom of the pecking order of society. That would come later.

During the height of the civil rights era Bob wrote, among other songs, "The Lonesome Death of Hattie Carroll," "The Death of Emmett Till," "The Ballad of Medgar Evers," and, of course "Blowing in the Wind," which became a kind of anthem. These songs are not just newspaper stories rewritten in rhyme; they speak to the human condition, and to human conditioning. That makes them timeless.

I met Bob Dylan on a hot day at the end of July 1961 at a marathon folk concert at Riverside Church in upper Manhattan, a big, all-day music festival organized to launch a radio station dedicated to folk music. Most of the musicians from the Village clubs were scheduled to play or to be part of the audience. It was a big deal. Dave Van Ronk, the Greenbriar Boys, Tom Paxton, Cynthia Gooding, and Bob Dylan were just a few of the people in the lineup. Pete had a car and drove a group of us uptown. Ramblin' Jack Elliott also performed that day. Jack was already a legendary troubadour, the first to follow in Woody Guthrie's footsteps before Bob Dylan came onto the scene. In fact, he had a reputation as "the son of Woody Guthrie" since he'd traveled around with Woody for some time and reproduced his style flawlessly. Since he and Bob had a good rapport, some friends called Bob "the son of Jack."

In addition to being a musician, Jack was a great storyteller, and he was in good form that day, regaling us with tales of his wanderings all over the United States and Europe. It was a very warm summer day, and we'd dressed accordingly. I was wearing a simple shift dress with thigh-high slits I'd recently made. Jack looked around and declared that his ambition after death was to come back as a sidewalk so women could walk all over him. Better than being walked all over by women in the manner he suffered in his life now, he said.

Whenever I looked around, Bobby was nearby. I thought he was oddly old-time looking, charming in a scraggly way. His jeans were as rumpled as his shirt and even in the hot weather he had on the black corduroy cap he always wore. He made me think of Harpo Marx, impish and approachable, but there was something about him that broadcast an intensity that was not to be taken lightly.

Though I'd seen Bob play at Gerde's in a duo with Mark Spoelstra, I was more aware of him when he was playing backup harp for other performers. I'd noticed him more then but didn't much think about it.

We started flirting and talking backstage at Riverside Church early in the day and didn't stop until the day was done. He was funny, engaging, intense, and he was persistent. These words completely describe who he was throughout the time we were together; only the order of the words would shift depending on mood or circumstance. If I drew a portrait of him, it would consist of words morphing into different shapes and sizes. He was not linear; he was quirky and jumpy, receptive to what was around him. As inexperienced as I was in the ways of love, I felt a strong attraction to this character. It was as if we knew each other already; we just needed time to get better acquainted. And so we did over the next four years.

After the marathon concert was over and the musicians were packing up their gear, tired but never too tired to party, word went out quickly that there was a gathering not too far from Riverside Church at the apartment of one of the folksingers and that is where everyone headed.

By then, Bob and I were pretty much glued to each other. When we needed a lift, it was for us as a couple, plus his guitar. Our private little world was taking shape.

As for the folk music radio station at Riverside Church, I don't know what became of it. Oscar Brand and Cynthia Gooding hosted the only two radio shows for the growing folk music scene in New York City. An appearance on these shows was a must for any ambitious folksinger. In a very short time, Bob Dylan got on both.

Riverside Radio Broadcasts All-Day Folk Music Program

By PETE KARMAN

A brimming potpourri of live folk music was served up to New Yorkers on Saturday when WRVR-FM, Riverside Radio, broadcast 12 hours of uninterrupted "singing and picking."

The station, the city's newest, is the voice of Riverside Church, 120th St. and Riverside Drive. The all-day folk music program was part of a campaign to return live, spontaneous radio to the estimated 7,000,000 FM listeners in the city.

THE FOLK FESTIVAL began at 9 a.m. with a "Panorama of Folk Music in New York," including taped visits to the "New Lost City Ramblers," Pete Seeger, a Washington Square Sunday songfest, and a night club that features folk music. These, and a discussion of present-day folk songs by a group of experts were the only pre-recorded portions of the program.

From noon on, the spotlight focused on fresh young folk talent, with a small army of ballad singers and instrumentalists parading across the stage of the church auditorium to perform before an appreciative studio audience and radio listeners.

The festival also demonstrated the wide variety and scope of folk music. Kenneth S. Goldstein, recording executive, called the program "A spectrum of different talents and music broad enough to offer something to everyone." Whole portions were given over to the blues, ballads and international folk songs.

Bob Yellin, banjo virtuoso of the "Greenbriar Boys," and Israel Young, of the Folklore Center, served as hosts. Yellin also performed.

John Cohen and Roger Sprung, both of noted folk trios, illustrated the old-fashioned Southern banjo style of "Cripple Creek" and "Old Joe Clark." Paul Cadwell and Sandy Bull, an old master and a young prodigy, offered intricate, deftly turned classical banjo pieces, while Yellin electrified the audience with his rendering of "Rawhide" a fast "bluegrass" number.

Performer at folk festival.

JAZZ AUTHOR Len Kunstadt emceed the blues portion, introducing singers Bob Fox, Bruce Langohorne, Dave Van Ronk and the Rev. Gary Davis. Every facet of the blues was displayed—city, rough country, work songs and commercial.

A nostalgic highpoint arrived when Victoria Spivey, former vocalist with Louis Armstrong, King Oliver and other jazz greats, teamed with W. C. Handy Jr., to perform his late father's classic, "St. Louis Blues."

Folksinger Cynthia Gooding was "international" hostess, introducing Greek and Middle Eastern melodies performed by singer Sahila Tekneci and instrumentalists George Mgrdichian and Thomas Tnthanasion.

Other young and often unheralded performers were heard. Just returned from five years in Europe where he was called the "most American" of U. S. folksingers, Rambling Jack Elliot, a New York-born, Western-bred singer, offered cowboy and outdoor tunes. Bob Dylan, of Gallup, N. M., played the guitar and harmonica simultaneously, and with rural gusto.

MANY of the audience sat through the entire 12 hours with undimmed pleasure. Often they broke into laughter at the antics of the performers. Listeners were urged throughout the day to come down to the church and join the fun.

Directors for Riverside Radio were Charles Dismukes and Virginia Riffaterre, assisted by some of the leading folk authorities in the country. Musicologists Alan Lomax and Moses Asch helped to prepare the show and others helped with auditions.

For WRVR, the purpose was to launch their venture into live, different programming offering music, live drama and discussion to suit all tastes. Later this month, another all-day session is scheduled for chamber and solo classical music. The performers will again be little-known but talented young people.

WRVR began broadcasting in January on the last open FM frequency in New York, 106.7, in studios newly built inside the vast complex of Riverside Church. The transmitting tower stands atop the church spire, 392 feet high, and the transmitter is the most powerful allowed.

Non-profit and non-commercial, it is operated on a special grant from the church on an experimental basis.

Pete Karman's report on the Riverside folk concert

After Bobby and I met at Riverside Church in July and slowly started getting to know each other, I was hesitant and avoided giving him a definite answer about where and when we would next meet. But that didn't last long. Initially we'd find each other in the evening at Gerde's or one of the other clubs and gathering places around the Village. When I wasn't working, we would spend afternoons together wandering here and there, engrossed in conversation.

At the Museum of Modern Art, I took him to see Picasso's *Guernica* and other much-loved paintings; then we'd sit outside in the sculpture garden and talk some more. Poetry, philosophy, art, and the horrors and injustices in the world—very earnest we were. He was also very funny and we made each other laugh. I felt good around him and I liked him sticking close by me or watching me from across a room. But I also liked that he could go inside himself so thoroughly and so completely that there was nothing else around but the music he was hearing in his head or the thoughts crossing his mind. He just disappeared for a spell. I admired his ability, his confidence, to do whatever he needed to do whenever he felt the need to do it.

He would withdraw anywhere at any time. It could happen in a noisy room full of people or when it was just the two of us alone together. I would observe him mentally go away and then come back. He didn't have to be present all the time. There was something so true about that that I did not feel excluded.

We discovered how much we had in common, including a mutual need for a comfortable place away from the chaos of life. We found in each other a kind of safe haven. Yet trouble between us slowly grew out of his facility for not telling the truth. The fact that he was evasive and secretive with me eventually created a rift. We were so very close, yet I felt insecure in not being able to trust him completely. He was vague about where he came from but open about anything that intrigued him. He was out and about collecting experiences, soaking up life right now in the present. Nobody was that bothered by or interested in where anyone came from, unless it was the topic at hand. Bobby wove tales and embellished on the truth, telling good stories, moving them along entertainingly. This was not untypical of anyone in that bohemian atmosphere and at the age we were, except that some of the tales he wove were out of sync with a previously woven one.

The sad story he told of being abandoned at a young age in New Mexico and then going to live with a traveling circus didn't jibe with his stories of growing up in Duluth. It became a running joke in a way—what would be the next version? There were suspicions about that Welsh last name, but nobody really gave a shit. At the end of the day, a good story was a good story. For Bob, where he came from held no sway on the young man he was becoming.

But as he became more known around the Village and beyond, interviewers and industry types asked questions and expected honest and coherent answers. He was on guard. His paranoia was palpable. It was as if he expected someone to show up and blow his cover and expose him. When we lived together, he didn't want people to just drop by unless he invited them himself.

When we met he was staying at different places and sleeping on couches. I was still house-sitting on Waverly Place, but that would end soon. We were both nomads with no fixed address. After he got a rave review in the *New York Times* in September, things changed for him. He got more paying work, for starters. And then Columbia Records signed him, delivering the first heady whiffs of fame. At last some decent money was in the offing, and he began looking for an apartment of his own. He went to see a few and then he called me to come check out a place he'd found on West Fourth Street.

161 West Fourth Street was a small four-story building just west of Sixth Avenue. The Door Store, a place that sold affordable unfinished furniture, occupied the ground floor, and O'Henry's, a relatively expensive Village restaurant with Tiffany lamps, oak tables and chairs, and sawdust artfully strewn around the floor, was down the street on the corner. Allan Block's sandal shop, the absolute best place for handmade leather sandals anywhere, and the Music Inn, an impossibly cluttered store that sold every kind of musical instrument ever made in the entire world, were just up the street. Allan Block played the fiddle, and folk musicians hung out at his store to jam the way they did at Izzy Young's Folklore Center a few blocks away on MacDougal Street. If one of them didn't have an instrument with him, he could always borrow something to strum or bang on at the Music Inn right next door. Directly across the street was a local

eatery called the Bagel where the cook worked in the window grilling hamburgers over a roaring flame. The burgers were charred on the outside, rare in the center, and served on crusty bread. There was a narrow counter with just a few stools and maybe two tiny tables on the opposite side. The place was small, dark, and dingy, but the food was good and the cook friendly. We went there often.

The apartment was a walk-up on the top floor of the building. The woman Bob rented it from was asking a nominal fee for the furnishings, and since it wasn't very big she didn't have much in it other than a bed, an armchair, and some crudely built shelves. The minuscule kitchen was against one wall with a bamboo curtain on a track in the ceiling that pulled across to hide it. She was leaving a few plates, glasses, and a pot or two. He paid her.

There was a tiny bedroom behind the main room and one closet that was to the left of the entrance door, which faced the bathroom. The floor was hardwood, but it was painted with a gray deck paint often used by landlords and tenants alike in old buildings to make the worn floors look better. The place was cozy and full of daylight, hot in summer and cold in winter. It faced the back of the building and overlooked an unkempt garden behind the pizza place in the adjacent building. A constant smell of overcooked tomato sauce wafted up through the windows. Because the bed took up the whole room, Bob would move it into the main room and put the couch—just a foam cushion on a wood platform with throw pillows that someone had given him—into the bedroom.

After a while he bought a secondhand black-and-white

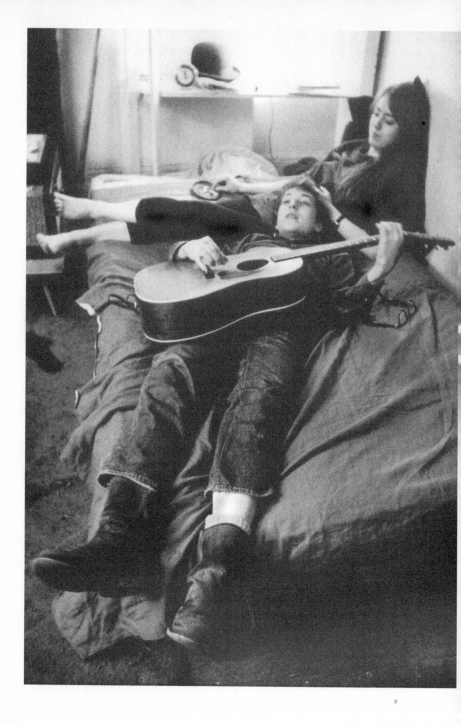

TV that was encased in a wood cabinet, a record player, and a radio from a guy named Francis who had an electronics shop on the corner of Tenth Street and Seventh Avenue South. The TV never worked very well, so Bob took it out of the cabinet and used the wood to build a decent coffee table and better shelves.

Francis was a neighborhood fixture, an electrician who could fix anything. His shop was in the basement of an apartment building and he spent time sitting out on the stoop working on something while watching the street. Whatever inventory he had—a radio, a TV, a turntable, a clock, a coffeemaker, you name it—it plugged in. Nothing had a battery, let alone a rechargeable battery, which probably didn't exist back then. And most of his inventory was secondhand, stuff he had repaired. He stockpiled anything that was hopelessly broken and scavenged it for parts. I don't think he had anything brand-new, and if he did have something it probably fell off a truck. The place was like a minigarage, with most of his stock on the floor or on rickety shelves. He had a huge pile of rabbit ear TV antennas off in a corner. If a customer came in complaining that a TV purchased from him didn't work, Francis would untangle an antenna from the pile and say, Take this and see if it doesn't solve the problem.

Once when Bob came back from a trip he brought me a battery-run portable clock radio not much bigger than a pack of cigarettes. It was a new product and at the time an unusual one. When the clock stopped working, I took it to Francis and he marveled at it. He sent me to a hardware store for a battery. There the clerks passed it around, puzzling over it. One of them put in a new battery, but it must have been the wrong voltage because now the radio didn't work, either. I think I ended up giving it to Francis.

$\mathcal{B}$ob and I had been talking about living together when he found an apartment of his own, but I could not officially move in with him until after my eighteenth birthday in November. There had been many discussions and much speculation about my moving in. Terri Thal and Dave Van Ronk were the oracles. I was underage and Bob was not; therefore he could be charged with something or other with a minor, they said gravely. But he wasn't twenty-one yet. We were both minors in that case and I would have to wait until I was twenty-one for us to be able to live together—eons away. Marriage was way too serious an option, not to be trifled with at our age. Once it was established that at eighteen I would be safely legal, all was well, and within a month or so I would be able to move in. To be on the safe side, Terri suggested, I should wait one day past my birthday.

My mother and her soon-to-be husband Fred, a humanities professor, had sublet a penthouse apartment in the Village, at 1 Sheridan Square. Fred had been in the navy and he must have looked good in the uniform, with his clear blue eyes and refined Anglo-Saxon demeanor. My mother's brother Al had introduced her to Fred, the father of the woman for whom he'd left his wife. Al thought it would be good for my mother, a widow, to meet him since he was also adjusting to life after a recent divorce. Or maybe Al just wanted the new woman in his life to meet someone from his family. In any case, the matchup worked out. Fred got on well with my mother. They began spending time together. He was very gentlemanly: he lit her cigarette, helped her with her coat, and held her chair when she sat down. He took her to the theater and to nice restaurants. She was not in the habit of being treated that way. It did her good.

She was secretive, however, about seeing Fred socially. Somehow it had an aura of incest, since he was the father of her brother's soon-to-be wife. My mother was reluctant to talk about the four of them socializing. There was also the problem of her relationship with Val. Even though my mother had been aware of Al's womanizing over the years, they had always been close. It was awkward for everyone involved.

Fred's divorce was still pending, so they couldn't get married until it came through. Fred did not want to "live in sin" at his home at the university where he was teaching. It wouldn't be proper, so they "lived in sin" in the penthouse sublet until his divorce was final. My sister and I had great fun with the hypocrisy of that one. We couldn't believe our mother, who had brought us up to reject bourgeois morality, was now going to marry it.

In those archaic times, couples living together without being married really were considered to be living in sin. If they had a child out of wedlock, the child was considered a bastard. If a single young woman got pregnant, it was a serious issue. Either the couple was forced to marry or the young woman was sent away somewhere until the baby was born and the infant was put up for adoption. To be a single mother was rough going, to say the least. Abortion was illegal and a highly risky choice. Women died. To choose to live in Greenwich Village meant more than just freedom to be an artist and run wild. Couples living in sin could rent an apartment, interracial couples had an easier time of it, and homosexuals, albeit still called fags and dykes, were pretty much let alone. The social upheavals of the 1960s, followed by the women's and gay pride movements, made dents in those other problems in the society at large. And after a long struggle the right to a safe and legal abortion became law.

The apartment on Sheridan Square that my mother and Fred sublet wasn't what I expected a penthouse to look like. In fact it was rather small, but it did have a terrace. The building was eight stories tall and the so-called penthouse was an apartment on the top floor. The terrace had a very high wall that pretty much blocked the view of the streets below, but there was sky to ponder. The place had one bedroom, a small kitchen, and a good-size dining room–living room. As part of the deal it offered another bedroom, without a bathroom but with its own entrance, on the same floor. My mother twisted my seventeen-year-old arm and persuaded me to live in that little room. Since I had to leave Waverly Place at the end of the month and I was still underage, I really didn't have a choice. I stayed there for the duration of their sublease and then the Ehrenbergs took me in again for a short stay past my eighteenth birthday. When I moved in with Bobby at the end of 1961 the fiction for Fred, at my mother's request, was that I had rented an apartment with my friend Janet. In the interim, since there was a separate entrance, Bobby and I could steal some time to engage in activities without the sanctity of marriage.

During that time Bob stayed off and on with Micki Isaacson, who had a one-bedroom apartment on a lower floor of 1 Sheridan Square. I didn't know much about Micki other than that she was always upbeat and welcoming—a Doris Day type. I don't remember if she had a job; she might have had a trust fund. It was as if Micki were running a hostel for folksingers—she became a kind of den mother. It seemed everyone was sleeping on her floor at some time or other, and it didn't bother her that if she had a party the guests never left. There were nights when Peter Yarrow, Jack Elliott, Jean Redpath, and Bobby were all camped out on her floor.

Those are just the people I remember, but I know there were more. It was a pajama party, only everyone slept in their clothes. I would stay with Bobby as long as I dared, then I would go upstairs to my lair at the penthouse, making sure I made enough noise walking through the place to the bathroom so my mother would know that I had arrived and that everything was as it should be.

It was at this sublet on Sheridan Square, with Bobby staying at Micki's a few floors below, that he and my mother got to know each other, so to speak. That wasn't necessarily a good thing. She, and my sister likewise, judged harshly. They had high standards. I might have felt inadequate around them, but Bob was under no obligation to play by their rules.

There were rumors and mumblings that the surname
Dylan was not his last name, but as I said, stuff like that was
no big deal. My mother had a hunch right off the bat that
the tales he told about himself, not to mention his name,
were bogus. When Bob needed a cabaret card to play his
first gig at Gerde's in 1961, Mike Porco helped him get one
and he claimed Dylan as his stage name. A cabaret card was
a license issued by the police department to entertainers so
they could work in places that served alcohol. Performers
who had arrest records for drugs or anything else had their
cards revoked or were not issued them in the first place.
Many were deprived of their livelihood for years, including
the great jazz musician Thelonious Monk, legendary singer
Billie Holiday, and Lord Buckley, a performance artist
before the category was invented. The cabaret card was
finally done away with in the mid-1960s. Rumors that
Zimmerman was Bob Dylan's real last name surfaced around
that time.

I guess I thought he would say something sooner or
later. I didn't give it much thought at the beginning of our
relationship. But as we got closer, and I moved in with him,
things like that took on more significance.

My father chose the name Susan for me when I was
born. He wanted something American since my mother had
chosen an Italian name, Carla Maria, for my older sister,
named after Karl Marx, no less.

Susan was a very common name for girls born in the

1940s. I used Sue for a time, but I preferred Susie. Having been given a name that lent itself to diminutives and varied spellings, I took the task seriously and went on a quest to find just the right version that would define me or at least distinguish me from the pack of Susans, Susies, and Sues I already knew and was bound to meet throughout my life. My school notebooks were full of variations on the spelling of Soozie. I certainly had been called Suze (Sooze) innumerable times but for some reason had never thought of it as a possibility.

One day in the early 1960s when leafing through an art book about Picasso, I came across a reproduction of his collage *Glass and Bottle of Suze*. Eureka. Suze was the name of a French liqueur. In addition I could pronounce it with two syllables or one, like the name Bette. Perfect. When I was in France a few years later I drank the liqueur and it wasn't half bad. Suze has a golden yellow color, not too sweet, with a faint citron flavor.

Whether Bob's motivation for name change was the same as mine or not, he went for the big time and kept the highly common first name of Robert (Bob, Bobby) and changed his last name instead. Now that was innovative.

I found out for sure that his name was Robert Allen Zimmerman when I saw his draft card. In spite of myself I was upset that he hadn't ever said anything about it.

Bobby had moved to West Fourth Street and I was staying there off and on before officially moving in. We came back to the apartment after a long night out and he was really drunk. When he clumsily removed his wallet from his pocket its contents fell on the floor and that is when I saw his name. We had been laughing, but when I picked up his draft card, my mood changed.

So Zimmerman is your real name after all? Yes? Well, why didn't you tell me?

The discovery of his birth name didn't have to be anything astounding or earth-shattering. I didn't mind his keeping secrets from others. I was accustomed to that, having grown up in the McCarthy era, when it was necessary to be wary of prying outsiders. But it was suddenly upsetting that he hadn't been open with me. I was hurt.

He was more forthcoming after that and he also learned how well I could keep secrets. Slowly the hurt wore off, but I couldn't shake feelings of doubt about him. I asked him never to lie to me. When I was in Italy the following summer, he sent letters telling me about himself with honesty and clarity that were unexpected after so much time together.

I called him Raz now and then, taken from his initials, just because I knew it annoyed him. After we saw the film *To Kill a Mockingbird*, I would call him Boo Radley, after the odd outsider character played by Robert Duvall. That one made him laugh, though.

Precious Time

I left the job at CORE because I was finding more paid work in the theater building sets and making props. A day job meant having to be alert during the day and since I was spending more time with Bob at night, wandering about listening to music, playing poker at the Van Ronks', going to parties, or just walking the streets with him until the sun came up, that was difficult.

The jail known as the Women's House of Detention sat on the triangle of land bordered by Sixth Avenue, Ninth Street, and Greenwich Avenue and was very much a part of the local Village scene. The building was a big, hulking edifice that dwarfed the delicacy of the Jefferson Market Courthouse next to it—today a public library.

The House of Detention windows faced Sixth Avenue and Greenwich Avenue. It had a fenced-in exercise yard on the roof from which the inmates would holler out taunts to passersby on the streets below. The jailed women's lovers, pimps, friends, and families, would line up in front of the shops along Greenwich Avenue and bellow up to them at all hours of the day and night. Anyone living in the neighborhood with a window open to catch an elusive breeze on summer nights never got much sleep.

Over on Bleecker and Thompson, which was still predominantly an Italian area, there was a store that sold live chickens in cages piled one on top of the other. It was a clean place, and the chickens were humanely kept in reasonably sized cages, with adequate space between them. I remember my grandfather Pop Rossi, whose chickens I cared for on his farm in Connecticut, telling me that chickens need to be kept clean and separated; otherwise they peck at one another viciously. They need adequate space or they become diseased. Even though I lived in the city, far from any farms, the information I learned from my grandfather about gardening and farming always stayed with me. I'd milked cows and taken care of chickens. I knew where meat and vegetables came from.

Pop Rossi made wine and grew beautiful juicy tomatoes that we would bite into like we did the apples on the tree out near the cow pasture. We ate homemade tortellini and pasta of all kinds, as well as risotto (but never polenta). My grandmother Cesarina baked bread in the wood-fired stove with the metal rings that she cooked on before they bought a modern gas stove. She made the butter she spread on the toast for breakfast in the morning and she gave us a little taste of coffee poured into a cup of milk fresh from the cows.

One summer morning I woke very early and looked out the bedroom window to see Pop holding a chicken down on a big tree stump with one hand. The chicken was making a hell of a noise. With his other hand, Pop raised an axe and thwacked the chicken. Its head went one way and its body the other, and with blood spurting from its neck it danced around the yard. The sight transfixed me. I was horrified to realize that the chickens I cared for so lovingly were the very same ones we ate for dinner in the evening. My poor grandmother, who was caring for me for an extended period, could not convince me to eat chicken or the broth with tortellini the rest of the time I was there.

The chicken coops on Thompson Street in the Village were well maintained. The chickens were healthy but not destined to live long, obviously. The customer picked out the chicken and it was taken in the back, where it was quietly and covertly killed, defeathered by scalding in hot water, and then butchered as the customer desired.

When Bob and I stayed up all night, which was not unusual for us, if we were in the vicinity of the south Village on our path toward home, we heard the roosters crowing at the break of dawn. We would wander up Bleecker Street across Sixth Avenue to Zito's Bakery. Zito's had a coal-fired brick oven in the basement and the night bakers readily handed out hot fresh bread to night Village wanderers on their way home. For us it was an inevitable pass-by. From Zito's we made a right from Bleecker onto Jones Street, practically perpendicular to the apartment on West Fourth. The bread was so good. We went upstairs and made coffee and stayed up some more or, completely exhausted, fell fast asleep, saving the bread for when we woke up, whatever time of day that was. I worked as a waitress in between theater jobs or just lived off my earnings for a stretch. Sometimes I was even eligible for unemployment insurance, if a job lasted long enough. Rents, food, and entertainment were not expensive back then. We were young and could live on very little. I bought my clothes at thrift shops or else made them. Books and records were for sale in the many secondhand shops around Manhattan. Usually someone you knew was working at some club or theater and you could get in free.

There were also many generous people who had food ready to feed hungry musicians and friends. Dave Van Ronk and Terri Thal were great cooks, as was Lillian Bailey, who with her husband, Mell, got to know Bob at Gerde's when he first arrived in the city. They always had something on the stove that was enough to feed whoever dropped by. We spent time with the MacKenzie family, Eve and Mac, and their teenage son. Bob was close to them and he was sleeping on their couch when I first met him. The door to their book-filled loft on West Twenty-eighth Street was always open to him and he stayed there off and on until he got his own place on West Fourth Street.

I'm not sure where I first encountered Dave Van Ronk. It might have been at the Gaslight or Gerde's or the bar the Kettle of Fish. On evenings when the weather was good and the music wasn't, a group of us would sit outside on the loading dock around the corner from the entrance to Gerde's talking, playing music, having a cigarette. At a certain point we'd walk over to the Gaslight or the Kettle of Fish to find Dave and Terri, and whoever else was around and up for roaming.

After wandering from club to coffeehouse we'd eventually head down to Chinatown for a meal at Sam Wo's, then end up at Dave and Terri's apartment on Waverly Place for an all-night poker game.

Dave would put a stack of LPs on the turntable, and under the thick cloud of smoke and whatever it was we were drinking, we'd knot our brows over heavy bets made in nickels and dimes.

It is hard to remember precisely who was playing poker on those nights because at the Van Ronks' apartment the door was always open. Besides Bobby and me, other rotating regulars included folksingers Pat Sky and Tom Paxton, with his soon-to-be wife, Midge, and Barry Kornfeld, who played a mean guitar—both the six- and twelve-string—and was a diverting storyteller. Barry would regale us with tales of his days escorting the blind bluesman Reverend Gary Davis from gig to gig. Gary Davis was a man with a commanding personality and voice, singing or talking. He would be in a room with a group of people and in the middle of a song or a conversation he'd suddenly stop dead and say: I smell a woman! A woman just walked in. Bring her to me.

At twenty-five, Van Ronk was well known and respected in the downtown music scene. He had been living in Greenwich Village and performing since the mid 1950s. Before he made a name for himself singing blues and folk music, he had played with Dixieland jazz bands.

Those were formative years for most of us, and Dave did a lot of the forming and teaching. It was amazing how much that man knew and how quick his wit.

Because I was younger than most of the people I was hanging out with, he kind of kept an eye on me. On the other hand Terri was responsible for an entirely different form of higher education. She was freewheeling, straight-talking, and like Dave, very political. When I first met them they lived on West Fifteenth Street, but not long after they moved to Waverly Place. The Van Ronk apartment at 190 Waverly quickly became the living room of the new generation of bohemians.

Bob Dylan brought me to their West Fifteenth Street place not long after we'd met at Riverside Church. He was intent on having me get to know the people he had become close to since coming to the city that winter, telling me how great they were, and how much he wanted me to meet them. When we'd arrive at the apartment, the café, the bar, the club, he'd bring me to that person, point to me and say, Hey, this is Suze. Remember when I was telling you about her?

It was a hot summer day when we went to Fifteenth Street and trudged up the stairs to their apartment on the top floor. Dave greeted us at the door. After a few minutes Terri walked out from the kitchen wearing only a bra and panties. Her underwear was white cotton—nothing lacy, frilly, or sexy about it, but that didn't make a bit of difference. At six feet tall, with the looks of a slightly offbeat and eccentric model, she made quite an impression. Her hair was dark brown, like her eyes, and she wore it very short, accentuating her long neck. She had a low voice and spoke in a heavy New York accent with the vocabulary of a sailor. I was in awe of her ways.

Terri managed Dave and a few other folksingers. To be a manager in the early days of folk music wasn't much of a profession. Folk music venues were small and informal places that didn't pay; performers passed around a basket for tips—hence the term *basket houses.*

Terri helped struggling folkies get gigs at the few clubs or coffeehouses that paid musicians. She was certainly more capable than they were at taking care of business. Both Dave and Terri seemed quite upstanding, despite their bohemian way of life. They were married, after all, and had a real apartment with real furniture in it.

There were not many females hanging out in their flat. It was mainly guys, musicians or politicos or both, who

Terri Thal and Dave Van Ronk, 1963

came and went, casually taking in Terri in her white underwear as she offered them things to eat or drink and then sat
down on the couch to join the conversation.

No one said a word about her clothes or lack of them,
taking the cue from Dave, who obviously felt her attire was
perfectly acceptable considering how hot the apartment
was in summer.

When Dave found out that my parents had been Communists, he felt it was his duty, as a Trotskyite, to work on
my politics. It did no good to tell him it wasn't my battle. He
would expound on the merits of the anarchists and Marxism
as interpreted by Trotsky, but he had absolutely no love for
Stalin and the American Communist Party.

Not being up on the details and the finer points of his

discourse, I'd nod and say I had no problem with that, but he looked skeptical. Even in the last conversation I had with him, just days before he died in 2002, among other things he said to me was, I'll see you soon, and I'll straighten out your politics.

Dave was not like others around the Village, both musicians and friends, who resented the attention focused on Bob—that was not his style. The only serious bad time and bad feeling that ever developed between Bob and Dave was over "House of the Rising Sun," a blues song out of New Orleans. It was a woman's lament but men tended to sing it. When Dave sang it, he gave the song such desolation and sorrow that no one else around the Village clubs sang it anymore. It was Dave's song. He owned it. His unique raspy, bluesy voice and the arrangement he created for the song added to its effectiveness. When Bob was recording songs for his first album on Columbia Records, he included "House of the Rising Sun," in Dave's version.

When Dave asked how the sessions were going at Columbia, Bob told him they were going fine. Then Dave told him about his plans for his own upcoming recording session.

I'm finally recording "House," he said.

Oops, said Bob, and confessed to Dave that he had just recorded it.

That did not go over well. Bob had done a traitorous thing, breaking the code of honor among thieves. He went to the session and sang the songs he knew, had recently learned, and just loved to sing. He insisted he did it all without thinking. He hadn't realized the error. Now he sorely did, but there was nothing to be done. The record had gone to press.

We were close with Dave and Terri by then. We hung out a lot together. Terri and I were intent on fixing the friendship because we knew it was important to both of them. We worked at it, going back and forth between them. It was a serious affront on Bob's part and Dave was angry for a long time.

Bobby felt really bad. The situation made him very nervous. Whether he was standing or sitting, his knees were bouncing, pumping the air as if he wanted to take off. He was not talking much, his brow was furrowed, and he was chain-smoking. He knew he'd crossed a line.

Eventually Terri and I prevailed and the rift was resolved via booze and food and poker games where Bobby lost often, as penance. Dave, however, had a bead on the new kid.

Once Bob's album came out, Dave stopped singing the song. He never recorded it. Personally, I think that is a loss. Bob's version on his first LP isn't bad at all, but all things considered, it's a copy of a lost original.

Bleecker Street was the Times Square of Greenwich Village because of all the tourists who gravitated to its numerous clubs and bars, especially on the weekends. The music club the Village Gate was just down the block from the Bitter End, with the Bleecker Street movie theater in between. Walking from one place to another with a detour onto MacDougal Street meant passing all those other clubs and coffeehouses: the Gaslight, the Figaro, Rienzi's, Fat Black Pussy Cat, Café Wha, and numerous others.

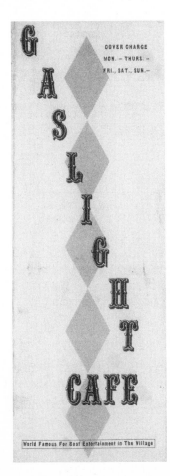

COVER CHARGE
MON. – THURS. –
FRI., SAT., SUN.,–

World Famous For Best Entertainment in The Village

The Gaslight was down a short flight of stairs from street level, in a basement with exposed pipes and a low ceiling. It lacked only the barflies and the liquor license necessary to accommodate them, but the Kettle of Fish bar was right up the stairs in the same building, so that wasn't too much of a problem. The Kettle became the "office," as in, Where is so and so? Upstairs in the office.

Dave, Terri, Bob, and I were at the Kettle often, particularly if Dave

The Street

ICED DRINKS

Tropicana	1.50
Mint Julep	1.50
Cider	.60
Coca-Cola	.60
Grenadine	.60
Grenadine Au Lait	.85
Limeade	.60
Orzato	.60
Pink Lemonade	.75
Lampone	.60
Papaya	.60
Papaya Au Lait	.85

COFFEES

Espresso	.60
Espresso Brandy	.65
Espresso Rum	.65
Espresso Romano	.65
Espresso Cinnamon	.65
Cafe Au Lait	.70
Cafe Royale	.85
Cappuccino	.75
Mocha	.75
Spiced Coffee	.70
Viennese Coffee	.70
Coffee Alexander (Frosted)	.85
American	.60

ALL ABOVE ICED ON REQUEST

...10 extra

HOT DRINKS

Brandy Chocolate	.75
Rum Chocolate	.75
Lime Chocolate	.75
Mint Chocolate	.75
Hawaiian Chocolate	.75
Ciocolatta	.75
Spiced Milk	.60
Cinnamon Stick Cider	.60

ICED ON REQUEST

...10 extra

TEAS

China Green	.60
Earl Grey	.60
English Breakfast	.60
Gun Powder	.60
Irish	.60
Jasmine	.60
Lap Sang Chouchang	.60
Ceylon Orange Pekee	.60
Spiced Tea	.75

ICED ON REQUEST

...10 extra

COVER CHARGE

MON. – THURS. –

FRI., SAT., SUN.–

and Bob both had a gig at the Gaslight. We would go upstairs between sets or at the end of the night and sit at a table with other performers on their way on or off stage. Inevitably the guys would begin telling bawdy stories, mocking the traditional folk ballads by replacing the plaintive lyrics with the

SODAS

Brandy	.85
Chocolate	.85
Mint	.85
Rum	.85
Grenadine	.85
Vanilla	.85
Papaya	.85

FRENCH ICE CREAM

Chocolate	.70
Coffee	.70
Vanilla	.70
Italian Ices	.60

SUNDAES

Mint	.95
Brandy	.95
Chocolate	.95
Nut	.95
Rum	.95
Vanilla	.95
Sundaes for two	1.75

SANDWICHES

American Cheese	.90
Grilled Cheese	.90
Doubleburger	1.75
Beefburger	1.10
Cheese Beefburger	1.25
Baconburger	1.25
Holland Ham	1.30
Holland Ham and Imported Swiss	1.50
Holland Ham and American Cheese	1.35
Imported Swiss	1.00

ABOVE SANDWICHES INCLUDE
LETTUCE, TOMATOE, PICKLES,
POTATO CHIPS

Cream Cheese & Date Nut Bread	.85
Assorted Pastries	.65
Assorted Cookies	.60
Pastry Ala Mode	.85

COVER CHARGE

MON. — THURS. —

FRI., SAT., SUN. —

filthy double entendres from
old raunchy blues songs (Dave
knew every single one ever written, word for word).

At one point Terri leaned over to me and said: I have a
good title for a ballad—I had a cunt nine inches long.

I looked at her, wide-eyed: I had never heard the word *cunt* before and could only guess what it meant. But I didn't want her to know that, so I laughed as she continued the "folk process" with this new ballad. My education expanded in every direction with Terri and Dave.

The Gaslight had a variety of performers taking turns on its tiny stage. Hugh Romney, later known as Wavy Gravy, was a hip philosopher–joker man–performance artist. Taylor Mead read, or more correctly, performed his poetry on a regular basis. He looked like one of the illustrations of a character in the Mother Goose book I had as a kid, a mischievous Jack Spratt with a whiny voice. The musicians were a more eclectic group than the nearly polished or the well-polished folk musicians hired for weeklong gigs at Gerde's or the Bitter End.

Peter Stampfel was the young Greenwich Village version of Grandpa Jones, the Grand Ole Opry performer with a banjo. I thought Peter was terrific. He played the fiddle, guitar, and banjo, stomping his feet and kicking his skinny legs out while he sang mostly off-key in a strong nasal tenor voice. I don't know why, but it worked. He could sing anything he wanted, and he did.

When he teamed up with Steve Weber to become the uniquely madcap Holy Modal Rounders, the two of them were a sight to behold. Peter was tall and skinny, but Weber was even taller and skinnier and could carry a tune. They wrote and covered a wide spectrum of songs, music with and without genre. Sui generis. The Rounders started out as a duo but expanded to include various musicians who came and went over time. They played with Sam Shepard and Tuli Kupferberg, who with the poet Ed Sanders were known as the Fugs, also in a class by themselves. It was mutating music–spoken word madness, neither ahead or behind the times. You could call it psycho-delic or psychedelic folk music, depending on your point of view.

As the unofficial gatekeeper of the Gaslight, it was Dave Van Ronk's job to have the tourists stay in their seats for a few sets on a slow night, or to hustle them in and out quickly in order to take in as much money as possible on weekends. The Bitter End seemed like a legitimate club by comparison. It was on street level, around the corner from the Gaslight, on the more touristy Bleecker Street, and had a bigger stage with a real backstage for the performers to hang out. If there was a pecking order to these up-and-coming folk and stand-up comedy places in the early 1960s, the Bitter End was just below the more established Village Gate, also on Bleecker. The Gate was primarily a jazz club where I first heard the Modern Jazz Quartet, Lionel Hampton, Mose Allison, and the truly unique Nina Simone—but it was dipping its toe into folk music.

The other places where musicians played were basket houses that attracted students and tourists and characters who sat all day and night, next to piles of papers and books, nursing stale cups of coffee. Everyone was prey for an old Village character named Maurice, the newspaper and magazine troubadour. Tall and bone thin, with a long white beard and white hair, he roamed the streets, cafés, and clubs of the Village selling old and new magazines and newspapers. He handed out free copies of a local paper, the *Villager*, for a cup of coffee and then regaled you with tales of the great writers and thinkers who had passed this way or that during his tenure. The only person who could best him on political history was Dave Van Ronk.

You're full of shit, Maurice, Dave would say to him affectionately but definitively, and that ended any further discussion on the topic.

Maurice, a Village character

Charlie Rothschild, who had a hand in booking the acts at Gerde's, was levelheaded and friendly, with a wry sense of humor. There is more to life than folk music, he'd say. He seemed to observe the antics and absurdities of the tightly knit, overwrought, often jealous, quasi-incestuous, and hermetic folk community of the Village with a sage detachment. All this gave me the impression that he had a life apart from folk music. He did have a day job—in folk music—working for the manager Albert Grossman. No matter: Charlie was capable of seeing beyond what was in front of him; I figured he had to have other interests.

Charlie started representing the singer Carolyn Hester as early as 1960 and got her signed with Columbia Records. From Waco, Texas, Carolyn possessed a lovely silky and slightly nasal soprano voice that didn't always get its due on recordings. She was luminous and beautiful on stage and off. I remember being thrilled when someone told me we looked like sisters, and she enjoyed it when people thought she was on the cover of Bob's *Freewheelin'* album.

Carolyn made songs come to life when she sang them. She could sing any genre of slow song and turn it into a haunting ballad. "Summertime" from George Gershwin's *Porgy and Bess* was an unusual choice for folk venues; but when she sang it you could hear a pin drop.

When I met Carolyn, she was married to Dick Fariña. Though Dick played music, he spoke of himself as a writer. He would read aloud from whatever he was working on—a book, a poem, or an article. He and Bobby got on very well. They would talk and laugh and riff on stuff to-gether. Dick said he was going to write about Bobby. I got you down, man, he'd say. Listen to this.

He read his description, focusing on the way Bob pumped the air with his knees, and Bobby loved it. He loved Dick's writing: You write like a poet, man, he told him.

Judy Collins was one of the female singers around the Vil-lage in the early years who evolved easily and gracefully from being typecast as a sixties folksinger to becoming a singer of all kinds of songs, including her own, later in her career. Charlie Rothschild began representing her in the late 1960s.

April 30, 1966, was the publication date of Dick Fariña's book *Been Down So Long It Looks Like Up to Me* and it was also the night he died. I was in the Limelight bar the next night as the news spread that he'd been killed in a motorcycle ac-cident on the West Coast. I ran into Judy, a close friend of Fariña's, and she was a wreck. I was without words. It was shattering news.

José Feliciano was about seventeen years old when he showed up at Gerde's and the other Village clubs and cof-feehouses. He was only two years younger than me but I still felt like his big sister; I looked out for him.

José was a vessel filled with music. He was physically compact and strong, with a mellifluous yet powerful voice. He was charming and scrappy and knew where to go and how to get there; being blind didn't hold him back. I used to help him up and down the steep flight of stairs from Gerde's basement onto the stage. He'd take my arm and pretend to guide me, so I'd know who was leading whom. Quietly he would ask me why I couldn't be his girl instead of that guy who talked funny, and then he'd do an imitation of Bob.

With someone I knew who had a car, we took José for a day trip to Coney Island. All the way there and back, in the manner of Bobby McFerrin, José made music with his voice, his feet, and both hands, tapping and slapping on every part of the car within his reach.

Jack Elliott was the son of Woody and Bob was the son of Jack—that's what folks said, and in a way it was true. For those who didn't know Woody Guthrie except from his recordings, his photographs, his books and those written about him, and the many stories people told about him, Jack Elliott was the one who animated those images. His story-telling, his singing style, and the folksiness he projected all came from his time traveling with Guthrie. But Jack never possessed the political fiber that Guthrie had woven into everything he produced. And Woody Guthrie was the real thing. Jack and Bob and whoever else was working on developing themselves in Guthrie's image had to do just that—develop an image and work it in with who they were, whether they came from Brooklyn, New York, Hibbing, Minnesota, or Anyplace, U.S.A.

Politics was not part of Jack's persona. He was a low-key, deadpan, very entertaining, funny man—he was wonderful to be around. He did ramble, but it was his way of talking rather than his geographical traveling that gave him the name Ramblin' Jack. He would start a story and wander all over the plains and tundra before the tale was concluded, or, more accurately, before he let his words trail off into the distance.

Jack was a good-looking man of average height with a warm and pleasant demeanor who smiled most of the time and was wonderfully off the wall. Jack may have been born in Brooklyn as Elliott Adnopoz, yet there was no trace of that in him, except that he knew his way around New York City really well. Ramblin' Jack Elliott was all cowpoke.

He would show up and hang around, then be off again to play a gig somewhere and return a few days or a few years later. When he hit New York City in 1961, rumors of anticipation preceded his arrival. He had been traveling around Europe for several years performing in clubs and on the streets with his buddy Derroll Adams and was finally returning to the States. By age thirty, he'd already recorded a number of record albums that bridged the gap between those of the legendary folk balladeers Cisco Houston, Pete Seeger, and of course Woody Guthrie.

Ramblin' Jack made music the way he told stories. He was always on stage, or maybe it is better to say he was never *on* stage. He was the same person whether he was on stage or off. Jack had no artifice in his art. That was his artistry: he was completely natural.

Bobby looked up to Jack and they bonded early on when folk music was making itself over, heading into the mainstream. Jack would call Bobby up on stage at Gerde's, where they would perform together more as a comedy duo than as serious folksingers. They played off each other's quirkiness. Later Bob went off on his quest and Jack was left unacknowledged in the dust of Bob's hard and fast drive out of the picture, as were others. There might have been some hurt feelings initially, but no animosity. It all worked itself out eventually, and they remained friends.

$\mathcal{B}$ruce Langhorne was a student at New York University and commuted to the Village from Harlem. He was an unassuming and charming man with an easy smile. His presence was strongly felt through his exceptional facility as a musician proficient on several instruments. He was Bob's vision for the Tambourine Man—a song written about a lonely night Bob had spent wandering the streets after the two of us had quarreled.

An unfortunate encounter with an exploding firecracker resulted in the loss of part of two fingers on Bruce's right hand. We used to kid around that Bruce was the American challenge to Django Reinhardt, the genius Gypsy guitarist whose left hand was badly burned in an accident when he was a child. Bruce was a guitar magician: though he was incredibly versatile, his sound was unmistakably his own. He was a highly sought-after accompanist at recording sessions and gigs for musicians working in any style.

$\mathcal{M}$y first sight of Odetta performing seared an image in my brain. She is standing in a circle of light with her guitar, and when she begins to sing the power of her voice obliterates everything else. All there is in the world is this one woman's voice. Behind her, slightly off to the side and also in a circle of light, is her bass player, Bill Lee. Except for his arms and fingers, he hardly appears to be moving. He is a small man and the bass is very big, but you know he rules it. Together they make music of no genre. It is jazz, it is blues, it is folk. Above all, it is dramatic. I was engulfed by Odetta's voice almost the same way I was when I first heard a John Lee Hooker record.

Many times in the years following I spent time with Odetta and watched her perform, but it was hard to lose my feeling of awe. She was soft-spoken, with a soothing voice that belied the profound power and depth of sound she could produce when she sang.

Bill Lee, the filmmaker Spike Lee's father, was primarily a jazz musician and he didn't appear to relate to this folk stuff easily. He was quiet and kept to himself, but Bob went over to talk to him, drawing him out, bringing him into the scene.

Odetta and her music might be unclassifiable, but she ran with the folkies probably because they embraced her musical diversity. The borders surrounding jazz were more defined. You couldn't sing, "The Water Is Wide," a traditional folk ballad, in a jazz setting in those years. The folk world included everything that wasn't easily classifiable. Folk music could be an amalgam of other genres: bluegrass to country to blues to gospel to traditional, and so on. Odetta could sing within and without all those styles, and then some. The folkies loved her.

Eric Weissberg played the banjo predominantly and Marshall Brickman the guitar. They played together in a bluegrass band and separately with other groups. What I remember most about them, however, is how funny they both were offstage. They could easily have been a comedy act. Marshall Brickman went on to work with Woody Allen and become a writer of Broadway shows. Eric will always be the best five-string banjo picker this side of Earl Scruggs. A fine musician all around, he is best known for the soundtrack of the movie *Deliverance*.

Bill Cosby was a stand-up comedian in the early sixties, one of many who performed at the Bitter End on Bleecker Street. Woody Allen, Dick Gregory, and Flip Wilson, and comedians who never made it as far as those guys did, honed their special genius straddling a stool in front of a brick wall at that club, the Gaslight, and the other venues on the street.

Noel Stookey, who became the Paul of Peter, Paul, and Mary, incorporated his stand-up routines into his musical sets. He was very funny and was famous for his sound effects, particularly a routine he did about flushing toilets. Woody Allen was incredibly nerdy and almost painful to watch as he clutched into himself, knees facing each other and elbows into his chest, his skinny fingers playing at his mouth as he tried to befriend the microphone. His eyes bugged behind his big eyeglasses as he whined his way through incongruous stories of incompetence and neurosis. The audience related, and loved him.

Bill Cosby was another matter, suave and good-looking and sure of himself. He made his observations about the trials of getting through life ridiculously funny almost because of his poised and self-assured manner. He and Bob bonded in ambition early on, but Cosby wasn't around long. He was not headed anywhere but up. He was not a downtown bohemian outsider; he was a cool dude making his way fast. One afternoon Bobby and I were lounging at an outdoor café and Cosby came into view driving a red convertible. He waved to us as he headed toward the West Side Highway and beyond to fame and fortune.

Another regular at Gerde's Folk City was the Flower Lady, a middle-aged woman with a stocky build and a heavy walk. She always wore the same clean and neatly pressed shirtwaist dress of no particular color. Her faded yellow hair was in a neat bun at her neck. She carried a big bouquet of red roses and silently went from table to table at the club, offering her flowers for sale. She never spoke and she never changed her blank expression. A few of us speculated that she didn't speak English. Now and then someone would try to engage her in conversation, but when nothing ever came of it, she was left alone.

"Here comes the Flower Lady" eventually gave way to no comments of any kind when she walked in the door, making her way past the bar to the customers sitting at the tables. One warm evening a few of us were sitting outside on the loading dock around the corner from Gerde's and we watched a sleek black Cadillac pull up to the curb. The door opened and the Flower Lady climbed out with her bunch of roses. She took no notice of us or of our dumbfounded expressions as she heavy-footed her way into the club to do her night's work.

There were so many talented people who practiced their art form and sharpened their skills during the period of the Greenwich Village renaissance of the sixties. To become a legend or a star wasn't always the point. Many did what they loved to do and became known for it far and wide, and others did what they loved to do and managed to make a living at it. Still others burned out and lost their way.

Behind the Music

The Lomaxes and Harry Smith, separately and in completely different ways, collected American old-time folk music. John Lomax and his son Alan did so through field recordings and Smith by obsessively collecting old commercial records wherever he found them.

The people who played and loved folk music from the 1940s on, and certainly in the 1960s, are indebted to Smith and the Lomaxes for the music they preserved and disseminated. It was through their work that this uniquely American music is available for all who love and are inspired by it.

Alan Lomax recorded folk music from around the world, also. His collection of Italian folk songs augmented what knowledge I had from the smattering of folk songs my sister and I learned hearing one of our uncles sing. My sister Carla worked for Lomax for a while and loved her job, but she noted that Alan wasn't always generous with crediting the people who worked for him. A larger issue is the way Lomax attributed credit to the original artists. The methods the Lomaxes used to finance their projects, and pay the performers they recorded and whose music they collected, was complicated and not for me to decipher. When I first heard old-time music I didn't think about who might have collected it or how; I just wanted to hear more. In the 1960s musicians around the Village were enthralled by the singers they heard on these records and the experience radically influenced the way they made music.

Above all, the Lomax field recordings and Harry Smith's *Anthology of American Folk Music* delivered this mu-

sic from back porches and local communities out into the world at large. They gave us an invaluable legacy: a musical heritage.

A group called the Friends of Old Time Music, founded by Israel Young, John Cohen, and Ralph Rinzler, was responsible for bringing into the urban folk fold Mississippi John Hurt, Roscoe Holcomb, Doc Watson, and many others. Following in the footsteps of Alan Lomax, they searched for the men and women who played and sang on the records they were captivated by and learning from. The musicians who were still around were pleased that a new young audience revered them and their music.

Ralph Rinzler played the mandolin with the Greenbriar Boys, a bluegrass group, and John Cohen was part of the New Lost City Ramblers, together with Mike Seeger and Tom Paley. The Ramblers sang folk songs from the Depression era, 1920s and 1930s Americana. They had great energy when they performed, and although they toured quite a bit and weren't around New York City much, their reputation was sizable.

I think I first encountered the Ramblers when I was about fifteen years old. We lived within a mile or so of La-Guardia Airport in Queens and the Ramblers had a plane to catch. Carla had been to a folk concert and had invited them to our apartment to hang out for a time before they were due at the airport. I peered in from the hallway and had a clear view of John Cohen sitting on the couch stomping his foot as he played and sang with the others, who were just out of my line of sight.

Pete Seeger, however, was the man behind the music. He was blacklisted from television and radio in the United States yet he sang everywhere and anywhere he could, from concert halls to schoolrooms to summer camps. Pete Seeger planted the seeds and taught us all to sing.

Accusations of plagiarism would always be a ball
and chain on Dylan's career as a songwriter, but especially
so in the early years, as his fame was growing. He was so
openly and nakedly searching for interesting music on albums, on the radio, in performance in a club that plagiarism was an easy gibe to make about him. His imitation
and emulation of Woody Guthrie was a case in point. Yet,
on the other hand, his intensity in his quest made people
want to help him. Everyone who knew him, whether they
were musicians or not, was sucked in by his fever to learn.
Friends voluntarily showed, played, or sang him something new or interesting they had or had heard about. And
he'd do the same when he discovered music that intrigued
him. It was a community until it wasn't anymore, but that
was inevitable. Artists grow and move on; some stabilize
in place, and others fall away.

My enthusiasms and passions encompassed the theater and art in addition to all kinds of music. Gerde's
wasn't considered an "artist's bar"—that was an entirely
different scene, as in the Cedar Tavern on University
Place, where the Abstract Expressionists hung out. But if
artists were into the music of the time, they hung out at
Gerde's. When Max's Kansas City opened later, at the end
of 1965, near Union Square, it attracted artists, writers,
and musicians who went to listen to music and hang out
despite the fact that it was north of the Fourteenth Street
"border."

I met the painter Brice Marden at Gerde's and we'd sit
and talk at the bar while watching Bob or another performer. I went to his place on Avenue C with an artist

friend of his wife, Pauline Baez, the middle Baez sister. Since Brice's studio seemed to take up most of the small railroad apartment, Pauline was confined to the kitchen with their baby son. I walked around looking at Brice's paintings, all of them in shades of gray. The paintings seemed morose, like an overcast sky or the remains of a building wall in an empty lot, quite a distance from the layered dancing lines of color that he painted later on. What they have in common is a certain reserve.

The Limelight, a large bar and restaurant on Seventh Avenue South just north of Bleecker Street, was a hangout for writers, theater people, and musicians—a typical Village crowd. A few doors away was a bar hangout for lesbians that I seem to remember was called Pom Pom's. Back then it was known as a bar for dykes, with no discrimination intended: the clientele defined a place. The nomenclature was casual—a biker bar, a beatnik bar, a hippie hangout, a place for dopers—and made no real difference, since most places catered to anyone who walked in the door. When two women I knew to be a couple broke up, one of them stayed with me when I lived on Avenue B. If there was any speculation about my sexuality because of this, I would have been surprised; I knew nothing of bisexuality. I learned of it only because the breakup was the result of one of the women's falling in love with a guy.

Live and learn. Very few people knew the two women were a couple in the first place; some things were closeted even in bohemia. If two women lived together, it was assumed they were friends. But two guys? They must be gay.

I was passionate about civil rights, banning the bomb, and any kind of injustice. Growing up in a politically conscious home during the Cold War and under McCarthyism, I had struggled through the issues of Communism, socialism, and the American way. I threw those interests out to Bob. I was exposed to a lot more than a kid from Hibbing, Minnesota, was, especially with my upbringing amid books and music and interesting, albeit difficult, people. And I was also from New York City. No contest there.

The learning process for artists of all stripes usually follows the path of imitate, assimilate, then innovate. If an artist is struck by something in his or her chosen art form, there is an all-consuming desire to absorb everything about it. During the process of assimilation the artist's output will be an imitation of the beloved form. In the end, for the uniquely gifted, there will be innovation. Sometimes if something proves impossible to replicate for some reason, the artist pushes to find another way—innovation by default. Dave Van Ronk said about his unique guitar style: I tried my damnedest to copy those old guys, but I just couldn't do it, so I had to come up with something.

It was obvious that Bob Dylan was an innovator. He worked hard to learn his craft, to make his art his own. And his art is entirely and originally his own, even if it is recognizable from or similar to something that was there before.

Now and then he acknowledged possible crossovers. One night he burst into the Kettle of Fish waving a piece of paper and announcing to Sylvia Tyson: Hey, you gotta listen to this song I just wrote! I just wrote it, or at least I think I wrote it, but maybe I heard it somewhere.

I'm not sure when I met Ian and Sylvia Tyson, but I think it was before I saw them perform as the Canadian folk duo Ian and Sylvia. Ian was movie-star handsome, Sylvia was stunning, and they had voices and musicianship to match their good looks. Ian came from the west coast of Canada and, having been a rodeo rider, had true cowboy credentials. He looked terrific in his cowboy getup of jeans, cowboy boots, well-cut cowboy shirt, and ten-gallon hat. Ian was hands down the best looking of all the cowboy dudes in Greenwich Village.

Sylvia had regal looks—tall and lean with long, straight dark brown hair. Her singing voice was bell-like and strong, with a sound that seemed to come down through the ages. Though she also wrote songs, in the early years she wasn't acknowledged for her writing abilities. Most people in and out of the music business just assumed that Ian was the writer and she was there to look lovely and sing beautifully.

Ian and Sylvia began playing music together in folk clubs around Toronto not long after they'd met. When they came to Greenwich Village in the 1960s, they were picked up by manager Albert Grossman and began recording for Vanguard Records, one of the premier folk labels. They were authentic in the way folk musicians had to be, yet it was obvious they would have commercial appeal.

The genius of Albert Grossman was to see early on that

Sylvia and Ian Tyson

there was a growing market for folk music and know just how to fill it. At the time he signed Ian and Sylvia he had just turned Peter Yarrow, Noel "Paul" Stookey, and Mary Travers into Peter, Paul, and Mary. Bob Dylan would be a little more complicated sell, but Albert believed he had the goods. His technique was to book his better-known acts at college venues and then insist they take Bob, too. He imposed Bob on his inevitable audience and they didn't take long to latch onto him. When Joan Baez took Dylan on tour with her, he was carried into the folk firmament.

I swear it was Ian Tyson who offered up the first taste of marijuana when Bob brought him to the flat one afternoon. Ian had a friend back home who had introduced him to this stuff you could smoke that would get you high. Bob didn't think I should try any until he had tested it, but later on I did.

I met Sylvia a few days later at Mell and Lillian Bailey's house, where our long friendship began. Once Ian and Sylvia signed with Albert Grossman, they were on tour quite a bit and I didn't see Sylvia as often as I would have liked, but they both came around to the apartment whenever they were in town. Bob would sprawl on the bed with his guitar and play a new song. Ian would listen and then would play something he or Sylvia had written. Sylvia would sing along intermittently while we all pondered the merits of new LPs we'd recently acquired or they had brought for us to hear. The cover of a Kingston Trio album earned scorn because the trio looked so collegiate and square in the photo. Unlike Van Ronk, who seemed to already know everything, we reveled in the joy of discovering something we had never heard before. And this wasn't just for music; it was about books and movies, too. We were a young and curious lot, but we all acted cool and hip and knowing.

$\mathcal{B}$obby was very close to Mell and Lillian Bailey, whom he'd gotten to know at Gerde's a few months after hitting town. Shortly after Bob and I met, he began telling me about them: he said I would love Lillian, especially. They

had an apartment on Avenue B and Third Street, in the East Village.

Mell and Lillian were older and married and had day jobs, but they were at Gerde's almost every evening. Mell was a music man, immersed in everything. Traditional music and bluegrass were his latest passion, which was unusual for a black man in those times because of the music's provenance.

The Baileys listened to classical music, jazz, blues, gospel, rhythm and blues, and folk music from around the world—everything from crooners to calypso. I had grown up with all kinds of music, including

Lillian Bailey (above)
and Mell Bailey

141

opera, so sifting through albums at their apartment felt like home to me. They might have had even more LPs than Van Ronk.

Mell played the guitar and sang some but wasn't serious about performing. Lillian was warm and outgoing and got right past my shyness. She looked a little like Sarah Vaughan if Sarah Vaughan had been a painter; Lillian had a way of putting together outfits that can only be described as elegant bohemian. We got on immediately. She was a visual artist like me and we shared the same sense of humor and the same birth date. Even though Lillian was thirty-three and I was seventeen when we met, we grew very close, and the friendship ended only with her death in 1994. When Bob and his family moved out of New York City a number of years later, he gave the Baileys his garden apartment on MacDougal Street for a very reasonable rent. Their one-bedroom on East Third Street was cramped after the birth of their son Drew in 1963.

Mell had a Wollensak reel-to-reel tape recorder, not a common piece of equipment for someone to have at home in the 1960s. Lillian and Mell had many friends who were musicians or artists of some kind. They had weekend gatherings that started in the day and would last into the evening, when Lillian would offer up delicious meals.

The musicians liked making recordings for Mell. Ian and Sylvia, Paul Clayton, and others came over to make tapes. Bob played and sang many songs into Mell's Wollensak, and he worked over his new material with Mell. Bob sang "Why Must I Be a Teenager in Love," traditional folk songs, and calypso duets with him. Cynthia Gooding, the folksinger who specialized in songs from around the world and had her own radio show, was a good friend of the Baileys, and they discussed potential artists for her program. Cynthia lived on Bleecker Street, a few blocks down from Gerde's, and she hosted some fine parties—living room concerts, really. Records were not played; musicians sang and played live as everyone milled about with their drinks and smokes.

The Bowery, the lower stretch of Third Avenue below St. Mark's Place, ending in Chinatown, was populated in those days by drunken bums, as they were called, who lived in flophouses, frequented cheap liquor stores and soup kitchens, and spent their days on the street cadging money for a bottle of sweet and lethal Thunderbird wine. Some made out better than others, on the strength of the stories they told to anyone who stopped to listen. The really good practitioners discussed politics, recited poetry, and quoted philosophy—their own included. They engaged the listener, but not to the point of conversation, because that would undermine the setting of performer and potential paying audience.

Huddled in doorways, sprawled casually in the gutter or on the litter-strewn sidewalks, hugging their booze bottles, they commented lazily or enthusiastically—depending on their level of alcohol intake—as people passed by. One evening I was engrossed in conversation with Mell Bailey while Bob and Lillian, trailing behind us, were talking together head to head as we made our way along the Bowery. A silhouetted figure of a man, using a building wall for support, watched us pass. Well, I'll be, he said, if that ain't integration, I don't know what is!

We didn't have parties at our place on West Fourth Street. The apartment was really small, and Bob didn't want a constant parade of people coming and going, like Terri and Dave had. We both liked privacy. One evening, however, there were many people at the place and much booze and wine, along with something to smoke. I don't remember who was there, but that might have to do more with what happened to me than with the passage of time.

After everyone left, I started feeling very strange. I had smoked and drunk some but not excessively. Suddenly I couldn't stand up; I felt as though my arms and legs were being yanked away from my body. My surroundings were barely recognizable. Light was strobe-like and ghosting and sound was echoing and coming at me from all directions. I sat on the floor trying to hold on to my legs, wrapping my arms tightly around them. I tried to explain to Bobby what was happening. I think I was crawling around—rolling.

He was terrified. He held me, trying to help me feel safe. I saw he was in a state, because somewhere deep down and distant a part of me was calm and collected. I observed the other part of me that was intensely occupied with the task of maintaining my body as a single unit with limbs attached. This continued for the rest of the night, but I had no sense of time passing. Bob telephoned Charlie Rothschild's brother Ed, who was a doctor. Ed told him not to worry, that by morning I should be OK.

As dawn was breaking, I stretched out my legs and arms. Whatever it was, it was over. We both fell asleep, exhausted. Someone had put something in my drink, as they say. We never found out who would do such a thing. I never voluntarily took LSD. That was it for me.

In the folk music world in the early days, it was a slow lope into marijuana use, and drug use in general. Booze was still it with the older crowd, and we were emulating them, but eventually drugs got equal billing. By the time the next group of Village explorers came on the scene, booze was on the way out, particularly with anyone who had been to college.

Downtown

The Off-Broadway theater called One Sheridan Square was located in the basement of the building where I had lived for a time with my mother and Fred before they got married. A production of the Irish playwright Brendan Behan's play *The Hostage* was playing at the theater and enjoying a long run. My sister Carla worked lights for the production and I had a job running the concession stand that was open before the show and during intermission. It was a great location, just up the street and around the corner from where Bobby and I were living on West Fourth Street.

I was standing in the back of the theater watching the play one evening when Behan himself wandered in. If Behan happened to be in the city where one of his plays was being put on, he had a habit of showing up and joining the performance. It made for interesting theater at times, especially when he engaged the actors in some improvisation. But he was a bit of a drinker and could completely disrupt the play if he was in his cups. I ran to the phone and called Bobby at home to tell him Brendan Behan was at the theater and he should come by.

Behan was very drunk. Listing left and right, he wandered onto the stage and, waving his hands about, made an incoherent speech to the actors. Then he abruptly teetered off the stage and out the door. He staggered up the stairs of the theater with Bob right behind him. Bob followed him to the White Horse, hoping for a conversation, but Behan was in no shape for anything remotely resembling talk and eventually passed out.

The rest of the evening and into the night at the infamous White Horse Tavern was as raucous as ever. The White Horse is known as the pub where, as legend has it, the Welsh poet Dylan Thomas drank himself to death in 1953 by consuming something like thirty-two shots of whiskey in one go. He performed this feat after being told by his doctor that even a single shot could kill him.

I first went to the White Horse with my older friend Pete and then hung out there on and off for many years after. At the White Horse I was introduced to the paralyzing effect of Irish whiskey when I drank Irish coffee, Ireland's cappuccino. Paddy, Tom, and Liam Clancy, the Irish folksingers who performed as the Clancy Brothers with Tommy Makem, occupied a table in the back room most nights. Already very well known, they sang and told stories and had a good time along with everyone else who ended their evenings at the White Horse. Tom Clancy chased my sister home one night all the way down Perry Street declaring his undying love. They were friends and she usually knew how to handle him, but he was particularly out of it that night and required some big guys from the bar to calm him down.

Most of the women at the White Horse knew that was the risk of staying too long at the bar when Tom Clancy was nearby and drinking heavily. He was the wildest of the brothers, and they were a wild bunch. Liam had the gift of a fine tenor voice and he truly knew how to use it. He could make you weep when he sang a ballad. Tom and Paddy were dramatic and forceful singers. Tommy Makem's liquid baritone had a tremulous vibrato and he carried the same kind of magic as Liam when he sang. I really liked Tommy. One of the songs in his repertoire that could hypnotize an audience was "The Cobbler," which began, "Oh, me name is Dick Darby, I'm a cobbler." Makem would put his foot up on a stool on the stage and proceed to rhythmically mime sewing a sole onto his shoe as he sang the song a cappella. It was mesmerizing. Together as a group the four sang traditional ballads, drinking songs, and Irish rebellion songs that made you want to take to the streets. These guys made singing a theatrical event: above all, the Clancy Brothers and Tommy Makem were actors who sang.

I used the Eighth Street Bookshop, at MacDougal, as a kind of library, reading books a little at a time, going back every few days to sneak in a few more chapters of a book I didn't have the money to buy. The very thin books of poetry were an easy read in one short visit. The Eighth Street Bookshop was known as the best bookstore in the neighborhood for new books. If you were buying old books or searching for bargains, the thing to do was to hunt and peck at the sec-ondhand bookstores and stalls along Fourth Avenue.

This was a time when bookstores weren't chain stores and had no chairs—let alone cafés—where customers could linger over books and magazines. Instead, people would lean against a shelf with a chosen book and try to be incon-spicuous. I would squeeze between display tables and scrunch down on the floor to read, hoping no one would no-tice. My friend Janet Kerr introduced me to *The Diary of Anaïs Nin*, and I read the first volume at the bookshop along with some Henry Miller novels.

Anaïs Nin kept a diary from childhood and wrote in it throughout her life. She lived in Spain, France, and the United States and recorded her many affairs, including a long liaison with Miller and his wife, June. She alluded to an incestuous relationship with her father. For Janet and me, she was a revelation. We were in awe of her feminine voice, an internal one that was mysterious, sensual, and tantalizingly illicit. We drank from it.

Janet and I met early on when she was going out with Johnny Herald, a good friend of Bobby's who was the lead singer and guitar player in the Greenbriar Boys. Johnny was lean, with chiseled features and black hair. For a city boy he had a true high lonesome sound—a gorgeous voice. "A leather-lunged tenor," said *New York Times* music critic Robert Shelton in the same article that placed Bob Dylan on the fast track to fame and fortune.

The September 29, 1961, *Times* review of Bob's performance at Gerde's was over-the-top exciting. We got the early edition of the paper late at night at the newspaper kiosk on Sheridan Square and went across the street to an all-night deli to read it. Then we went back and bought more copies.

Though the photograph was unflattering, the article wasn't by any means. The review was glorious, a true coup. Robert Shelton had been around the clubs and bars for ages, seeing every new and old performer, but he'd never written a review quite like the one he wrote for Bobby. "Resembling a cross between a choir boy and a beatnik" and "bursting at the seams with talent" were highlights. "Mr. Dylan is vague about his antecedents and birthplace, but it matters less

Shelton's breakthrough review

THE NEW YORK TIMES, FRIDAY,

Bob Dylan: A Distinctive

20-Year-Old Singer Is Bright New Face at Gerde's Club

By ROBERT SHELTON

A bright new face in folk music is appearing at Gerde's Folk City. Although only 20 years old, Bob Dylan is one of the most distinctive stylists to play in a Manhattan cabaret in months.

Resembling a cross between a choir boy and a beatnik, Mr. Dylan has a cherubic look and a mop of tousled hair he partly covers with a Huck Finn black corduroy cap. His clothes may need a bit of tailoring, but when he works his guitar, harmonica or piano and composes new songs faster than he can remember them, there is no doubt that he is bursting at the seams with talent.

Mr. Dylan's voice is anything but pretty. He is consciously trying to recapture the rude beauty of a Southern field hand musing in melody on his porch. All the "husk and bark" are left on his notes and a searing intensity pervades his songs.

Slow-Motion Mood

Mr. Dylan is both comedian and tragedian. Like a vaudeville actor on the rural circuit, he offers a variety of droll musical monologues: "Talking Bear Mountain" lampoons the overcrowding of an excursion boat, "Talking New York" satirizes his troubles in gaining recognition and "Talking Havah Nagilah" burlesques the folk-music craze and the singer himself.

In his serious vein, Mr. Dylan seems to be performing in a slow-motion film. Elasticized phrases are drawn out until you think they may snap. He rocks his head and body, closes his

Bob Dylan

eyes in reverie and seems to be groping for a word or a mood, then resolves the tension benevolently by finding the word and the mood.

He may mumble the text of "House of the Rising Sun" in a scarcely understandable growl or sob, or clearly enunciate the poetic poignancy of a Blind Lemon Jefferson blues: "One

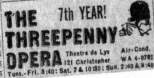

Folk-Song Stylist

Greenbriar Boys Are Also on Bill With Bluegrass Music

kind favor I ask of you—See that my grave is kept clean."

Mr. Dylan's highly personalized approach toward folk song is still evolving. He has been sopping up influences like a sponge. At times, the drama he aims at is off-target melodrama and his stylization threatens to topple over as a mannered excess.

But if not for every taste, his music-making has the mark of originality and inspiration, all the more noteworthy for his youth. Mr. Dylan is vague about his antecedents and birthplace, but it matters less where he has been than where he is going, and that would seem to be straight up.

If Mr. Dylan's pace is slow, the other half of the show at Folk City compensates for it. A whirlwind trio, the Greenbriar Boys, whips up some of the fastest, most tempestuous Bluegrass music this side of Nashville on eight cylinders and don blue collars and black string-bow ties. They join Mr. Herald, a leather-lunged tenor whose athletic, high-range country yodeling is a thing of wonder.

The fourth member of the group, a Virginia fiddler, Buddy nineteen strings. (Five strings on Bob Yellin's banjo, six on John Herald's guitar and eight on Ralph Rinzler's mandolin.)

The Greenbriar Boys were the first Bluegrass band to play regularly in a New York night club. Messrs. Yellin and Rinzler take off their executive white collars each evening to Pendleton, appeared with them recently at the coffee-serving One Sheridan Square, but his Pentacostal Baptist upbringing forbids his working in, let alone patronizing, a saloon.

Bluegrass is a heady, vibrant sort of hoedown music, the contemporary successor to the old-time country tunes of the New Lost City Ramblers. As this trio performs it, Bluegrass is a springy, tightly arranged instrumental and vocal ensemble style that is frequently very funny and always fresh. The trio's large granary includes virtuoso pieces like "Rawhide," baleful ditties such as "Farewell, Amelia Earhart, First Lady of the Air" and gospel admonitions on the order of "We Need a Whole Lot More of Jesus and a Lot Less Rock 'n' Roll."

where he has been than where he is going, and that would seem to be straight up" was another insightful line.

The Greenbriar Boys were the headliners at Gerde's, and although they were very favorably reviewed, clearly the article's focus was on Bob. Nearly all of his pay for the two-week gig went right back into Gerde's coffers, however. He

had one hell of a bar tab, and now it was obvious he was going to have the money to pay it.

Janet Kerr had left Seattle for New York City sometime in
the late 1950s, and although she was in her early twenties
when we met in 1961, she'd already been married and was in
the process of getting a divorce. She had blond hair and
jewel-like bright blue eyes with thick black lashes. Unlike
the other girls around the Village, Janet wore red lipstick
and blush on her cheeks in addition to the eye makeup we
all wore. She invited me to her apartment on East Eighty-

first Street near her job at
the Metropolitan Museum
of Art, and I was really impressed with her creativity.
She'd crafted a lovely home
for herself out of odds and
ends that she'd found on
the street or had made herself. A short time later she
moved to Johnny's apart-
ment in the Village, and
since Bobby and Johnny
were pals the four of us
went around together. Or
the two guys would go off
someplace, and Janet and I
would go someplace else.
Then we'd all meet later.

Janet Kerr

One night Johnny, Janet, Bobby, and I were at the White Horse when Bob Shelton, who had a penchant for protesting that "it is the shank of the evening" whenever there was a sign of things winding down, invited everyone back to his apartment on Waverly Place. The four of us finished our drinks and managed the walk from Hudson Street to Waverly Place without incident. Once there, despite the state we were already in, we accepted the offer of more to drink. Bobby, clasping the stem of a full glass of wine in his hand, slumped on the couch and within minutes fell fast asleep. The party went on around him, with everyone speculating as to when he would let go of his glass. When he woke up some time later, the glass was still upright in his hand and not so much as a drop had spilled—a remarkable sight to all assembled. I stared at him in amazement. What? he mumbled as he took a swig.

The Greenbriar Boys played a lot at Gerde's so Janet was around for the music as often as I was. She sang and knew how to play the autoharp, but back then she didn't let on that she could. Janet was inventive with clothing the way I was and we used to haunt the thrift shops looking for interesting stuff to wear. We both made our own clothes and we'd often roam the fabric stores in search of good remnants. We didn't really like to sew per se, but we loved making things.

The dusty secondhand bookshops and the junk stores along Canal Street were great places to find inspiration and precious treasures. Eventually we made and sold art-to-wear jewelry that we constructed out of bits of our cut-up paintings, papier-mâché mounted on tin can lids, and other found objects. We came up with the idea of making jewelry that would clip on and then dangle from the tops of our boots. We called our line Suja-baubles, from Suze and Janet.

We printed up business cards and made portable display cases for our wares out of old file boxes. It was a little too soon for stores to con-template a line of hippie or bohemian clothing, let alone jewelry of the handmade sort. We were thrilled when we managed to get an appointment with the accessories buyer for Bloomingdale's. But the woman did not bother to hide her disdain as we earnestly showed her our jewelry and demonstrated how to dress up a pair of boots with a Suja-bauble.

Offended that someone in her position could be so blatantly rude, we left the store and headed back downtown to think of other stores to try. We managed to make a little money here and there, but it certainly wasn't a living, which is what we were hoping for.

We did have fun trying though.

One of my favorite Bob Dylan songs is one I first heard Willie Nelson sing on his CD *Across the Borderline:* "What Was It You Wanted?" I had a sense right away that only he could have written it.

To me, this song is the essence of Bob Dylan. It showcases his acerbic wit and his ability to twist multiple meanings around his finger. The old songs, from the early time of his life in which I participated, are so recognizable, so naked, that I cannot listen to them easily. They bring back everything. There is nothing mysterious or shrouded with hidden meaning for me. They are raw, intense, and clear.

When he started out, Bob was playful, a mix of Harpo Marx and Woody Guthrie, with a big dose of himself as a binding ingredient. Onstage he moved around a lot, removing the harmonicas from his pockets and placing them on a nearby stool, fiddling with the capo on his guitar and the corduroy cap on his head. Then he would adjust or change the harmonica in the holder around his neck, retune his guitar, and go back to organizing the harmonicas on the stool.

He rarely said anything. He might give a quick grin or grimace and make the little noises of someone who was working hard. When he finally began to play, he had the audience's attention and he knew it. All that fumbling around was the warm-up for a set that was either very down home or hypnotic and distant. From the very beginning he was a charismatic performer.

Though he was developing a persona and absorbing many influences, he was always his own self. There were people who saw him as needing guidance and tried to mold and teach him. He went along, glad to get the input, the information, and the help; but he knew his own way to be. He sorted and sifted and took only what he needed. Ultimately much of the rancor many felt as he moved on and up and away, taking everything within him and leaving them behind, was due to the fact that these people wanted acknowledgment for what they had given him. He would not be who he is if it weren't for me, they'd said.

He was not the person they thought he was. He kept going; he moved on. Look what happened to Lot's wife when she looked back.

> What was it you wanted?
> Tell me again I forgot.
>
> Whatever you wanted
> What could it be
> Did somebody tell you
> That you could get it from me,
> Is it something that comes natural
> Is it easy to say,
> Why do you want it,
> Who are you anyway?

Bob's reaction to being signed by Columbia Records in the fall of 1961—handpicked by the legendary producer John Hammond, no less—was exuberant. The *New York Times* review was having an immediate and positive effect. Bobby had performed some songs for Hammond during a rehearsal for the recording session when he played backup harmonica for the singer Carolyn Hester, and Hammond recognized something special in the raw, unblemished sound. It was John Hammond who got recording contracts for the young Billie Holiday, Teddy Wilson, Benny Goodman, and Count Basie, among others. Hammond had a reputation for finding gold. He'd signed Aretha Franklin. There was money to be made in folk music and a growing flock of very good musicians were available for the record companies to pick from. Most companies were hunting for the next Kingston Trio or another Joan Baez. Instead Hammond was struck by something he saw in Bob while he was producing Carolyn Hester's album. Hammond was intrigued by the unpolished yet confident style that this unique young performer managed to exude.

After he secured Bob Dylan for Columbia Records, John Hammond went on to sign Bruce Springsteen and Stevie Ray Vaughan. Tricky to predict the future, but John Hammond obviously had an ear for it.

That a big, prestigious company like Columbia rather than Folkways or Vanguard wanted to sign Bob was true recognition of his talent. The road to where he knew he was headed was being paved. Each newly paved part brought his destiny closer to the present. There were no back roads to retrace, no side roads to follow—only forward, only ahead.

Quietly Bob said: This is the beginning of what I have always known. I am going to be big.

He said it calmly and knowingly, and it was true. No bragging, no Look at me, no Ain't I grand. That was not his way. He spoke only what he knew to be true. He would not have said so otherwise.

Out on the street and in the clubs he celebrated with excitement and maybe even displayed a "drinks on me" joviality, though he was not known for his generosity. The inevitable envy and resentment of other folksingers were to be deflected if at all possible. Many who knew Bobby felt he would be successful, although no one knew how huge he would become. Certainly Dave Van Ronk and Izzy Young knew Bob would be culled from the crop of performers on the street. Early on they and others saw, as Hammond did, that Bob possessed something more, that he stood out in some rough-edged way.

Performers who had been on the scene longer and had their niche carved out on the folk circuit were aghast at the audacity of this young upstart punk. The malicious underbelly of the folk music beast was revealed, and it was positively an unpleasant sight.

Bob was serious about the work he intended to do and paid ill-wishers no mind. He was ready to set down on record the music that he had accumulated within himself up to that point.

I had never been in a recording studio before and it was exhilarating. The speakers were huge and the playback sound enveloped the studio, giving me the sensation that I was inside the music—listening to sound from the inside out. When the album came out and I read the liner notes by "Stacey Williams," an alternate moniker for Bob Shelton, I laughed at his description of me as sitting "devotedly and wide-eyed through the recording session" and Bob as fretting his guitar on "In My Time of Dyin' " with my lipstick holder. I didn't wear lipstick and how typical of a guy to translate my reaction to being in a recording studio for the first time as devotion. At least he got "wide-eyed" right.

During the sessions, John Hammond did not interfere with Bob's process but watched and listened, letting Bob do as he wished. Columbia planned to rush his album into stores within two months, believing Dylan to be the next big thing. I watched Bob as he sang and saw his focus, his loyalty to the work at hand, the art he was making. Bob was intense, both sure and not sure of what he was doing. Afterward he'd ask: What do you think, what do you think?

$\mathcal{B}$ob wanted a shearling jacket to wear for his picture on the cover of the album, but there was no way he could afford a real one. We had a hard time finding a jacket that looked right. We finally found a synthetic shearling in a shop on Sixth Avenue in the Village that looked pretty good—almost like the real thing—and had a price to match.

Bob carefully adjusted the collar, just so. He was ready for his self-titled close-up.

I zzy Young produced a concert by Bob Dylan at Carnegie Chapter Hall, one of the smaller stages within Carnegie Hall, on November 4, 1961. Izzy said that Albert Grossman put him up to it but that he didn't mind, because he thought Bob Dylan was great. It was a mystery why only fifty-three people showed up. Bob was better known downtown, yet between the *New York Times* review and a contract with Columbia Records (the album wasn't released until March 1962), his reputation was rapidly growing all over town. Maybe the paltry turnout had to do with the venue on Fifty-seventh Street, so far above Fourteenth Street, the northernmost border of Greenwich Village.

Bob sang traditional folk songs and blues and casually wandered around the big stage in the nearly empty hall as if he were in a downtown coffeehouse. He was not discouraged by the low turnout; he liked to perform, and every performance helped him develop his chops and work his repertoire. Though Izzy lost money, he paid Bobby ten or twenty dollars, because as he said, you always pay the workingman for his efforts.

Van Ronk called Paul Clayton "Pablo" for reasons I no longer remember—or maybe there was no reason other than the translation of his name to Spanish and Dave's penchant for nicknames. Back in those days, the study of the origins of traditional music was a passion among musicians. Some folksingers believed they had to perform a song authentically in the traditional style with no deviation from the way the original singer sang it on the scratchy old LPs they listened to, taken primarily from Harry Smith's *Anthology of American Folk Music*; those recordings were the Holy Grail. A folksinger who dared reinterpret a traditional song by adding a personal inflection of some sort was scorned as inauthentic. Yet most of these performers were about as authentic as Las Vegas. They were middle-class city or suburban kids who had never been near a backwoods except at summer camp. This same purist attitude was at the root of the problem when Dylan went electric.

Paul Clayton was one of the people around the Village with a vast knowledge of American folk music. He had studied at the University of Virginia with a well-known folklorist, Arthur Kyle Davis, and had done a lot of traveling to collect songs. Paul was also a folksinger with a smooth voice and clean guitar style, and he performed far and wide, starting in the 1950s. He and Bob hit it off and spent a lot of time together. Paul really cared for Bob, and when Bob planned a cross-country trip in February 1964 he asked Paul to come with him along with his buddy and bodyguard, Victor Maimudes, and Pete Karman.

In May 1962, two months after Bob's first album was

released, Bob, Paul, and I went on a trip south. The final destination was Paul's log cabin in Brown's Cove, Virginia, not far from Charlottesville. We drove into Virginia through the beautiful landscape of the Blue Ridge Mountains. Paul was the driver and I sat with him in the front seat while Bob sprawled in the back playing his guitar, working on songs. It was the first road trip for me since the car accident I'd been in, and I was overcome by fear, sitting upright with my foot on an imaginary brake.

When Paul asked me why I was so tense, I mumbled something about the accident. He looked straight at me with his liquid blue eyes and said: That is a terrible trauma. Tell me what happened.

Revealing personal information wasn't something that came easily to me and I was getting good at deflecting questions that came too close, but his approach was so direct and sincere that I began to talk. He listened and asked questions until the whole tale was told. He said he had wondered about my scar.

Talking about a traumatic car accident while driving in a car had an odd relaxing effect and I was fine for the rest of the trip, relieved that Paul had pulled the story out of me.

I think we ended up telling horrible accident stories for a time, and maybe even singing a few, as Paul drove the mountain roads with nary a screeching tire on any of the curves.

When we got to Charlottesville we stayed with friends of Paul's before taking off to meet some old-time blues musicians he knew from his travels. We hoped to visit Etta Baker, the great blues guitar player famous for her song "Rail-

road Bill," but it never happened. To impress the folkies
back in New York, Bob joked, we should say we met her,
anyway, but we never did. You could blow your cool by not
being cool about things like that.

Since I had never been south of Washington, D.C., the
trip was a revelation. Though I'd seen photographs and films
of dirt-poor and segregated America, actually being in it
was something else. Clean, tree-lined streets with painted
white houses gave way to dusty roads with few trees and run-
down shacks made of wood boards or tin. At the first house
where we stopped, Paul and Bob didn't think it would be a
good idea for me to go in, the living conditions were grim,
so I waited in the car.

I went in with him and Bob at the next house, though,
and it made me wonder what the first one must have been
like inside. This shack was windowless and smaller than a
New York City studio apartment. It was wide enough for a
twin bed against one wall and a chair or two tight against the
opposite wall with hardly any walking space in between.
Coming in from the bright sunshine, I couldn't see a thing
at first.

After a minute I made out a figure sitting on the bed. He
seemed very old and thin and when he smiled he had no
teeth. I don't remember if he played something first or if
Bob did. I don't even remember what Bob played.

But the reaction of the man on the bed was indelible.
When Bob finished playing, the old blues man leaned forward and he said: You got it, boy. You got it.

After we'd gone outside, more people came by to listen and the old guy said again, stomping his feet in time to Bob's playing: That boy's got it. The boy's got his music in him.

$\mathcal{B}$ack in Charlottesville Paul Clayton threw a party for Bob's twenty-first birthday. We had a real good time listening to music and making music at Steve Wilson's house. Steve was an old buddy of Paul's and the friendship opened to include us. When Steve moved up to New York City at some point we saw a lot of each other and he became a close friend of Van Ronk's. I think Steve played a Dobro, although I'm not sure how because he only had one arm.

After the birthday we all got into the car to go to Paul's cabin. We bought food to make a big stew to cook outside on the fire. There was a brook running on his property that was clean, cold, and clear as glass—delicious water for drinking. When I went to the brook to wash and peel the carrots, I reveled in the sound of the water rushing over the stones as it chugged down from the far-off mountains. It reminded me of the brook near my grandparents' farm.

As I scraped away at the carrots and popped a few pieces in my mouth, I felt my eyes starting to itch. So I rubbed them. When I wet them with water from the brook, they only itched more. By the time I got back to the cabin my eyes were nearly swollen shut and itched like mad. The back of my throat began to feel scratchy and I was in a bit of a stupor. When I could no longer see and was having trouble breathing, it got a little scary. A decision was made to take me to the nearest hospital, which meant driving back to Charlottesville—and that made me feel even worse because I was ruining the weekend.

At the hospital I was given a shot of cortisone and told I probably had an allergic reaction to the carrots. Out of nowhere I had developed a serious raw carrot allergy. I had a feeling it had something to do with what's in the ground they grow in and the pesticides used, but what do I know?

I waited a year and then tasted a tiny drop of organic carrot juice. Immediately my throat began to itch, and that was it for raw carrots and me forever.

Back in New York City by the end of May it was time for me to get ready to leave for Europe on June 9. I had to pick up my passport in Midtown, at Rockefeller Center. Sylvia Tyson came with me and, as we walked up Fifth Avenue, at some point my pocket got picked. The running joke among Villagers is that it is never safe to travel above Fourteenth Street. I came back downtown swearing that this was true and wondering if crossing the Atlantic fell into the same category.

P a r t   T w o

Fate

> Small tall fragile still
>
> climbing upward down a hill
>
> legs that carry body prone
>
> hands that linger soft like stone
>
> at the bottom glad to find
>
> feet to rest with more to climb
>
> (NOTEBOOK ENTRY, 1962)

Italy and Indecision

My mother and Fred, who had married earlier in the year and had moved to his place in New Jersey, were planning a trip to France and Italy in June 1962 and my mother decided to take me with her. She wanted to revive the plans she had made for me to go to school in Italy after I graduated from high school—plans that had been destroyed by the car accident in March 1961.

But my life had changed in the last year.

Now it was a difficult choice for me: going to Italy meant leaving Bob and the life I was living in New York. It was a big decision, and no matter which choice I made, it would have a lasting impact. If I stayed, I might regret the opportunity missed for the second time. Before the car accident wiped out the dream of going to live in Italy, I had really relished the idea, but things were different now. I would be away from my love and my life.

I drove friends nuts asking them what they thought I should do. Terri Thal and Sylvia Tyson said the same thing: It's a good opportunity to go to Europe, and if you don't take it you might regret it. You will be back, and if this relationship is meant to last it will, even if you are gone for a time.

I wrung my hands and agonized. Bob waited me out. He tried not to make it difficult for me by pushing me to stay. It was my decision, he said, but he would much rather I didn't go. He was really angry at Terri, though, for not reinforcing his view that I not leave him.

My mother did the opposite. When she pushed for me to go, I was nonplussed by her sudden interest in my life and well-being. My history with her made it hard to believe she was sincere. But I told myself that maybe I should accept her sincerity since she seemed genuinely happy with Fred and finally had financial security after some very hard times. She might be all right for real.

On the other hand, I wondered if her motivation to yank me out of my life might be to show her new husband that she was concerned about her wayward eighteen-year-old daughter. Fred knew where I was living but had no inkling I was "living in sin" with Bob. He was a respectable professor and an ex-navy officer who was no doubt put off by the freewheeling life her youngest daughter led. In any case, I knew my mother did not approve of Bob at all. He paid her no homage and she paid him none. They saw through each other in some way that had nothing to do with me.

In the end, I went mainly to stop the chatter of indecision inside my head. The tickets, reservations, and plans for a school in Perugia that had been made, confirmed, and paid for mostly by Fred were also hard to turn down, even though they'd been presented to me as a fait accompli. Fred and my mother had booked passage on the *Rotterdam*, leaving New York on June 9, 1962, and arriving in Le Havre, France, a week later. After a few days in Paris (Paris!), we would drive down to a town in the south of France where Fred's son and daughter-in-law and her family lived. We'd spend a day or two with them, then drive through Switzerland to Italy over the Alps. It was an enticing itinerary but also a very long trip, and I had lingering worries about spending all that time with my mother and Fred.

Neither Bob nor I quite realized the implications of a departure that would lead to a long separation. We joked about the passengers I would have to spend a week with on a floating hotel. When the ship was ready to sail and it was time for visitors to disembark, we were still joking as we said good-bye. But wisps of sadness and foreboding enveloped me as I watched him walk to the stairs, then turn and smile and wave. The ship's foghorn sounded over and over as the ocean liner began slowly pulling away from the dock, sliding out to sea toward the horizon. The people waving from shore were getting smaller and smaller until they were no longer visible.

I spent most of the voyage in a state of numbness. I wandered about the ship looking at the ocean during the day and watching it change color as the sky slipped into afternoon and into evening and into night. I watched the stars take over the sky and fill the horizon as the ocean turned an opaque black that made it look menacing and primordial.

I kept to myself, reading or drawing. I crawled out of my shell when I wandered into a group of kids my age listening to a young man play the guitar and sing folk songs. I hung out with them a bit and attempted to teach the guitar player the song Bob had written recently called "Blowin' in the Wind." Even though I stumbled over some of the words, I remembered the melody well enough to sing it to him, but since I can't carry a tune he didn't really learn it.

In Paris I was so happy to find a letter from Bob waiting for me at the hotel. I answered it right away. He described the ship sailing off and watching me, as I had watched him, getting smaller and smaller.

The drive through the French countryside was beautiful, but I barely noticed it. My spirits lifted during the time we spent with the French family Fred's son had married into. They lived well. I remember sitting at a long table with other people in addition to the three of us and being served endless dishes of delicious food. A different wine was poured for each course and a sorbet to cleanse the palate was eaten between the meat and the fish courses. What a glorious way to live!

On the drive from France into Switzerland, my mother told stories from the time she lived in Paris toward the end of the 1930s, before the Second World War. It was after her first husband had drowned and she didn't care about anything anymore and was willing to take risks with her own life. She went to Paris to work with a group of young Communists who were helping Italians escape from Fascist Italy. American passports donated by Italian Americans were altered and then smuggled into Italy. She became a courier, delivering the forged passports to a contact in Spain or in Italy. Italian partisans who wanted to join the International Brigades going to Spain to fight against Franco in the Spanish Civil War also used the passports.

As we got closer to the Swiss town of Montreux, the

THE PENGUIN POETS
D 26
LORD BYRON

To you From
I, me, Bob
on this holy day
I give to you

this (penguin) here
present that
I purchased
for you in

the New York
rain

Hatfully
Loving
You,
Lord Byron Dylan
1962

An inscribed gift from Bob

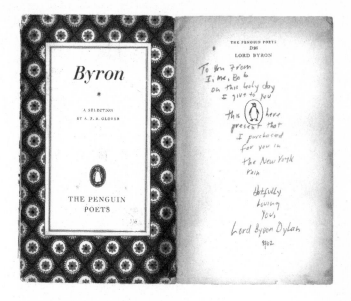

THE PENGUIN POETS
D59
LORD BYRON

*To you from
I, me, Bob
on this holy day
I give to you

this Ⓟ here
present that
I purchased
for you in
the New York
rain

Hotfully
Loving
You,
Lord Byron Dylan
1962*

subject switched to poetry. Because my mother had read poetry to me as a child, I sensed the rhythm in language before I could understand the meaning of the words. The dramatic and romantic poems of Lord Byron became one of my youthful favorites. On a rocky island rising out of the water on Lake Léman in Montreux stood the twelfth-century castle of Chillon. Byron had written a poem called "The Prisoner of Chillon," about a political prisoner held in the dungeons below the castle, and I wanted to visit it.

That day we seemed to have the castle to ourselves. I recited what I could remember of "The Prisoner of Chillon" and, although it was hardly fitting, "She Walks in Beauty," the only other Byron poem I knew by heart. The prisons were dank dungeons carved from the rock that supported the castle's foundation; prisoners were chained there for years on end. Byron's poem was about a real person, François Bonivard, a lay official at a priory in Geneva who spoke out in favor of the Reformation and was rewarded by the Duke of Savoy with a sentence of six years shackled to a stone pillar. "The Prisoner of Chillon" spoke of the glory of sacrifice for a cause.

The words of Byron, Shelley, Keats and of the many other writers who had traveled to Italy in the nineteenth century and the early twentieth were good company as we drove over the Alps and into Italy.

After traveling through landscapes I had seen reproduced in Renaissance paintings my whole life, we stayed in Florence, where I nearly fainted before the powerful unfinished sculptures by Michelangelo, not to mention the actual statue of David at the Galleria dell'Accademia. As I walked over one of the bridges that cross the Arno River, I thought of my uncle Peter and his recitations of Dante encountering his adored Beatrice.

Finally we made it to the medieval hill town of Perugia, in the center of Italy, between Florence and Rome. Perugia has a long history of hard and bloody battles fought against various popes. In the 1500s tall towers and spires were constructed by the nobility and the wealthy commercial class as symbols of their wealth and power, the same reasons skyscrapers are built today (Trump Tower in New York City is an example). The nobility were contesting the power of the Vatican, which ruled the Papal States, so the Church as a reprisal destroyed the towers, dismantling them and using the stones to build an underground city cum fortress. This would serve as fortification against future invaders who dared threaten its omnipotence. The Papal States and the states controlled by the great noble families—the Medici, the Sforza, and in Umbria the Baglioni—were constantly at war over power and control of the land that would become a united Italy about three centuries later, thanks to Garibaldi.

It is also interesting to note that in the regions of Umbria—of which Perugia is the capital—and Tuscany, unsalted bread is made to this day. The citizens refused to use salt when the Vatican levied a hefty tax on it in the 1540s. For the Papal States to tax salt, a prime resource that was as vital to food preservation as refrigeration became in the nineteenth century, was enough to provoke rebellion.

My mother and Fred were on their way to Sardinia. Fred was a devout Italophile who hoped to live in Italy when he retired from teaching. The decorous gentleman with his Anglo-Saxon ways had found his Anna Magnani, and he desired nothing but to live in her country of origin. He planned to buy a house in Sardinia and arrange to teach for half the year in semiretirement in the United States and live the other six months in Italy. Their plan now was to leave me in Perugia and continue their trip after the day or two it took to get me settled. They did just that.

The road trip was over, and suddenly I found myself in a strange town, with a room in a *pensione* on a street named

Corso Garibaldi. I was enrolled in a three-month Italian language course at L'Università per Stranieri, the University for Foreigners.

Students came here from all over the world to learn Italian and take courses in Italian history and culture. Classes were conducted entirely in Italian, an excellent method of learning a language by complete immersion. The Italian course I was enrolled in would begin in a week. In the interim I would find my way as best I could. I had a sinking sensation that I had fallen for my mother's wicked scheme to get me away from Bob—whom she hated, I now saw clearly—and away from my vagabond life with him in Greenwich Village, just to impress her new straight-up, Waspy professor husband. I felt sick.

Meals were included at the *pensione* and served at specific times, the signora who ran it explained before I went off to my room to unpack. I must have done some unpacking, but suddenly I was overcome by a feeling of anxiety that left me unable to move. I sat frozen on the edge of the bed with my hands in my lap like dead weights. My feet didn't feel as though they were part of my body. I must have sat like that for hours.

Mealtimes came and went. At some point that day, or maybe the next morning, someone knocked on my door and asked me if I was all right. I wasn't, but I said I was, *grazie*, and then like a zombie I went to the meal that was being served then—whatever it was. After sitting quietly and watching everyone having a fine time together, I excused myself and went back to my room to sleep.

Three days passed this way. By the fourth, I felt less numb: a sense of place and surroundings crept back in. Life was reentering my body. I had no towel and was in need of one. My hair was dirty. I was hungry. I wanted to write to Bob and let him know where I was. I missed him terribly. The shock of being on my own in this strange place where I had only a limited knowledge of the language and knew absolutely no one was terrifying. It is as if everything that had happened in my entire life came to a full stop in this little room in this medieval hill town in the country of Italy, the homeland of my family.

I looked up the word *towel* in my pocket dictionary: *asciugamano*. Oh my—how could I possibly pronounce that? I wasn't sure I would be able to speak at all, so I underlined the word and, clutching the dictionary, I went out into the street, where everywhere people were going about their business. I joined the flow of people walking in one direction, hoping I would eventually pass a store with an *asciugamano* in the window that I could just point to rather than ask for.

After a while I saw a store that seemed the kind of place that would sell a thing such as a towel. When I walked in the door of the shop everyone stopped speaking and turned to look at me. The attention was unexpected but not unfriendly. When I opened my dictionary and showed it to the woman closest to me, she peered at the underlined word. *Asciugamano*, she said and smiled. Sì, sì.

After a discussion with the other customers, the saleswoman showed me an array of brightly colored striped towels.

I chose one and offered my wallet to her. She took some bills and then gave me change and a neatly wrapped package with my precious towel. I nodded and smiled at everyone and left. I never said a word. I'm sure they thought I was a deaf mute.

The next step was to find a place to buy stamps so I could mail my letter home to Bob.

The letters Bob wrote to me in 1962 during the eight months I was away are letters written by a young writer on the rise who is in love. They are very personal, full of pain, humor, and storytelling. The writing is raw at times yet they are wonderful letters:

> Nothing much is happening here I guess—Bob Shelton is waiting for Jean—the dogs are waiting to go out, the thiefs are waiting for an old lady—little kids are waiting for school—the cop is waiting to beat up on someone—them lousey bums are waiting for money—Grove Street is waiting for Bedford Street—the dirty are waiting to be cleaned—Everybody is waiting for cooler weather—and I am just waiting for you—.

I hope I recognized back then how good the letters were, but when you are in love you don't always notice such things. Noticing the quality of the writing would have required a degree of detachment I couldn't muster. It was difficult to see beyond the back-and-forth conversation we were having.

He wrote to tell me about what he was doing, where he was going, and who he was seeing:

sort of unconsiously got very tired — I couldn't
think of anything to say — Seeing all the
headlines about War and Cuba and even once
sitting in the Figaro all nite waiting for the
world to end (the 1st nite Kennedy talked and
The Prussian ships were getting nearer Cuba —)
I honestly to God thought it was all over —
Not that I gave a shit any more then the
next guy (that's a lie I guess) but it was
interesting waiting for the bombs to fall and
Kill you — And it really seemed that way —
If the world did end that nite, all I
wanted was to be with you — And it was im —
possible cause you're so far away — And

I saw another great movie—"The Magnificent
Seven"—oh I just couldn't believe it—I hate to
say it but I'm Yul Brynner—Gawd am I ever him—
I'm a gun man—I cleaned up a Mexican peon
town with six other gunmen—I shot Eli Wallach—
I thought for a minute I coulda been Eli Wallach
but after seeing Yul—I just knew I was him—nobody ever had to tell me—I just knew it right off
the bat.

I finally cleaned up the house—I shoved out all
the pigs—threw out all the cat shit and shoveled
the horse manure out in the hall—it's cleaner
now—.

Some of the words he wrote in the letters became song lyrics, others he put in quotes so I would know they were from a newly written song:

> I had another recording session you know—I sang six more songs—you're in two of them—Bob Dy-lan's Blues and Down The Highway ("All you five

& ten cent women with nothing in your heads I
got a real gal I'm loving and I'll lover her 'til I'm
dead so get away from my door and my window
too—right now"). Anyway you're in those two
songs specifically—and another one too—"I'm in
the Mood for You"—which is for you but I don't
mention your name. . . .

I wrote a song about that statue we saw in
Washington of Tom Jefferson—you're in it.

The letters and the songs have the same rhythm. He is
always recognizable because he writes true to what he feels
and sees in the world.

REVELATIONS

While in Italy I read Françoise Gilot's memoir, *Life with
Picasso*. I expected to learn about Picasso, an artist I loved,
but instead the book turned into something entirely different. It made me think about Bob. I forgot all about Picasso.
I felt I was reading a book of revelations, lessons, warnings.
Even though Picasso was a much older man than Bob and
had experienced a lot more, their personalities were so similar it was astounding.

Picasso did as he pleased, not worrying about the consequences for the people around him or the effect his actions
had on them. He took no responsibility, clarified nothing,
came to no decisions and did nothing that would have made
it possible or easier for the various women he was involved

with to leave him and get on with their lives. He was a magnet, and the force field surrounding him was so strong it was not easy to pull away.

His art was the main function of his life. At the end of his arm was a brush.

I was floored. The same feeling kicked in that I had felt in New York: that men could always have it both ways. They were born into a society that gave them permission to do as they pleased. Women, on the other hand, were sidelined.

And for the male artist (Picasso, Bob) it didn't matter what others expected or felt or thought of them or their work; they just did it. I could identify with that all I wanted, but at that time I could not live it outright. Permission was not granted. Females were guests, not participants.

In her memoir Gilot wrote about what it meant to be around "genius." At eighteen, I was not mature enough to understand what it meant to nurture genius. Or rather, I knew what it meant, but I was young and in love with this guy Bob. I didn't think of him that way—as an abstraction, a genius, someone to handle with care, to treat in some special way. We would nurture each other as needed and as equals.

All the talk in the Village about his incredible talent, his uniqueness—did that mean I should treat him differently? Wouldn't that be detrimental in the long and short run for both of us, no matter his gifts or the outcome of this love story? More mulling, more confusion only made it harder for me to think straight. I read the book through twice, searching for an arrow to point me somewhere.

When I was away from him all those months, he chan-
neled what he was feeling into a very creative time. He
wrote many songs at a fevered clip. He was in white heat. He
performed often and well and wrote beautiful songs about
many things, including the pain caused by a lover who is far
away. A recording from that time of him singing the traditional ballad "Barbara Allen" tears at the heartstrings.

In my youthful confusion I was still struggling for permission to be. All that was offered to a musician's girlfriend
in the early 1960s was a role as her boyfriend's "chick," a
string on his guitar. And in the case of Bob's rising fame, I
would be a gatekeeper—one step closer to an idol. People
would want to know me just to get closer to him. My significance would be based on his greater significance. That idea
did not entice.

I tried to sort out the feelings I had as a female in a man's
world, without having any of the vocabulary to do so. I tried
to figure out this guy who was calling me to come home to
him, writing letters full of love; yet when I was with him, he
seemed to take my presence for granted. I was expected just
to be there by his side as he went about his business.
Women and girls were permitted to sit at the table, where
they would be served without any hesitation, but they were
not to ask for any more. The concept of equality between
men and women was unheard of.

I saw no way to reconcile the larger world I was discovering in Italy and what would be required of me if I went
back to New York. So I stayed on in Italy; I tried to explain
why to Bob.

I loved him and he loved me, but I had doubts about him, his honesty, and the way life would be. I hadn't gone to college and in Italy I was living that experience. As soon as I found out there was an art school in Perugia, I enrolled. At the Accademia di Belle Arti and certainly at the University for Foreigners, I was around people my age from different countries: I was learning, learning, learning. There were no dark, smoky clubs like in New York, but there was conversation and music at outdoor cafés and in the piazzas.

I took long walks out into the country with a drawing pad and books of poetry. I sat under ancient olive trees to draw them in their soft, lolling landscape and tried to read French and Italian poetry in the original. I smoked gritty Italian-brand cigarettes that you could purchase a few at a time with a packet of waxy matches and listened to the music of Yves Montand, Jacques Brel, Charles Aznavour, and weird Italian Elvis imitators.

I decided to cut my nearly waist-length hair to a more manageable length. Cutting it was also a reaction to the grown-up stylishness of the Italian and other European women and my desire not to look so obviously foreign.

Bob's response was:

> Yes maybe I wish maybe you didn't cut your hair—
> it's so good—it was the only blond hair that didn't
> look like hay—it'll grow back tho huh? Maybe
> you won't cut it no more then. . . .
>
> I think I'll go out now and get a crew cut—no I
> won't—yes I will—who knows—

Matricola N. 341.

TESSERA DI IMMATRICOLAZIONE

Sig. na ROTOLO S. Justine
nato a New York city
il 20 novembre 1943
di nazionalità U.S.A.
Passaporto N. B/135413
è stato immatricolato studente nei Corsi
Estivi di Pittura e Scultura per Cittadini
Stranieri nell'Anno Accademico 1961/62
per il Corso di Pittura
il giorno 1.9.62

IL DIRETTORE   IL PRESIDENTE

IL DIRETTORE AMM.VO

FIRMA DELLO STUDENTE
Justine Rotolo

The pastime of the young men in Perugia was to engage the foreign women who paraded by them all summer long in their miniskirts. They were unrelenting and the easiest way to have them leave you alone was to give in to an introduction and an exchange of names. On the ship I had started reading Lawrence Durrell's *Alexandria Quartet*, and in Perugia I began giving my name to anyone who stopped me as "Justine," after the title character of the first volume. Somehow I liked the idea and used that name all the time, claiming it was my middle name (it wasn't). That was that.

I had a Swiss friend, Rosemarie, who was an outsider like me and also avoided the organized cultural activities the University for Foreigners promoted. She spoke German, French, and English and was now learning Italian. I loved to hear Rosemarie count in German, even though she carefully explained to me that it was Swiss German, not German German. I made her say the number 555 over and over; I found all those "foonfy" sounds strung together hysterically funny. She made me say "thirty-three and a third" in English over and over for all the lispy "th, th, th" sounds.

At the university there was a dignified elderly man who handled the complicated needs of the students, a kind of concierge at a multilingual establishment. He was especially attentive, in a fatherly way, toward me and I repaid him by publicly embarrassing him in front of the crowd of students and instructors who were always hovering around him. I was picking up Italian rapidly and felt more confident every day. And when I was in doubt about a word, I would Italianize an English one. Sometimes it worked well enough. And sometimes it did not, to unfortunate effect.

When this reserved man offered to help me once again with something, I said to him quite audibly in the big room with reverberating acoustics, Ma Signore, Lei non mi deve spoiliare così. When he looked at me oddly and the gaggle of people in the immediate vicinity went silent, I smiled and, thinking he hadn't heard me, repeated it.

He looked away as Rosemarie yanked my arm and told me to be quiet. Pulling me aside, she explained that *spogliare* meant "to undress" in Italian, and I had said to him, But sir, you mustn't continue to undress me like that, and not that he mustn't continue to spoil me.

I was so mortified, I avoided going back to the school for several days, afraid to see him.

During the summer, my friend Janet Kerr came to visit me and stayed awhile in the *pensione* before going on to France. She also was enchanted by Perugia, its dreamlike qualities such an enormous contrast with the way life was lived in New York City.

Perugia is landlocked and built like a medieval fortress

With Janet Kerr in Perugia

about 1,600 feet above sea level. It is all steep hills, with many streets that are literally flights of stone stairs that lead up to the only level part of the city, its center.

When the Etruscans, a people about whom very little is known, originally settled the area, they left traces of their civilization all over Umbria and Tuscany. Their alphabet is decipherable, yet the vocabulary is not. There seems to be no final agreement among historians as to why a seafaring people would settle so far from the sea.

They were exquisite artisans, making fine gold jewelry and beautiful miniature figures that looked like mini Giacometti statues. The walls they built withstood wars and earthquakes over long centuries to the present time. The Etruscans carved stone to a precision fit and did not use mortar. The Romans, who conquered them, did not destroy anything; instead they built their arches and walls above and around what the Etruscans had constructed.

Janet sat in the garden of the *pensione* and played her autoharp and sang folk songs in her sultry voice. The tourists and students staying there were enthralled and marveled at the strange instrument. Within a short time she met a young Frenchman named Bernard and ended up traveling to France with him.

At the one theater in town, the Morlacchi, where concerts, opera, and plays were presented, I was an extra in a production of an opera. An announcement had been posted at the University for Foreigners that nonsinging extras were needed for the production. Many foreign students showed up for the audition at the theater, including Rosemarie and me. The director, who seemed very important because he had everyone heeding his every demand, instructed us to line up on the newly constructed set. He explained that we were to look desperate and pleading.

Stretch out your hands and beg with every fiber of your being, he said, as the King and his court strode by. He looked at each of us intently, pointed, and said, You, yes. You, no.

No, he told Rosemarie.

When he turned to me, I returned his gaze with intensity. I soulfully implored. I stretched out my hands and beseeched.

You, he said, pointing at me. Yes, you.

Our costumes were gray rags and we were made up to look dirty and red-eyed. I believe the opera ran for only a few performances, but I had a great time.

The grass-covered cloister inside the art school had an ancient well in the center of it. We sat with our drawing pads under the arched walkway surrounding the grounds and drew each other, the cloister, and the building we were in. We worked with our various art supplies in a room that was cluttered with gesso molds of limbs, hands, and heads on shelves and hanging on the walls. We learned anatomy by drawing from full-scale replicas of statues by Michelangelo and Donatello.

Summer was endless and the coolness of the approaching fall inviting. I kept postponing the time to go home.

In September I moved to the Pensione Arco Etrusco. This one didn't include meals and therefore cost less. My allowance from my mother and the money I had saved from various jobs would last longer. By now I knew my way around. There were many places to eat well for very little; it was a university town, after all. Several local *trattorie* (informal home-style restaurants) served three-course meals for a few dollars, with a small supplement for a quarter liter of wine. They offered pasta, followed by meat and vegetables and then a serving of fruit and cheese—not at all like the sort of eating places that cluster around university campuses in the United States.

Lithograph, Italy 1962

I had a room right on top of the Etruscan Arch, one of the main tourist attractions in Perugia. Built by the Etruscans and modified by Caesar Augustus, it is pictured on every postcard. My room was big, dank, and dark, with only one window, but that window was over the arch and had a tiny balcony. I sent a postcard to Bob and he wrote back:

Got your postcard showing that arch you live at—
God it's like that balcony in Romeo and Juliet—
Nobody calls to you and sings to you like in that
tho, do they??

The room had a big cement sink with only a cold-water
faucet. There was a trap door in the middle of the floor,
which I was disappointed to discover was nailed securely
shut when I tried to pull it open in search of the history that
might be stored there.

I sent Bob a shirt I bought for him at the local market.
He is wearing it in some of those publicity stills taken some
time later:

> You sent me a great shirt—I wear it in the
> house . . . but not outside cause I don't want no
> one to see me in it before you see me in it—please
> come back and see me in the shirt—then I'll be
> able to wear it outside.

Despite the good time I was having and the new people
I was meeting, I agonized continually over what I wanted to
do and over my feelings for Bob. It was not easy. I pleaded
for time and he pleaded for that time to end:

> There is a Peter Sellers movie on at 5 o'clock—I
> promised myself that I would see Taylor Mead's
> movie "The Flower Thief" . . . don't think I'm
> really loving movies—It's just that I'm hating
> time—I'm trying to push it by—I'm trying to stab
> it—stomp on it—throw it on the ground and kick
> it—bend it and twist it with griting teeth and
> burning eyes—I hate it I love you—

Without the summer sun to warm the walls of the Etruscan
Arch, my room got colder and danker. There was no heat of any
kind. I moved one more time, in early October, to a *pensione*
that offered a room with a gas heater and an improvised kitchen
with a hot plate and a small sink. It was on Via della Gabbia,
Street of the Cage. It wasn't much of a *pensione* since the owner,
a signora, rented out the two extra rooms in her home. The improvised kitchen was behind a heavy red brocade curtain tied
back with thick gold cords, very much like in a theater.

In front of the curtain were a bed, a desk, a bookcase, and a window that looked out onto the street. I loved the room and I liked the signora. She was full of energy, walleyed, and squat. When she walked the lower half of her body appeared to be on time delay, showing up a few seconds later. She rented out *bombole,* gas canisters used for kitchen stoves and heaters because Perugia didn't have piped-in city gas lines at that time. The signora also collected and restored clothing for antique dolls, *bambole.* I named her home *La Casa delle Bombole e Bambole.*

The signora was always in a flurry of activity. The phone rang constantly. She assumed I would answer it and take messages for her. She would place her fingers on her lips to say I'm not here, no matter who called. She never seemed to be able to deliver the *bombole* on time or to finish sewing the clothes for the *bambole.* She also had two young children to take care of and a husband who was there sometimes but not often, preferring the outside world to the constant chaos at home. He did show up for meals and to change into a newly pressed shirt, however.

The signora spent an inordinate amount of time ironing everything in sight. The towels in the bathroom were stiff and as flat as boards as a result. I used my colorful striped towel that I had bought when I first arrived in Perugia in July. When she offered to iron it for me, I politely told her it wasn't necessary, but *grazie* all the same.

The spell broke around the time cold weather blew in from the surrounding mountains. It was October 1962, and on the nineteenth the Cuban missile crisis exploded. I was in a café in Perugia watching Kennedy on TV. It was very tense. People were crowded around the television in stunned silence. Everyone thought the world was on the brink of nuclear annihilation. Life as we knew it was about to end. A letter from Bob arrived on October 29, after the worst of the crisis was over and the worst conceivable horror had been avoided. He wrote that in the time leading up to the face-off between the United States and the Soviet Union, he felt that: "the maniacs were really going to do it this time," and he recounted his passive acceptance of the inevitability of dying. He only hoped that he would "die quick and not have to put up with radiation."

Bob wearing the Italian shirt

Sitting in the Figaro all nite waiting for the world to end (the first nite Kennedy talked and the Russian ships were getting nearer Cuba—). I honest to God thought it was all over—Not that I gave a shit any more then the next guy (that's a lie I guess) but it was interesting waiting for the bombs to fall and kill you—and it really seemed that way—

If the world did end that nite, all I wanted was to be with you—And it was impossible cause you're so far away—And that was why it seemed so hopeless.

I felt the same way. What was I doing so far away? Suddenly I was desperately homesick. All the indecision and the conflicted feelings had disappeared. I knew where I wanted to be.

The political crisis may have passed, but that didn't bring the return of a feeling of security. Quite the contrary—the smell of devastation charged the future. A line had been crossed, and there was no going back. I made a decision to finish out the time at the Accademia and be home by Christmas, less than two months away.

In December I sailed for home from Naples on the *Cristoforo Colombo*. I had a cabin somewhere in the vicinity of the ship's engines and about the size of a closet. Big pipes ran along the walls and they, as well as the entire cabin, were thick with layers of crusty white paint. I thought that if I scraped the paint down to the first layer the cabin would be

twice as big and the pipes as thin as wire. It felt like steer-
age, which seemed an appropriate way to travel to the
United States, my home. Even the name of the ship seemed
right—the Christopher Columbus. Remember where you
come from, and you will know who you are.

Grapevines have a tendency to grow every which way but straight. They dip, curve, and curl tightly in a tangled web. For sound to travel along such a vine and be reproduced without distortion is impossible: that is how rumors and gossip travel.

Bob was in England to do a television show, with a side trip to Italy, as I was returning by ship to New York City at the end of 1962. Our letters had crossed in the mail. The dates and plans made with an element of surprise for each other backfired and by the time my ship docked in New York he had already left. We wouldn't reconnect until mid-January.

I spent a short time in New Jersey with my mother and Fred and then headed to the apartment in the Village. I was excited to see everyone after such a long absence.

Just being in the little Fourth Street apartment again brought me to tears. I couldn't wait to see Bobby. I didn't regret the long separation, but I had suffered it. I had no idea, though, of the extent to which he'd suffered it in public.

When I went around to some of the clubs, I did not get a friendly reception. Instead I was greeted with accusations that I was cold and indifferent to someone who loved me. I was not there for Dylan when he needed me most. Some deliberately sang songs he had written about his heartache as well as any ballad that pointed a finger at a cruel lover.

The gossipy insinuations by the folkies around the Village hit hard. Bob had suffered publicly and as a result I was the villain, the Barbara Allen to his Sweet William.

I did not handle public involvement in my private life well. I had been looking forward to reconnecting with people and had not expected this unwelcome home. It was as if every letter Bob had written to me and every phone call he had made had been performed in a theater in front of an audience. Now I was the second act, standing alone on the stage after intermission; it was open season on my performance. I was booed and panned, while the guy from the first act had received a standing ovation.

Intimate friends like Lillian and Mell Bailey didn't treat me this way. Truly close friends who knew Bob and me understood not to judge. They paid no attention to the twists along the grapevine. With these friends I spent real quality time until Bob got back a week or so later in January, when we made up for lost time.

Bob and I were right back together again, absorbing the changes that had happened to both of us during our separation. I was more confident and he was more open. Whatever it was that held us together hadn't dissipated. He wanted to be part of my world as much as he wanted me in his.

He had traveling tales to tell me, opinions to express, more songs to sing, and I had found other artists, poets, and music to add to my roster of enthusiasms to share. I was reading poetry by Rimbaud and it piqued his interest. We went back and forth, feeding each other's curiosity. When Bob searched for more, Allen Ginsberg took him further with his great spontaneous knowledge of all the poets.

After the events of the past October the fear of a political confrontation leading to the use of nuclear weapons hovered over every day more than anyone wanted to contemplate. There was no doubt how profoundly scary the threat of nuclear war had seemed. While in England Bob had written "Masters of War," and shortly after his return he sang the new song in an interview with Alan Lomax. His conversation was upbeat in contrast to the emotion in his singing voice. He cited Soviet premier Khrushchev's response to an English reporter who asked who had won the conflict over Cuba. Khrushchev had replied, as quoted by Bob, Kennedy didn't win, I didn't win. Humanity won. He's a poet, Bob added, laughing.

Izzy Young decided to put together a songbook about the bomb and asked for contributions from Bob and other songwriters. The same sentiment that provoked "Masters of War" was behind the song Bob gave Izzy but the tone was entirely different. Despite our anxiety about the world around us we were in good spirits and happy to be together. The song displayed the black humor and the surrealist tone we communicated in:

> I hate the letters in yer word—B that means bad
>> yer so bad that even
> A dead hog in the sun would get up an' run O that
>> stands for orrible
> Yer so orrible that the word drops it's first letter
>> and runs M
> That stands for morgue an' all them folks in it 're
>> feelin' lucky

The bomb songbook idea was one of many projects initiated by Izzy Young but it never went anywhere in the end. Izzy, who never threw anything away if it had writing on it, filed the song among his papers for 1963 and forgot about it. It was only recently he came across Bob's "Go Away You Bomb," given to him so long ago for a book that was never published.

Growing up, I loved Shakespeare, and the poetry of Edna St. Vincent Millay and Lord Byron. When I found Bertolt Brecht and later the Beat poets, once I got over the jolt of the staccato rhythms—so different from Byron's rhyming lyricism—I was all ears for the harsh sound and the straight talk. Visual art was another story. When I was still in high school, I saw an exhibit of new American artists at the Museum of Modern Art, with Coke bottles embedded in the paintings and large, sloppy-looking canvases slathered with swaths of what looked like house paint, not oil paint.

The 1950s were a formal time—no one sat on the floor of museums or any other institutions. But I was so struck by what I was seeing that I slid to the floor to stare at the paintings, especially the one with the Coke bottles in it. I thought it was absurd. What was all this?

I grew up looking at the great artists of the Italian Renaissance and the Dutch masters. I loved Picasso, Cézanne, Van Gogh, and Derain. It was all about beauty. The art in this show was unexpected and unsettling. I didn't know what to make of it.

The art off the walls was hard for me to comprehend also. The first time I encountered the combines of Robert Rauschenberg—specifically the goat with the tire around its middle—I thought it was ugly. I didn't understand the lack of beauty. Where did "art" go?

On the other hand, the joy of youth is not to be bothered by where things might've gone but to find out where things are going.

I needed to take more time looking in order to develop my ability to see, but I got there. I think the transitional link for me was Wassily Kandinsky, whose work I was drawn to because of its vibrant colors and woozy shapes but didn't like at first. His paintings appeared cartoonlike and flimsy to me. I made myself go and see everything he'd done, to find out why I didn't like his work, and then of course I began to like it. I was learning the language of seeing.

I was lucky to live in New York, a city filled with galleries and bookstores, where I could take my time and look for free. The Metropolitan Museum of Art, with its accessible pay-what-you-wish policy, became my university.

Somewhere in my gallery wanderings I came upon a box by Joseph Cornell, and the effect it had on me was so strong that I had to look away. I thought I might harm the piece if I looked at it too closely. I walked around the gallery, waiting until I settled down a bit before going back to look at it again. I don't remember any other work of art ever capturing me in quite this way. I felt that his work was mine alone, and I could not speak to anyone about him for some time, it was such a private sensation.

The work of the brilliant and witty Red Grooms was an accessible link between old and new. I could see how he descended from the art I was accustomed to. The spirit of Picasso, Derain, and the Dada pranksters was apparent in his paintings and constructions.

Another seminal show that furthered my art education was *The Art of Assemblage* at the Museum of Modern Art. By then I was with Bob and we went to see it together. Bob was as critical and curious about visual art as he was about the written word. It pleased me that he was able to look at something for as long as I could.

The exhibit was rich with art on and off the walls that was horrible and exciting and ugly and beautiful all at once. I was still a sucker for beauty, but I was discovering what beauty could be made of. By the time I encountered Nam June Paik's video screens and his weirdly wired TV sets, some years later, I was fine. These artists were to the art world what the Beats were to the written word. But for me, Joseph Cornell was a time-stopping poet in a place all his own.

Theater and film were other grounds ready for new plantings. During the early sixties Off Broadway was thriving, and Off-Off Broadway was just starting up. Plays were put on in coffeehouses and in church basements. New plays were performed and old plays were given new interpretations. I worked with different crews of people making sets and props for many productions. Most of the people I worked with were artists, actors, and writers, happy to do this work rather than wait on tables or drive cabs. The best memories I have of that period are the countless hours spent with others making and painting lightweight replicas for the stage: a Russian coat of arms, antique furniture, brick walls, rock piles, forests, and a Noah's ark for productions most of whose names I no longer recall. The last, however, was for a production of the opera *Noye's Fludde* by Benjamin Britten, and the first was for a play based on *War and Peace*.

We built these things out of chicken wire, canvas, and special molding products similar to papier-mâché; and we painstakingly painted in all details by hand. To give walls and rocks texture, we used uncooked oatmeal and farina. Being artists, we invented and improvised ways to do things and then spent many hours making it all work. We pored over books that had photographs of the objects we were replicating. I learned many techniques that came in handy over the years for my own artwork.

Quinton Raines was the overseer, so to speak, in this freewheeling atmosphere. He was the man who found the jobs, hired the crew, and was part of it himself. We all worked closely with the set designer, if there was one. Sometimes Quinton rented a basement or a loft space for us to work in, but many times we built everything from scratch in the theater itself. I spent so much time at the Theatre de Lys (renamed the Lucille Lortel in 1981) on Christopher Street and the Cherry Lane on Commerce Street that they began to feel like second homes.

LeRoi Jones, later known as Amiri Baraka, was an up-and-coming playwright and poet in the mid-1960s, and Carla and I both worked with Quinton on the production of his play *Dutchman,* along with Edward Albee's *American Dream,* both directed by Alan Schneider, at the Cherry Lane. I remember Jones sitting in the back of the theater during rehearsals or walking around the set, saying little. His demeanor was always very serious and focused.

I also worked at Zeller Studios, a bigger and more established set construction company located in a loft way over by the East River on Avenue D. In addition to building sets for theater productions, Gary, the owner, also made sets for industrial shows held at fancy hotels in the general metropolitan area. Our mad crew of artists and actors would drive to the hotel location in the studio's van and wheel in the big canvas carriers covered with tarps and filled with props, as well as the set to be assembled and the tools and supplies with which to do it all.

Metal frames wrapped in heavy-duty canvas, the carriers were like cloth Dumpsters on wheels. When we left, we loaded them up, covering everything with the tarps and putting it all in the van. We no longer had the sets, just supplies and tools that we placed carefully on top of the assortment of hotel flatware, tableware, and tablecloths we'd take back to the studio on Avenue D. Nobody had much money, and the temptation to have a nice platter or silver-plated salad forks was overwhelming at times.

Letter from Bob, October 1962:

> I saw this play called A Man is A Man in which Steve Israel (you might know him) played the lead—the best thing in it tho was Judith Malina— Steve invited me to come cause he plays the lead just one nite a week, the slowest nite, the Sunday one—anyhow he's beautiful but no Gary Cooper (or Cary Grant)—(just kidding). That Judith Malina was great tho—you've got to see her act sometime—

When I got back from Italy and Bob was back from England, and we were once again united and settled into a life together in the apartment on West Fourth Street, we went to see the Living Theater production of *The Brig* at its space on Fourteenth Street. Founded by Julian Beck and Judith Malina in the late 1940s, the Living Theater was revolutionary in its day. Beck and Malina's approach to theater was based somewhat on Antonin Artaud and the Surrealists' ideas for the Theater of Cruelty in France during the 1930s. The theatrical philosophy of the Living Theater was to break the fourth wall, to eliminate the separation between audience and actors. The company performed the works of American and European experimental writers like Gertrude Stein and Jean Cocteau, in addition to contemporary playwrights.

The Brig was about ritual cruelty in Marine Corps prisons. It was a powerful production exposing to civilians (the audience) the culture of the military. As I remember it, the entire stage was a chain-link cage with barbed wire and loudspeakers on top of poles. The "play" consisted of barking commands from guards to the prisoners, who in turn shouted requests for permission to move forward, sit, or step across an arbitrary line. The dialogue was incomprehensible a lot of the time, but the degradation of the men was jarring and the dehumanization of the prison system overall was shocking. The unrelenting verbal assaults of the guards and the general din left audiences with a feeling of exhaustion and defeat equal to that of prisoners confined to the brig. We were both blown away by the force of the production.

As a result of the success of *The Brig* and the relative success of equally controversial and abrasive previous productions, the Living Theater was constantly harassed by its landlords or the city for some infraction or other. Inevitably, it would lose the lease on its performance space. It became a nomadic theater group. When the IRS came down on Beck and Malina during the production of *The Brig*, they fled to Europe.

As unlikely as it may sound, it was at the Living Theater space on Fourteenth Street that Bob and I first saw Tiny Tim perform. When he first showed up in the Village in search of gigs, Tiny Tim was an anomaly, singing songs from the late nineteenth century and playing a plastic ukulele. What was he doing tiptoeing around deliberate bohemians, hard drinkers, poets, wisecracking satirical standup comedians, and folk, blues, and bluegrass singers in coffeehouses and bars?

Contrary to Tiny Tim's reputation for fastidiousness, he tended to look disheveled in his baggy black suit and white shirt. He wore a dusty-looking black hat over greasy ringlets of black hair. His skin was pasty; he didn't look healthy. But then he would get up and sing those silly songs in his whiny, trembling falsetto and you had to love him, if just for his courage. He was really knowledgeable about the music he sang and was completely committed to the work he set out to do. It made no difference to him if he was being ridiculed or appreciated. He reveled in both—attention meant an audience, which meant everything to him. He never stepped out of character. He was always Tiny Tim, though he did look a little spiffier by the time he hit it big on national television in the late sixties.

Popular music and Hollywood movies were bland in the same way during the fifties and early sixties. Most popular music was about as exciting as a Doris Day and Rock Hudson movie. Finally music was evolving into something else, and movies shortly followed.

The Village movie theaters showed "art movies," code for foreign films. There was even a theater on Eighth Street called the Art Theater. Bob and I saw *Pull My Daisy* in one of those Village theaters. It was unlike any other movie we'd seen, an abstract black-and-white American film by and about the Beat Generation that had more in common with the French New Wave than anything out of Hollywood. The characters were a wild bunch of crazy poets, painters, and music makers. Jack Kerouac narrated the short film, whose cast included Allen Ginsberg, Gregory Corso, Peter Orlovsky, Larry Rivers, Alice Neel, and David Amram. Alfred Leslie, a painter, and the great photographer Robert Frank directed and filmed it. *Pull My Daisy* had no story and no plot. There was something familiar about the way it was off-balance, unknown, and freewheeling. It was oddly discombobulating to see a movie that made you feel you were in the next room.

I identified with the men in the film, not the women, who seemed insignificant in the midst of these wild, funny, and offbeat guys. I wanted to be them but didn't know how. I envied their freedom.

Many years later when I saw the film again, I was shaken by that memory. This time I was cognizant of the women and their role in the story. They were inconsequential and extraneous in the way a prop is part of a set. At worst they were nags, ruining all the fun with their talk. In the narration the men have names, but the women are Wife and Sister. I saw the female characters as recognizing and accepting their sidekick role in the lives of their men. It was depressing. It was beyond imagining that women could be part of wild, free craziness, too.

Marx Brothers movies were the favored un–Hollywood Technicolor extravaganzas. In those years, Hollywood films played in the big palacelike theaters around Forty-second Street. The only movie theater like that in the Village was the Loew's at Greenwich Avenue and Twelfth Street, now long gone. Weeklong festivals of Marx Brothers movies were held at the New Yorker theater on the Upper West Side. Up until then I had only seen their movies on a small TV so it was great fun to see them on a big screen.

The downtown theaters such as the Bleecker Street Cinema had festivals of Japanese, French, and Italian movies. And there were artists, or maybe they saw themselves as filmmakers, who scratched and painted directly on film stock and then showed the results at obscure venues in the East Village. Some of these were fascinating and others were sleep inducing, but all of them set the groundwork for Andy Warhol and his endless films. I remember going with Bob to a loft somewhere and watching one of Warhol's films, a work in progress. Bob didn't think much of the film or of Warhol. His taste in movies could be quite conventional. Storytelling was important.

The New Wave films from France were a revelation. It was important to see François Truffaut's first feature film, *The 400 Blows*, and Alfred Hitchcock's *Psycho*, which came out the same year and were filmed in black and white. The shower scene in *Psycho* was so over-the-top shocking that the blood pouring down the bathtub drain appeared to be truly red.

When Bob and I saw Truffaut's *Shoot the Piano Player*, we were both transfixed. We loved it. The film is sad, a tragedy, yet it is not bleak; it is also absurd and very funny. The story moves with the rhythm of life: slow and hesitant followed by bursts of frenzy, without resolution. So true—life just goes on. I have seen it many times over the years and it is still one of my favorite movies. Charles Aznavour, the French singer whose records I later heard in Italy, played the main character with a heartbreaking acceptance of how things are in the world.

Not long after we saw *Shoot the Piano Player* we went to see *Last Year at Marienbad* by another French filmmaker of the New Wave, Alain Resnais. That film was totally incomprehensible, and as we walked out of the movie theater Bob said that in the last scene the camera should have slowly pulled away to reveal a sign over an entrance gate: "Marienbad Insane Asylum."

That would've saved the movie, he suggested.

SUBTEXT

Had my father not died when my sister and I were still young girls, he would have expanded on what he'd already taught us—to value ourselves—and possibly equipped us with some practical knowledge on how to manage our lives. At least that is what I thought having a father meant. But it was not to be. So off we went into our adulthoods armed with what we had learned so far.

Carla and I had similar interests and similar talents, but

our approaches to living our lives were very different. We looked out for each other, each in our own way, but she couldn't handle my way unless it was hers. She was smart and tough but also fanciful. I was fanciful and unbound but also centered. We were told as children that I took after my father in looks and temperament while Carla and my mother were two peas in a pod. Carla did receive the gift of a beautiful singing voice from my father, though, whereas I got stuck with my mother's really good ear but without the ability to reproduce what I heard. I grew taller than my big sister and inherited the blond hair and blue green eyes that came from my father's Sicilian family, while Carla inherited my mother's dark hair and big dark eyes. Although many people said we looked exactly alike despite our coloring, there were just as many who saw no resemblance at all.

I did not learn how to walk in the world from my mother but I did learn from her how to revel in my imagination. Having never finished high school, she was entirely self-educated and forever curious, and she passed on her curiosity. She showed her daughters the world of books, music, and art. She read the great poets of the world to us as well as *Winnie the Pooh* and *The Wizard of Oz.* My favorite book, which I carried around like a Bible wherever I went in those nomadic years, was her 1910 edition of *Twelve Centuries of English Poetry and Prose.* When we could read on our own, we did so with gusto because of her enthusiasm. That was an important gift worth treasuring.

Because my mother was also very political, she taught us about equality, that all men are created equal, and instilled in us a sense of justice. Her belief in Communism was based in these beliefs, and neither she nor my father was doctrinaire or an apologist for Stalin. They were far more freewheeling in their following of Communism, but the repressive climate of the forties and fifties meant there was no place for people like them to discuss the theories of Karl Marx and how those theories were put into practice in the Soviet Union. Many who might have made a difference in the direction of the American Communist Party either got fed up and quit or kept quiet and toed the party line. A siege mentality prevailed; a united front was necessary.

As the Cold War raged, the postwar economy was booming. Men went to work and women were happy homemakers who smoked, drank cocktails, raised children, and wore girdles. Working-class families aspired to move to the suburbs and have a two-car garage. Everything was hunky-dory. Meanwhile, the fear of a nuclear war was ever present: children wore dog tags around their necks and every school had "duck and cover" air raid drills. Loyalty oaths had to be signed in workplaces and schools.

Segregation was a way of life. In the South, water fountains were clearly marked For White and For Colored. Black and white musicians on tour in the same band couldn't stay in the same hotel. Even hugely successful African American performers were subjected to these indignities.

I grew up in that 1950s lockdown on anything that deviated from the pastel norm. Fear of "the other," that dark cloud looming over the shiny chrome of a sleek new car, ready to sully it, ruled the day. Communists were behind Negroes' demands for equality. Rhythm and blues and rock and roll were torrid and sweaty the way Pat Boone and his ilk could never be. Beat poets and James Dean were stoking rebellion and delivering angst to an eager audience. For a kid like me, who grew up hiding, knowing I came from "the other," it was a relief to find some company on the big screen and in the streets. And those who knew in their lonely souls that something else had to be out there finally found what they were looking for and shed their pastels for indigo.

The times would soon be a-changin':

> The line it is drawn
> The curse it is cast
> The slow one now
> Will later be fast
> As the present now
> Will later be past
> The order is
> Rapidly fadin'.
> And the first one now
> Will later be last
> For the times, they are a-changin'.

Record Time

The *Freewheelin' Bob Dylan* cover photograph came about rather casually; it certainly wasn't planned or produced in any way. Columbia Records was sending a photographer to the apartment on West Fourth Street to take pictures of Bob for publicity purposes and possibly for the cover of his new, as-yet-untitled second album. We got up early that morning to make sure the place would be in order when the photographer and Billy James, a publicist at Columbia, showed up.

Bob chose his rumpled clothes carefully. I put on a sweater and on top of that a sweater that was a bulky knit belonging to Bob. As usual, the apartment was cold. It had snowed a few days earlier and it was one of those damp New York City winter days that chill to the bone.

Billy James arrived with the photographer, Don Hunstein, who was on staff at Columbia Records. Billy always wore suits even when he was hanging out downtown, or at least that is how I remember him. Despite the formality of his clothing, he fit in wherever he went. He was a genial and honest guy. Bob liked him, and so did I.

The apartment was tiny and there really wasn't anyplace to go to get out of the way. While Don Hunstein was setting up his equipment, Billy showed me one of his cameras, a Hasselblad, which was beautiful to look at, and into. I loved peering down into the big square viewfinder that showed the crisply framed scene in front of me.

Don took some shots of Bob with and without his guitar, sitting on the big, faded gold-colored stuffed armchair that was a street find. It could have been Billy or Don, or possibly Bob, who suggested I get in the picture

while Bob played and sang. I felt self-conscious and a bit silly, but Billy knew how to make an awkward situation feel natural, and I relaxed some. In any case, Bob and I related to each other intensely; that was hard not to pick up on.

We were all having a good time, and after a bit Don suggested we go outside. Bob put on his suede jacket. It was an "image" choice because that jacket was not remotely suited for the weather. I don't care that he was from the cold North Country—he was bound to freeze going out in that—but maybe we wouldn't be outside for very long. When I was in Italy I had bought a loden green coat that I loved dearly, even though I knew it wasn't suitable for a New York winter. I put it on over the big bulky sweater and tightly tied the belt of the coat around me for warmth. I felt like an Italian sausage. Out we all went.

I huddled next to Bob as we walked up and down Jones Street

per instructions from Don and encouraging smiles from Billy. Bob stuck his hands in the pockets of his jeans and leaned into me. We walked the length of Jones Street facing West Fourth with Bleecker Street at our backs. The snow on the streets was slushy and filthy from the traffic. The sidewalks were icy and slippery, but at least there wasn't much of a wind blowing. To keep warm we started horsing around. Don kept clicking away. A delivery van pulled up and parked, so we turned onto West Fourth Street. In some of the outtakes it is obvious that by then we were freezing; certainly Bob was, in that thin jacket. But image was all.

Taking a break to warm up some, I ran up the front steps of the apartment building and watched from behind the front door with Billy James while Don took some shots of Bob on West Fourth Street by himself.

My guess is the day ended with a warm meal on Columbia Record's tab. It was much later that decisions were made about the cover. I don't recall that Bob had any control over the photo they chose, but I know he was happy with it. I was surprised they didn't use one of Bob by himself.

I remember discussions about the title but I don't remember who suggested it. The choice of the word *freewheeling* sounds like something either John Hammond or Albert Grossman might have come up with. But the spelling, with the dropped *g* at the end, is all Bob. During his early years, he was adamant about writing down words as spoken by every-day people. He chopped off the ends of words like a hiker hacking a path through the woods, machete in hand.

Early in his career, Bob didn't have much control over how his work was presented and marketed. The people at Columbia certainly listened to his opinions and Albert could fight for a change or a compromise; but Bob didn't have the kind of power he would have in years to come. As for me, I was never given a release to sign or paid anything. It never dawned on me to ask. No one gave it a thought back in 1963. Don Hunstein was on the payroll of Columbia Records so I believe he just got paid for a good day's work.

Looking back from the present, the age of über-marketing, the story of how the cover came about seems genuinely innocent, bordering on sweet. But it is one of those cultural markers that influenced the look of album covers precisely because of its casual, down-home spon-taneity and sensibility. Most album covers were carefully staged and controlled, to terrific effect on the Blue Note jazz album covers, with their snappy graphics and beautiful black-and-white photographs, and to not-so-great effect on the perfectly posed and clean-cut pop and folk albums. Whoever was ultimately responsible for choosing that par-ticular photograph for *The Freewheelin' Bob Dylan* really had an eye for a new look.

The album spoke the time-honored language of youth

and rebellion against the status quo, and the cover embodied the image. The songs had something to say. It was folk music, but it was really rock and roll.

COLUMBIA CONVENTIONS

As *The Freewheelin' Bob Dylan* was about to be released, Bob was scheduled to appear on *The Ed Sullivan Show*. He was very excited about the album and gave away a few copies of the first pressing to close friends.

Freewheelin' included a satirical song Bob had written about the John Birch Society, a right-wing group that believed insidious Communists had infiltrated every facet of American life. At Columbia Records, the inclusion of the song, "Talkin' John Birch Paranoid Blues," was a controversial one, considering the wintry politics of the Cold War.

Bob decided to sing the song for the *Ed Sullivan Show* appearance. He sang it at the afternoon rehearsal for the evening show. It was a humorous Woody Guthrie–style talking-blues song in the voice of a John Birch Society member who is searching for Communists—investigating everything and everyone—and ends up investigating himself, hoping he won't find anything. CBS exerted pressure and Ed Sullivan apologetically but firmly suggested that Bob sing something else.

Bob was furious. He had spent some time with a blacklisted performer, John Henry Faulk, who had recently won a case against CBS and written a book about his ordeal called *Fear on Trial*. Bob was very interested in the subject of the blacklist and censorship, whose repercussions and absurdities were still apparent in the popularity of groups like the John Birch Society. He called me from the rehearsal studio in a fit. With remnants of McCarthy-era political censorship still in place in 1963, Bob Dylan refused to appear on the *Ed Sullivan Show*. That was that.

The fiasco over Bob's actions created problems for Columbia, but Albert Grossman, a wise and thorough manager, handled the situation deftly. He huddled with Bob and Columbia and worked out a compromise that removed the "controversial" John Birch song from a new version of *Freewheelin'* that would be released instead. Bob was content to substitute "Rambling Gambling Willie" and "Let Me Die in My Footsteps" for songs he had written and recorded more recently: "Masters of War," "Talkin' World War III Blues," and "Bob Dylan's Dream." And so he agreed to cut the John Birch song from the final version of the album, which was officially released in May.

In July, when the incident was pretty much over and done with, Bob was to attend a one-week Columbia Records convention in Puerto Rico. Bob and I were booked at the Americana Hotel as Mr. and Mrs. Dylan because that was the only way we could have a room together. It became a running gag; we called each other "wife" and "husband" and had a hard time keeping a straight face when the hotel staff addressed us as "Mr." or "Mrs." We felt like naughty kids who had gotten away with something.

We were under the impression that we'd spend most of

our time hanging out at the hotel pool in bathing suits, drinking things with tiny paper umbrellas in them, until it was time for Bob to perform for the movers and shakers who had come to see the new talent Columbia had signed. The point of the convention was to introduce the new talent to the sales force. There was a huge blowup of the cover of the *Freewheelin'* album in the lobby of the Americana Hotel.

Village bohemian that I was, I didn't bring the right clothes or shoes for the convention and the various functions with Columbia Record executives and sales people that it turned out we were expected to attend. The early 1960s were still under the auspices of the 1950s dress code. People were expected to dress properly for the occasion. Women and girls did not wear pants—let alone blue jeans—to restaurants, offices, theaters, schools, or the dentist's office. It was unheard of. Men wore suits and ties pretty much everywhere. If you lived in the outer boroughs, you dressed up to go into Manhattan. If you lived downtown, you dressed up to go uptown. The whole point of living in Greenwich Village was that you didn't have to cater to conventions of this sort. And we didn't.

The only dress I'd packed was a short and simple summer shift I had made, and the only shoes I had with me were a pair of Allan Block sandals. The sandals were beautifully handmade, but they were not delicate or elegant in any way. They had thick leather soles molded to the contour of the foot, with dark leather straps the width of fettuccine that laced up the ankle. Goddard Lieberson, the head of Columbia Records, had invited us to dinner at a fancy restaurant and I didn't have anything but those sandals to wear with my dress. I hadn't given any thought to the social requirements before leaving the city, but suddenly at the convention I became uncomfortably aware of them.

My sister, who had lobbied hard to come with us to Puerto Rico, had packed the right kind of clothes and shoes and therefore was prepared to go anywhere. She told me: If you wear a pair of high heels, pretty much any dress will pass muster.

That was a lesson given too late—here we were, after all—and there wasn't much I could do about it. It was advice I never would have heeded, anyway. I was capable of following convention when necessary, but I was—and am—one of those women who could never manage to walk in high heels.

Goddard Lieberson was a very worldly, genteel man yet quite down to earth. If he minded the way Bobby and I looked, and no doubt acted, he never let on. In fact, I think he enjoyed it on some level. My sister made a good impression on him that evening; he was charmed by her vast knowledge of music, and when she went back to New York he sent her a collection of classical music albums. Carla—Bobby called her Carla-in-law—had nothing but disdain for the way Bob comported himself. He didn't schmooze with the suits—didn't make small talk with the executives or salesmen. In her eyes, he made no effort of any kind to be polite to anyone. As for me, her baby sister, well, what could she expect from someone who chose to be with a boy who behaved as Bob did?

Tony Bennett, walking by with a Columbia bigwig in the hotel lobby, both of them wearing suits and ties, pointed to

Bob, in scruffy jeans and shirt and most likely Allan Block sandals, and asked who he was.

The Columbia executive said something like: Oh, he is the new young singer that John Hammond signed.

No doubt puzzled, Bennett nodded as they continued on their way.

Who knows what went through Bennett's mind that evening when Bob got up with his acoustic guitar and performed a few songs from his new album? "Hammond's folly" was what many in the record industry thought for a time. Bob's first album, which Hammond had also produced, had sold poorly and Bob was totally out of sync with the suave and classy artists recording on the Columbia label. The *Freewheelin'* album, however, was catching on in a way that none of them could have predicted.

ART

One evening Peter Yarrow came over to eat with us on West Fourth Street. I was grilling steaks—nothing special—and Peter offered to bring a bottle of wine.

Great, I said.

In those days, it was possible to find a decent enough bottle for a buck, and a few of us became connoisseurs of one-dollar wines. Peter knew something about wine, and he was a generous man. He awakened my taste buds to the glory of wines from France when he ceremoniously uncorked the bottle of Médoc he brought with him. It was exquisite, and it changed our whole perspective. No longer would that dollar Chianti or Rioja satisfy. It was uphill from there.

As the times changed economically for Bob, he was wide open to partaking of the finer things of life, and so was I. With Peter and Albert Grossman we went to several uptown restaurants. They had special knowledge to pass on, and we wined and dined really well. Not long after I returned from Italy—where my own knowledge of the good things in life had flourished—and Bob from England, we had flown to Toronto with Albert. Ian and Sylvia, whom Albert also managed, were there and it was great to be reunited with them. All of us had such a fine time wining and dining around the city that I have no recollection of any daytime hours, and even my recollections of nighttime are foggy.

Whenever we spent time in Woodstock, New York, where Peter's mother owned a cabin, we drank Médoc,

Saint-Émilion, and good-quality Italian wines. Peter and I did most of the cooking.

I came from economically working-class but culturally sophisticated people. Without money, however, there was more talk of fine wines than actual buying and drinking of them. I don't think Bob thought about it much, but he certainly recognized good quality when it came his way. In all things, he was a fast learner.

My grandfather on my mother's side of the family, Pop Rossi, made his own wine from the vines he grew on his farm in northwestern Connecticut, near Torrington. There were several Italians who settled in the area because of the good farmland and the beauty of the landscape.

Everyone in the area envied Pop's wine. They planted the same vines that produced the same grapes and tended them with the same methods he used, but their wine was never as good as his, they said, and they wanted to know his secret. Why was his wine exceptional and theirs merely good? When Pop pointed to the sky and said, *la luna*, the moon, they would laugh him off: Yes, yes, loony. C'mon, tell us the truth.

Pop Rossi's secret was that he would look at the moon every night during the harvest season and when he saw that the moon was in the right phase he would harvest his grapes the following day.

Sometimes science can explain why peasant knowledge makes sense. In the case of Pop Rossi's harvesting theories, it's not difficult. The moon affects tides and also the water content in grapes. Pop knew when his grapes were plump enough with water and ready for harvesting by watching the cycle of the moon. But the other vintners refused to believe that this was how he did it. And although I grew up revering his wine because the grown-ups said it was so, I have no real memory of how it tasted since we kids drank it in a glass that had mostly water in it.

Pop stopped making wine at ninety. At ninety-two, he had an operation on one of his toes, and although he recovered quickly for a man his age, I remember him saying to me, I can't dance anymore and I can't make wine anymore. What is the point of living?

And then he laughed.

There were no bottles of Pop Rossi's vino left for me to try when I was old enough to comprehend the glory of good wine, so the nature of his bounty remains a family myth.

I did have a working knowledge of Italian wines by the time I was living in the Village, however, and it was sufficient for my economic reality. In those days the neighborhood wine stores imported basic table wines from Europe. There was no fuss—restaurants would put a candle in empty straw-encased Chianti bottles and place them on the red-and-white-checked tablecloths that dressed the tables.

Peter invited us to stay with him in the cabin in Woodstock sometime in late May, before the Newport Folk Festival. Peter and I went to the Art Students League to draw from a live model (he was an artist as well as a musician) while Bobby stayed at the cabin to write.

I loved to draw with pen and ink. There was nothing more satisfying than making a drawing with one flowing continuous line—like peeling an apple with a knife and removing the skin in one long, unbroken slice. I brought watercolors with me to Woodstock to wean myself from my preoccupation with the line, but I hated everything I did.

There was an upright piano in the cabin and Bobby spent most of the time playing it even when he wasn't working on songs. I had no idea he could play the piano so well and I was truly impressed by his ability. At Gerde's he would play now and then, but otherwise he didn't have everyday access to one.

At the cabin he kept a notebook beside him on the piano bench as he worked on songs, which were coming out of him rapid fire, his focus and skill almost making the work seem effortless. The music flowed from him like the pen line in my drawing books. My appreciation of his extraordinary musicianship deepened.

Peter was very pleased to give Bobby the chance to get away from the pressures that were building around him as a result of the success of *Freewheelin'*. Peter also needed a break from his hectic life as part of the very popular Peter, Paul, and Mary. He was recognized everywhere he went. A woman stopped him in Woodstock to say that she couldn't help noticing how close he and Mary were when she'd seen them walking around town the day before. She had in fact seen me and assumed I was Mary.

At times Peter and Bob would horse around, playing and singing anything that came into their heads, while I read or drew. Times were good and it was refreshing to be away from the Village scene for a while. I was very fond of Peter; we had been friends before Albert Grossman created Peter, Paul, and Mary, when Peter was a performer playing solo in clubs and coffeehouses and crashing at Micki Isaacson's apartment at 1 Sheridan Square. We had a lot of fun together.

MUSIC

From midnight to 5:00 a.m. Mondays to Fridays, an actor by the name of Bob Fass hosted a radio show called *Radio Unnameable* on WBAI, a listener-supported alternative station in New York City. It was a free-form collage of music and talk. Fass chatted, played records, welcomed visitors to the studio; if listeners called in with interesting or apt comments, he would deliver those opinions on the air.

A reaction from a guest or a caller to something Fass played or said might tilt him in still another direction and spur more discourse or discord until the approach of dawn and the end of his program.

The eclectic records Fass played and the stories he told made it difficult to leave the radio or shut it off. I would fall asleep, only to be jolted awake at the dusty, scratchy hour of 5:00 a.m. by the program's signature signoff of a baby girl yelling into the microphone, "Bye bye, bye BYE!!"

Right after the first pressing of *Freewheelin'* on acetate in March 1963, Bobby, Johnny Herald of the Greenbriar Boys, and I went up to the WBAI studios to play it.

After announcing the arrival of Bob Dylan and friends, Fass encouraged us to talk. What ensued was spontaneous silliness, very much in tune with the time of night that leans toward morning. Making up names, Bobby said we were the Naked Theater looking for a performance space, and later we were proprietors and designers of Authentic Folk Music Suits, the only acceptable attire for concert arenas, clubs, and out along the highway. Johnny Herald recited poetry as a "genius poet of the folk." In between the banter, Fass played a few cuts from the record interspersed with his usual cornucopia. The title and the release date of the *Free-wheelin'* album were never even mentioned.

In August I went to the March on Washington on the same Actors Equity bus as Bob Fass.

Sometime in late spring or early summer, before the 1963 Newport Folk Festival, someone came back to the Village from out West with a bullwhip as a present for Bob; I don't remember who it was for sure: it may have been Jack Elliott, Harry Jackson, Ian Tyson, or Peter La Farge, since they were the cowboys of the Village at that time.

Even though Jack, né Elliott Adnopoz, was a cowboy from Brooklyn, a bullwhip was not his style, nor was it Ian's. I will hazard a guess that La Farge, a folksinger with more of a tough-guy presence than the others, gave Bobby the bull-whip and instructed him in how to snap and crack it properly.

Harry Jackson had real cowboy credentials. He was a painter and sculptor from Cody, Wyoming, who sang cowboy songs and painted large epic cowboy paintings. A thickset man in his late thirties, Harry was full of the energy of life.

He took a liking to Bob, said he was the real thing, and wanted to paint his portrait. Harry's studio was on Broome Street, an industrial area below Houston Street where artists could rent large lofts for next to nothing. By the mid-1970s the area had been given the name SoHo (for South of Houston), and eventually the artists got priced out by upscale stores and galleries. Back in the 1960s, there was nothing trendy about the area, which was barely a neighborhood; there were warehouses and small manufacturing and artists' lofts. Harry had a big, dark live-in studio space with a round table in the center he'd made out of a large electrical company cable spool found on the street. It was wood, maybe ten feet in diameter, and perfect table height. Many afternoons and evenings were spent around that table in Harry's studio listening to his stories and songs as he worked on Bob's portrait. I recall the painting as dark with light from above hitting the figure of Bob sitting in a chair playing his guitar. The painting had a lonely look to it. Harry was a cowboy Titian.

$\mathcal{B}$obby practiced cracking that bullwhip whenever he found the space. He took the whip with him to the Newport Folk Festival in 1963 and cracked it for hours backstage or around the pool, cigarette dangling from his mouth, kicking up dust. He got real good at it. During the day we spent a lot of time at the pool. Bob liked using the diving board in addition to thwacking the bullwhip.

There was a mix of musicians at the Folk Festival that year: Pete Seeger, Joan Baez, Judy Collins, Dave Van Ronk,

[Newport 1963]

Jack Elliott, Ian and Sylvia, Mississippi John Hurt, and many others. People in the music business—managers, record company executives and scouts—were also in attendance.

The sense of business hovering—the sound of money, mixed with the prospect of record deals and fame—was exciting for the up-and-coming folk musicians hoping for a break. There was a lot going on. Photographers David Gahr and Jim Marshall were everywhere at once, snapping away. Bob was all business and all fun at the same time. Cracking that bullwhip. Shaking up the ground.

We had flown from New York to Providence, Rhode Island, with Albert Grossman and Peter, Paul, and Mary. From Providence we flew to Newport in a small private plane. When we arrived in Newport I went off with Mary to a hair salon to get our hair washed and fussed over. I was a bit intimidated because I had never been to a fancy hair salon before and wasn't sure what to do, so I kept an eye on what Mary did and let them fuss.

There were gatherings in the various hotel rooms, and musicians sang and played music together informally. Joan Baez came to Newport with the person she was involved with, who, like me, was not a musician, so the two of us hung out together at some of those jam sessions. Joan was a big star in the folk music world and the center of attention. Bob was the new, fast-rising star and after his performance at the festival it was clear that the folk world was his oyster. Bob's songs were in the folk idiom yet they were definitely and undeniably written in the present. The writing was timeless and timely—explosively so—and the audience gasped in recognition. It was inevitable that he and Baez would create electricity. I got a few sidelong glances whenever they sang together.

Their voices were so disparate—her extraordinary soprano crosshatching with his intense and unpretty sound—but the dissonance thrilled people. Their convergence was predictable; for folk music, it was a mandate. Professionally, Baez would be good for Dylan. She was a woman who knew what she wanted and set out to get it. She wanted to get his songs to her audience. She was a political person and to continue singing woeful old-time ballads in woeful times wouldn't work for much longer.

The festival was energizing because the music was so good and the feeling of being on the brink of something big was in the air. Folk music had won the day, moving out to unite discontented kids everywhere who were waiting for a ticket to ride. On the dramatic closing night of the festival when the performers linked arms together on the stage and movingly sang "We Shall Overcome," the entire audience was on its feet, singing with them.

After Newport, Baez and Dylan's professional appearances together were exciting and provoked gossip about an affair. At first it was just gossip—then, of course, it wasn't. What was especially hard for me was dealing with what was private becoming public.

In the late spring of 1963, I'd begun work on a production of *Brecht on Brecht,* a play by George Tabori scheduled to open in July at the Sheridan Square Playhouse. It had been produced a few years earlier at the Theatre de Lys with Lotte Lenya in the cast. The new production, directed by Gene Frankel, was bare bones. Subtitled *An Improvisation,* it was made up of excerpts from Brecht's writings and songs, interspersed with taped readings from his appearance before the House Un-American Activities Committee in 1947. The cast consisted of six actors, three male and three female, who recited monologues or sang or both.

There wasn't much of a set to speak of—just a few chairs and maybe a table and a large photo of Brecht on a scrim in the background. The Sheridan Square Playhouse didn't have a raised stage. The audience seating was in front and to the left and right of the performance area, which was in front of the theater's back wall. There was a backstage room off to one side.

I was the assistant to the stage manager and set designer, Quinton Raines. Quinton was originally from the South and in his late twenties, or early thirties. He was an aspiring playwright, and I later acted in a few showcase productions of one of his plays. He was also a capable carpenter who, as noted previously, would put together crews of artists, actors, and writers to build sets and props for Off- and Off-Off-Broadway plays. There was a regulation that theaters with seating under a certain number could hire a nonunion crew. I learned to use power tools and was extremely proud of the muscles I developed as a result.

Quinton was a bit obsessed with Bobby and would insist on talking with him about philosophy and writing. Quinton had a tendency to pry into people's lives, especially when he had had too much to drink; he never knew when to back off. I had a hard time with people who drank and soul-talked at me, which was obviously a holdover from experience with my mother. I would get sucked into the situation and not see a way out. Otherwise, Quinton was all right.

Brecht on Brecht was a very spare production overall: there were the actors, the director, a lighting technician, Quinton, and me. I was thrilled to be working on this play; Brecht had captivated me for some time. I was intrigued by what he had to say and the rhythm of his language.

I wanted to share with Bob my interest in Brecht and my preoccupation with his dilemma as an artist living under both autocratic Communism and democratic capitalism. There is no doubt Bob had heard of Brecht, as Brecht was known in those years, but he might not have read anything by him or seen his plays.

I told him to meet me at the theater earlier than usual so he could catch a few rehearsals. I really wanted him to see the play and one performance in particular: the actress Micki Grant singing "Pirate Jenny." The song is a tale of the toil and trouble of a hotel maid constantly ordered about by everyone. She sings her song of revenge as the Pirate Jenny on a great ship, the Black Freighter, where all her tormentors are taken prisoner. One by one, she sends them to their death. The hour of her ship had come in.

It is a compelling song of revenge and as sung by Micki Grant, a black woman, it took on another dimension. This was the civil rights era, and listening to her sing the song was a powerful piece of living theater. I knew Bob should not miss it. He sat still and quiet. Didn't even jiggle his leg. Brecht would be part of him now, as would the performance of Micki Grant as Pirate Jenny.

My fascination with Brecht had begun with the cast album of the *Threepenny Opera* that my parents owned. *Threepenny* opened at the Theatre de Lys in 1954 and played there for a long time. I would sit on the floor in front of the cabinet my father had built to hold their record albums and stare at the cover, disappearing into it, the way a child does. The cast was pictured there in costumes of reds, blacks, oranges, and yellows—very fiery. In the picture Lotte Lenya's hair was orange and her makeup exaggerated; she has a mean expression on her face. The other woman on the cover was prettier but done up the same way, wearing a form-fitting, vibrantly colored dress. There seemed to be something naughty about them. They certainly didn't look like the women I saw walking around the streets in Queens. The music was raw and raucous and had nothing to do with opera as far as I could tell.

Some years later when I read John Gay's *Beggar's Opera*, on which Brecht based his *Threepenny Opera,* one thing led to another and I began to read a lot of Brecht and to learn about his life. Brecht left Germany because of the rise of Nazism and lived in various countries before eventually coming to the United States. Once here he got to know other expatriates and refugees from Nazism and Fascism who worked in Hollywood as writers, and he, too, headed West to join their ranks.

McCarthyism was on the rise, and Brecht was suspected of being a Communist, as were so many others working in Hollywood. Brecht was certainly a Marxist, but he never joined the Communist Party and he wasn't a U.S. citizen. He was issued a subpoena to appear before the House Un-American Activities Committee in October 1947. Immediately after giving testimony but not names, he left for Europe, wanting no part of an American Inquisition. He went to live in East Germany, only to have his theatrical ideas stifled under the dogma of Communism. Where could he live to pursue his work without interference from the government? His dilemma fueled my questions about what it would be like to live under Communism.

Brecht became a symbol for me during the Cold War. In all the discussions of communism versus capitalism, I was obsessed with the restrictions and censorship imposed on the artist and free thinker by both Western and Eastern governments. I couldn't see why someone who believed in open expression and an equitable society could be in conflict with the ideals of democracy and Marxism.

I was intrigued by the Cuban revolution of 1959, figuring that a Latin culture might give artists more leeway under Communism—in other words, play up the "party" in Communist Party. The Cuban revolutionaries would add color and soul and a democratic structure to the worthy ideas of Karl Marx. I thought that the ice-cold rule of Stalinism could not survive the warmth of the Cuban sun.

Most of the people I knew, and had known ever since I could remember, were engaged with the discourse of the day, which meant listening to voices coming from everywhere talking about Cuba, civil rights, the threat of nuclear war, and the escalating war in Vietnam. The revolution in Cuba looked like hope for those of us who grew up with the orthodoxy of the old left. Red-diaper babies or not, something was off; the old ways were not working, and the Soviet Union was definitely not the answer. It was in this context that I explored the life and work of Bertolt Brecht.

Intellectually, I understood the hard times American Communists had endured surviving McCarthyism and the blacklist, as had people on the left with whom I identified. Just a flicker of suspicion could get you fired from a job. If you knew someone who might be associated with Communist Party members or you had a name similar to that of someone who might be or were married to or a relative of someone, you were suspect. Many lives were ruined as a result.

As an example close to home, I remember the Hollywood actress Karen Morley (*Scarface, Pride and Prejudice,* and numerous other films of the 1930s and 1940s) and her husband, the actor Lloyd Gough (*Body and Soul, Sunset Boulevard,* and many others), coming around our apartment in Queens when I was a child. They had both been blacklisted in Hollywood because of their membership in the Communist Party (or maybe just an affiliation with it—the subject was always so hush-hush, nothing was ever known for sure). They moved to New York City, where the blacklist still hadn't taken a firm hold, to look for theater and television work.

In 1954 Karen Morley actually ran for lieutenant governor of New York on the American Labor Party ticket, the progressive political party that was discounted as merely a front for the Communist Party. The ALP was the

My mother on the stump for Vito
Marcantonio, Harlem congressman

party of the popular congressman Vito Marcantonio, who had been a protégé of Fiorello La Guardia. Years earlier my mother had worked for Marc, as he was known, giving speeches and writing articles for his campaigns. When we were young children, she took my sister and me with her to Marc's district office in East Harlem, then predominantly an Italian neighborhood, where we helped stuff envelopes for mailings to his constituents.

When Lloyd Gough, Karen's husband, came over to our house he would tell us stories, play the concertina, and sing drinking songs and sea chanties. My sister and I always demanded more, and he usually obliged.

Years later I saw an announcement that Lloyd was one of many performers playing at a club in the Village. I was eager to introduce him to Bob; I had talked him up a great deal because he was such a happy memory from my early childhood. But to my chagrin Lloyd wasn't at all friendly; he brushed me off, as if he were ashamed of being seen playing in a folk club. Because of his political beliefs, he had been denied his livelihood as an actor. He was in the dumps— more than a decade of being blacklisted had been very rough for him.

I thought of the Communists as regimented and doctrinaire, albeit honest and genuine in their desire for a better world. Being immersed in politics meant being a strategist, and that I was not. Bottom line: I knew that I could never sign on to any political organization. It wasn't in my nature to follow a party line. I would participate, but I would never join anything.

With the election of John F. Kennedy in 1960, America had a young president who seemed ready and able to look at the problems at home and in the world in new ways. There was hope that the times would be changing. But the more things change, the more they stay the same. Politics are politics, and progress moves at an excruciatingly slow pace.

The civil rights movement was tearing apart the old patterns of society and stitching up new ones while the escalating war in Vietnam was ripping into the fabric of American society in what seemed like irreparable ways. A cultural war was about to break out in many arenas.

Rock and roll was approaching adolescence and kids who had grown up with one foot in folk music and the other in rock were unsteady in their loyalties. Rock was tied to commercialism and selling out. Elvis was a flagrant reminder of that.

A musician will censure and judge music, but not by genre. Bob and I listened to rock and roll, which was part of the musical landscape. He didn't separate music into categories of worthiness; nor did I. I had grown up listening to all kinds of music. Bob soaked up everything and glommed onto whatever taught him something new. At the height of the folk boom, a variety of music was still being offered in the Village clubs. Jazz, although sidelined by folk music and rhythm and blues, was easy to find at the Vanguard, occasionally at the Village Gate, and at the often relocating Five

Spot. Like Beat poetry, jazz was not trendy in the 1960s, but the music was ensconced within the culture. And like the folkies some years down the line, jazz musicians struggled to survive on fewer gigs.

For a time, the Five Spot was up and running on the corner of St. Mark's Place and Third Avenue. It was a small and smoky club. One night on our way someplace else, Bob and I stopped in to see Charlie Mingus play with his quartet. That night, the piano player was white and female. The band was in full swing when Mingus, still playing his bass, started to comment aloud to the pianist as she played. His voice got louder and more insistent as he critiqued her abilities.

Go ahead bitch, show me what you can't do; white lady wanna play jazz: He was vicious and he didn't let up. I watched, mortified for her. But she continued playing like a pro, her face betraying nothing but concentration. She hit those keys, swung those notes as if her life depended on it. Mingus tormented her to the very end of the set and then said no more. In the sparsely crowded club, people stared into their drinks, pretending nothing out of the ordinary had happened. After some applause, Bobby and I left in silence. It took a while to get a grip on what we'd just witnessed.

I wasn't attentive to the comings and goings of the business world of folk music, and I didn't pay much attention to the intrigues of the musicians either, until I was involved with

Bobby. The more I saw, the less I wanted to be involved. I was always wary of the confinement of being a member of a scene. I was loyal to friends, no matter their standing in a pecking order. The in-depth discussions about who and what was truly traditional or who and what fit in some category or other were not that important to me, but I did love discovering, and learning about, all kinds of American music. I absorbed the music that grew from the loamy American soil—through cross-pollination over continents—viscerally during that period of my life. I cherish and love it. I grew up prepared to listen and see, and I did just that.

Later on, when Bob caused an uproar by going electric at the Newport Folk Festival of 1965 and at the concert in Forest Hills that year, I wondered who was doing all the booing. It is perfectly understandable that when your favorite artist, musician, or writer does something different from an established format, fans will be shaken. It will take time for the audience to accept the new work.

But I had an uncomfortable feeling about the strong objections to the new music Bob was making. He was abandoning "protest" music, folk music, and going commercial—selling out—to rock and roll, people said. I heard dogma and orthodoxy in all the discussions going on about his new direction—his betrayal, as many called it. There was more behind those condemnations than merely the reactions of an audience of shocked fans. It made me think about Brecht and the censoring of artists.

Anyone who was capable of writing the songs Dylan wrote had not abandoned anything at all. He continued writing about what was on his mind. Adding a band and play-

ing an electric guitar was an exploratory passage musi-
cally—after all, music is about sound. He had grown as a
person and as a writer since coming to New York City in the
winter of 1961. Four volatile and intensely lived years had
gone by in which he'd experienced much more in his life.
He wrote about those things. How many times must a person write the song he has already written?

Bob always did as he saw fit. He was rarely swayed by
outside demands or requests. He went where he wanted to
go, even if it meant alienating his public, fans, friends, and
lovers. He did not make anything easy for anyone, or for
himself.

Gil Turner followed Pete Seeger the way Jack Elliott and Bobby followed Woody Guthrie. He was a big, sincere man who in addition to his music worked in the civil rights movement, as did many other folk performers. Gil, Happy Traum, and Rob Cohen formed a group called the New World Singers and in July 1963, with Pete Seeger and Bob, they put together a concert in Greenwood, Mississippi, in support of the voter registration drive. I was working on *Brecht on Brecht* and couldn't go, so I organized a clothing drive and before they left I loaded the car with donations.

For a time Gil was an emcee at Gerde's and, like others, he pushed Mike Porco to hire Bob for a solo gig. Gil was one of the first folksingers to champion Bob as a songwriter. He encouraged Bob to show him more of his songs, which was all Bob needed to hear. He latched on to anyone who understood where he was headed.

I believe it was Gil who introduced Bob to *Broadside* magazine. Sis Cunningham and Gordon Friesen started *Broadside* as an alternative to *Singout!*, the self-described "magazine for folk music." *Broadside* would focus solely on songwriters who wrote about the concerns and troubles of the times in the mode of Guthrie and Seeger.

Len Chandler, one of the folk musicians involved in the burgeoning civil rights movement, had his songs printed in *Broadside.* Bob spent time with Len and when I met his wife, Nancy, who was also an artist, we hit it off just fine.

The *Broadside* meetings were held at Sis and Gordon's uptown apartment, where the singers would gather to sing their latest songs into a tape recorder. Either Sis or Gordon would then type out the lyrics and handwrite the musical notes—with guitar chords—and print copies of the magazine on their mimeograph machine. They were the first to print a song by Bob Dylan.

This was the time when the appellation *singer-songwriter* and the term *protest singer* were coined. Both labels seemed confining to me. There were many performers really good at interpreting songs written by others who weren't necessarily good at writing songs (protest or otherwise) themselves. It was unfortunate that it became de rigueur for all singers to write songs instead of interpreting the work of other, better songwriters. To cite the wisdom of Dave Van Ronk: singers have been covering songs by Puccini and Verdi for ages to great effect. No one would have expected Luciano Pavarotti to write his own arias.

Songwriters of all stripes came and went at the *Broadside* gatherings. I remember everyone as very earnest and dedicated, and Sis was more than happy to showcase the talents of Bob Dylan. Certainly I was happy to have my drawings illustrate Bobby's songs in the magazine.

After Bob had moved on, he wrote a letter to Gordon and Sis. In it he recounted his conflicted feelings about his growing fame, lamenting that some of his fellow musicians were still undeservedly unrecognized and struggling economically. He wrote about morality, fear, and love, which was very touching. Gordon and Sis published it in the January 1964 issue.

When Phil Ochs arrived at *Broadside* he made a notable difference. He had a fine tenor voice with a Joan Baez–like vibrato. His songs were good and he was already a polished performer. Phil's songs were journalistic, restricted to a specified subject or event. To write topical songs is risky because as time passes the songs lose their relevance: they have a built-in expiration date. But that doesn't lessen the validity of a well-written song; it serves its purpose within its designated shelf life. Phil was good at what he did.

Bobby and Phil had respect for each other as writers; they shared an affinity and a rivalry they both reveled in for a time. But their friendship was complicated. Phil Ochs came to know his limitations as a songwriter in the context of his admiration for what he believed were the unlimited abilities of Bob Dylan. At first they challenged each other, but as time went by, Phil was in awe of each new song Bob wrote. As Bob's fame grew, he in turn would chide Phil for confining himself within a genre. Phil, like Baez, was politically active; he used his talent and popularity to promote his political beliefs. Dylan worked outside the border.

Phil was living with his girlfriend, Alice, in a roomy apartment on Bleecker Street at the corner of Thompson. It was another Village hangout, and the four of us spent a lot of time together. Alice never seemed to mind people showing up whenever and staying until all hours of the night, even into the morning. She was relaxed and easygoing. The location of the apartment, in the midst of all the music clubs, became problematic as Bobby became more well known. He took to leaving via the fire escape in the back of

BROADSIDE
P.O.BOX 193
CATHEDRAL
STATION
NEW YORK 25
N. Y.

BROADSIDE #23

LATE
MARCH
1963
PRICE
35¢

Train a-travelin-

ILLUSTRATION
By
SUSIE ROTOLO

by
BOB DYLAN

There's an iron train a-travelin' that's been a
rollin' thru the years, With a firebox of hatred & a
furnace full of fears.   If you e- ver heard it's
sound or seen it's blood-red broken frame, Then you
heard my voice a-singin' & you know my name. —

CONT'D →

BROADSIDE #20

PO Box 193 Cathedral Sta., NY 25 NY

FEBRUARY, 1963
35 cents

MASTERS of WAR
by BOB DYLAN
Illustrated by Susie Rotolo

© 1963, Author

Come you masters of war —,

You that build all the guns

You that build the death planes—

You that build the big bombs

You that hide behind walls— You that hide behind desks, I just

want you to know I can see thru your masks.

You that never 've done nothing but build to destroy
You play with my world like it's your little toy
You put a gun in my hand then you hide from my eyes
And you turn and run farther when the fast bullets fly.

Like Judas of old you lie and deceive
A world war can be won you want me to believe
But I see thru your eyes & I see thru your brain
Like I see thru the water that runs down my drain.

You fasten the triggers for the others to fire
Then you sit back and watch as the death count gets higher
You hide in your mansions as the young peoples' blood
Flows out of their bodies and is buried in the mud.

CONT'D →

the building to avoid being recognized by the people wandering from club to club along Bleecker Street.

When Phil and Alice got married I was a witness at their wedding. By then Alice was visibly pregnant, and both of them were very nervous and giddy. During the ceremony at City Hall, we tried to stifle our giggles. The justice of the peace had to interrupt the proceedings to chastise us for not taking the situation seriously. No one was more serious about what they were doing than Alice and Phil. But that is precisely why it struck all of us as so funny.

I last saw Phil toward the end of 1966, when I ran into him at the Limelight one night before I left New York for Italy again. He was drinking a lot by then and he was bloated and disheveled, volatile and dark.

Phil began telling me a long, convoluted tale that made no sense. He laughed and cried and his manner frightened me. I tried to act as if nothing was wrong with his behavior or appearance. I gave him my address in Italy and half begged him to get away, take a long break, and come visit me. Phil Ochs had a good career and people who loved him but the demons he struggled with eventually engulfed and overpowered him. He committed suicide in 1976 at the age of thirty-six.

H i d e
and
S e e k

In youth loneliness is but the discovery of life
<small>(NOTEBOOK ENTRY, 1962)</small>

Bob's parents were ordinary in a way that he was not. He didn't feel he came from the right place considering how he felt about himself in the world.

Quite a few of the folk musicians playing in the Village had grown up in the suburbs in middle-class families and didn't advertise it. Some of them were from left-wing families that owned albums by Pete Seeger, Woody Guthrie, and Josh White but had to be quiet about it because of Red baiting and McCarthyism. There were also many in the Village who felt the same about their families as Bob did about his—that they were just plain ordinary folks; they were not talking about their backgrounds any more than he was. When my mother was around, she was trouble, but in all fairness she was interesting and nothing about the way I grew up was ordinary. Yet I didn't feel like talking about my family, either. Those were the times; everyone was busy reinventing his or her wheels. Families were baggage.

When I was in Italy Bob wrote me letters about his family, his feelings growing up, his name change, and about truth and lies. He spoke of his family's goodness—how well they treated him—and how bad he felt when he could not please them in a traditional manner, as his younger brother could.

Bob didn't keep his parents informed about his life in

New York City. Having read in some newspaper or magazine that Albert Grossman was his manager, his father called Albert's office in New York asking Bob to get in touch. John Court, Albert's partner, relayed the message and Bob, although not pleased, called home.

When he was ready for his parents to see who he had become, and he was ready to have me know them, he brought them to New York for the Town Hall concert in April 1963, which had been scheduled before the release of the *Freewheelin' Bob Dylan* album. There wasn't a big turnout, but the concert was definitely a success. It was clear that Bob had the goods to perform beyond the clubs and halls on the folk circuit. He had written so many very good songs, and his assurance as a performer was evident in his perfectly timed stumbles, jerks, and groans. It was ever more apparent how clearly he saw himself and his work, despite his loose-change manner. Watching Bob in the spotlight alone on the stage, with his guitar and harmonica, his voice and his words, I felt the power he had. Seeing him out of the context of the Village, on the Town Hall stage, it was evident that he owned it. I was happy for him and proud. So were his parents.

We went to dinner together at a restaurant near their hotel on the West Side of Manhattan in the Forties. His parents were very pleasant. In hindsight, I'm sure they wished I hadn't been there so they could have visited with their son alone.

The evening went smoothly, no bumps, no apparent tension. Bob did not prep me beforehand.

Mr. and Mrs. Zimmerman were soft-spoken and his

FOLK SONGS DRAW CARNEGIE CHEERS

Bob Dylan Appears as an 'Angry Young' Recitalist

10-28-63

In contrast to the simple naïveté of most folk-music concerts, the solo program by Bob Dylan at Carnegie Hall Saturday night left his listeners stirred, thinking and cheering for more.

The capacity audience, mostly of high school age, was restless until Mr. Dylan began to perform 20 of his songs and adaptations in the folk vein. Then they were caught up in the passionate, eloquent, icon-smashing musical statements of a 22-year-old minstrel who is quite unlike any poet or song writer to be heard today.

To regard Mr. Dylan as merely an entertainer is to slight his importance. Rather, he is a moralist, a pamphleteer, an angry young man with a guitar, a social protest poet, a latter-day James Dean who knows what he is rebelling against, perhaps an American Yevtushenko (the Russian poet).

Mr. Dylan is far from being a "finished" artist. Some of his songs were almost speeches delivered to guitar chording. Some of his lyrics have been left unwrought. The first half of the program lagged in pacing.

But these were trifles in the face of overwhelming emotional impact and provocation to thought made by an incredibly gifted and courageous writer. Even if the words torn from a newspaper, "The Lonesome Death of Hattie Carroll," lacked melodic profile, the passion of their cry against injustice transcended questions of form and craft.

Other songs had the ring of classics. "The Times, They Are a'Changing" serves notice on parents to understand their children or to move out of their path; "With God on Our Side" hurls a challenge at pious platitudes of history; "Only a Pawn in Their Game" laments the death of Medgar Evers, but goes on to analyze the social factors that caused his murder.

Several songs—of love, reform school and a writer's despair—were as personal as the country blues. Mr. Dylan's contempt for censorship was disclosed in his "Talking John Birch," which has been barred from television and recording. He also spoke derisively against political blacklisting of artists.

All this added up to the fact that Mr. Dylan is much more than an entertainer. His poetry, for all its topical urgency and lack of polish, will probably outlive much of the writing by the "professionals." He is assuming the role of radical spokesman, with music as his vehicle. The adulatory reception of his listeners indicated that he was speaking for them, too.

ROBERT SHELTON.

New York Times *review of the Carnegie Hall concert*

mother, especially, was friendly while his father was more reserved. I see the scene as a series of photographs; no dialogue comes to me. We are sitting at a round table, Bob next to me, me next to his father, and his father next to his mother, his mother next to Bob.

They came to New York again for his Carnegie Hall concert in October, and the next day *Newsweek* wrote about his true identity as Robert Zimmerman from Hibbing, Minnesota. His parents were interviewed for the piece.

It was a relief to have that done with at last, but the article was a very nasty piece of work implying with relish that the young man whose "finger was on the pulse of a generation" was a fake. He was just a middle-class kid from the Midwest escaping a nondescript background. The tone belittled the significance of his work and it was disturbing for him to be portrayed that way. Bob was extremely angry; he felt violated and his parents, proud of their son and not wishing to hurt him, were very upset.

Woman Troubles

There was an attitude toward musicians' girlfriends—
"chicks," as we were called, or "old lady," if a wife—that I
couldn't tolerate. Since this was before there was a feminist
vocabulary, I had no framework for those feelings yet they
were very strong. I couldn't define it, but the word *chick*
made me feel as if I weren't a whole being. I was a possession
of this person, Bob, who was the center of attention—that
was supposed to be my validation.

A lot of the problems women, married or not, had in
their relationships in the 1960s probably stemmed from
confusion over who they were and where they fit. Many
women were relegated to the background because that
was the way it was, not because men were bad. Make the
coffee, serve the drinks, sit down and listen, was the tune.
The side effects of this scenario made for feelings of inse-
curity and doubt, which snowballed into dissatisfaction
and unhappiness that were difficult to articulate.

I couldn't find my way with anyone, really. Everything
was centered on folk music, which was fine, because music was a big part of my life, but it wasn't my life's work.
The politics of the time were what we all had in common,
pretty much, but no one was choosing politics as a profession. Politics were the foundation upon which many other
things were built. But I was also interested in the theater,
where I was involved with productions that were breaking
new ground, and curious about art that was erupting into
something no one except Marcel Duchamp and the
Dadaists, perhaps, could have foreseen. I was very young,
I was still forming myself, but I did know I wasn't a musi-

cian, nor was I a musician's "chick." And you could bet the neck of a Gibson I had no desire to graduate to "old lady."

The Carnegie Hall concert in October 1963 was the culmination of a series of high steps up the ladder of success for Bob. In August the Newport Folk Festival had been a big deal, but it was a folk festival. The audience at Carnegie expanded to encompass a much bigger group of people. Peter, Paul, and Mary had a huge hit single with Bob's song "Blowin' in the Wind," and the *Freewheelin'* album was getting attention. Word had spread. Outside of the hall there were blowups of the cover of the album in black and white. Bob's reaction to seeing those larger-than-life pictures in the middle of Fifty-seventh Street was a surprised and embarrassed laugh, while I was amazed and self-conscious at the same time.

During the concert, the audience hung on every word Bob spoke and sang, and when it was over they gave him a raucous standing ovation. Backstage with Albert Grossman, Dave Van Ronk, Terri Thal, and others, I watched and absorbed what was happening. We all sensed a sea change and it was exhilarating.

At the end of the concert, there was a huge mob waiting for Bob at the stage door, and Albert was concerned that he get into the rented limo in one piece.

Acting as decoys, Terri and I diverted some of the fans by walking in the opposite direction, while Bob and the others jumped into the waiting limo. Those in the crowd who hadn't fallen for the ruse got to the limo just as Bob was sliding into it. Terri and I ducked around the cars to circle back, and as the crowd surged around us we clambered in the door Albert held open.

I remember being very frightened by the energy of the crowd. They literally charged the limousine, pounding on the roof and slapping at the windows, yelling to get Bob's attention. He gave a few staccato waves and then turned away.

As the car slowly moved out into traffic, we gradually lost the fans, who ran behind us. Albert had a Mona Lisa smile on his face. We were all pretty quiet, except for the odd quip, because it was both exciting and scary. Bob was in the right place at the right time with the right stuff. This truly was the beginning of his future: Bobby had become Dylan.

Pete Seeger called me after the Carnegie Hall concert. We were on the phone for a long time and he did most of the talking. He said I was a muse to an exceptional songwriter and artist. He talked about his philosophy of life. He talked about his wife, Toshi. He talked about many things, but above all he wanted to tell me how special Bob was and how I was an important part of that. He wanted to acknowledge my role since I, too, was a rare soul. I felt honored by his call and warmed by his words. His thoughtfulness in making the call, his regard for how I might be feeling in this whirlwind time of rising fame for Bob, was generous and genuinely helpful. Even though he saw me in the role of the woman behind the great man, I was not offended.

Alan Lomax also gave me what was intended as a compliment. He believed I was exceptional because, in so many words, I stood by the poet, the genius. I unselfishly tended to his needs and desires. I put him first. I was a rare girl for these times.

I was offended and found nothing complimentary in that description. I didn't see myself as subservient to my boyfriend or anyone else—nor was this what I aspired to be. I seriously doubted Bob saw me that way, either. We live within our own time and at that time, prefeminism, not many gave a thought to equality between men and women. Striving for equality meant fighting to integrate lunch counters and schools. Equality was a goal for blacks within a whites-only society.

I chafed at the notion of devoting my young self to serving somebody, since I was still curious about life— questing. I hated being thought of as so-and-so's chick: I did not want to be a string on Bob Dylan's guitar. Because I was with my boyfriend didn't mean I had to walk a few paces behind, picking up his tossed-off candy wrappers.

But I didn't know where to put that frustration. This was before the women's liberation movement of the 1970s, when many of these issues were articulated. I resented not being able to wander off by myself and sit in a café to draw, read, or write the way the guys could, without getting hit on. And forget about going to a movie alone. A girl at the movies by herself meant she was fair game, asking for trouble. And she usually got it.

Between theater jobs, I was working as a waitress in a kosher deli on Avenue B, up the street from Tompkins

Square Park. Long and narrow, with the deli counter at the front and table service in back, it was a busy place at lunchtime. My first day at work the owner took me to the kitchen to show me the lay of the land. He said I must never let the customers see me take the milk from the same refrigerator where the meat was kept. He didn't keep separate dishes, either, yet the place was advertised as strictly kosher.

On top of my clothes I had to wear a silly white milk-maid type of apron. As I walked down the narrow aisle taking or serving orders, inevitably a man would yank the tie on my apron or tug at the pocket, pretending to put money in. Though it was maddening, I had to smile; these were regular customers and I needed the job. The owner used to holler from the front for them to lay off but it meant nothing really—just the old "between guys" game going on.

After I had worked there a few weeks, a young man began coming in often and paying attention to me. He said he knew I had to be more than "just a waitress" and tried to engage me in conversation. He left really nice tips and pestered me for my phone number. The owner didn't like this at all. One day he made a loud speech about men harassing his hired help and threw the man out. Though the owner never seemed to mind true harassment of his hired help, he was happy to grandstand with the friendly customer who even berated the old men who yanked at my apron strings.

As a birthday present to myself, I quit. I would think about the future in a few days. But two days later Kennedy was shot, and the future suddenly had a different meaning.

I had moved out of the West Fourth Street apartment in August 1963 because I could no longer cope with all the pressure, gossip, truth, and lies that living with Bob entailed. I was unable to find solid ground—I was on quicksand and very vulnerable. I felt pulled every which way by well-meaning people with good and bad advice. But there were those who were not well-meaning at all. Someone who fit the latter profile called me one night when Bob wasn't home and began to speculate about Bob and about me. He hinted, questioned, and then judged our behavior and abilities; he gossiped and then played the therapist. He succeeded in further scrambling my already scrambled brains. It was a bad night.

In the end the solution was to move out. I got an apartment with my sister on Avenue B. I needed to get my bearings. I began taking classes at the School of Visual Arts at night and struck up friendships with a few artists. With them I spent time talking about many things, none of which involved the world of folk music.

The Avenue B apartment was a floor-through railroad flat. Certain tenement apartments in New York City were called railroad flats because one room was behind the other and the passage from room to room was a narrow corridor.

The front room—the living room in this apartment—had an exposed brick wall and two windows that looked out onto the avenue, followed by two "bedrooms" with no doors, no windows, and an airshaft between them. The kitchen, with windows facing the back of the building, was the next room in the line and had a bathtub next to the sink. Off to the side was a minuscule room with a toilet. There was no privacy because there were no doors except the one to the so-called bathroom. The ceilings were high, but the rent wasn't.

The building was on the corner of East Seventh Street, across from Tompkins Square Park. On one side of the entrance door was an old dark bar and on the other a Pentecostal church. That made for a nice contrast of rousing church music by day and rowdy bar noises by night.

Bob and I got along better when we weren't under the same roof and came together when we both felt like it. At least it seemed that way. When he was in New York, he was always at the Avenue B apartment, which was rough on Carla. They didn't get along well and she felt I was better off without the lyin' cheatin' manipulatin' bastard.

She had a valid point but, alas, I was caught in the whirlpool of indecision that is tortured young love. And we sure tortured and young loved each other to distraction. I didn't manage to get away from him for a long time—and not for want of trying, either.

November 22, 1963, was a day that yanked the rug out from under us all in a way that even the Cuban missile crisis of the previous year hadn't. It is hard to place anybody in a specific location when the news of John F. Kennedy's assassination began to spread. Nothing seemed real, and everything seemed to be happening either in slow motion or speeded up. There was disbelief and shock. It didn't seem conceivable that a president of the United States could be assassinated in the time you were living in; such things were the horrors of history. The days following the assassination were even more shocking.

Bobby, Carla, and I were together at the Avenue B apartment sitting on the rickety wicker couch, cigarettes in hand, in front of the old black-and-white television set to watch Lee Harvey Oswald, the alleged lone assassin, be arraigned. We watched him get shot right there, live, on national TV. If we'd turned to flick an ash, we would have missed it.

Chaos ensued, both on TV and everyplace else.

Did you see that?!

The three of us froze and went deadly serious. There was no instant replay; these were the days before video cameras. The attack had been captured on film. The news commentators would have to explain what they saw or knew until the film was processed. Bob barely spoke and could not leave the TV. He was fastened to it. Everyone was.

Would it ever end—the endless speculation, the endless funeral, the endless questions, the endless mourning, in the endless, endless, upside-down, fear-filled world?

Later that month Bob and I, with Pete Karman and his girlfriend, went to see Lenny Bruce at the Village Theater (later known as the Fillmore East) on Second Avenue and Sixth Street. The place was packed and expectations were high for every reason you could think of, but especially in anticipation of what Bruce would make of the Kennedy assassination and the murder on live TV of Lee Harvey Oswald by Jack Ruby.

But Bruce was not ready to face his public that night. We were getting rowdy, stomping our feet, applauding, yelling encouragement for him to come out from behind the heavy red curtain and speak to us. He would peek out and then withdraw behind it. Someone would announce something, and then we had to wait some more.

At that time, Lenny Bruce was being hounded by lawsuits and lawyers, fighting obscenity charges filed against him from coast to coast. He had enough paperwork for an archive and when he finally walked hesitantly out in front of the curtain, he was clutching a big part of it. Discombobulated, he began shuffling the pages and reading from his trial transcripts. When the crowd got restless, he said, He is dead, he is dead, it is done, and went back to reading and commenting wryly on the legal absurdities overwhelming and destroying him.

I don't know what we expected from Lenny Bruce that evening, but it wasn't that. No one could put anything back on a recognizable, definable path. Whatever had been set in motion by the assassination and murder was as yet undefined. Chaos wasn't necessarily pandemonium; chaos could just be formless. The performance Bruce gave that night reinforced that feeling.

POLITICS AS USUAL

In December 1963, the Emergency Civil Liberties Committee, ECLC, presented Dylan with the annual Tom Paine
Award in "recognition of distinguished service in the fight
for civil liberty."

Bob's acceptance speech was akin to performance art.
He was very uncomfortable with the formality of the situation and uneasy about making a speech. It was a fiasco in
many ways. Most of what he said was misconstrued by the
members in attendance at the ceremony. He jumped from
one thing to another like a grasshopper, yet there was a
point to it all.

Bob was twenty-two and had shot to fame meteorically
since the release of *The Freewheelin' Bob Dylan* in May. In the
course of the year that was about to end, JFK had been assassinated, the battles for civil rights were still being
fought, and the huge March on Washington with the now
legendary speech given by Martin Luther King had taken
place in August. Bob had been to Mississippi in June with
Pete Seeger and others to support a voting rights campaign,
and he had had a breakthrough appearance at the Newport
Folk Festival in July. He had performed at Town Hall to a
small but enthusiastic audience a month before the release
of his album; in October he'd been mobbed by fans after his
concert at Carnegie Hall. Then there had been the snide
story in *Newsweek* "outing" him as Robert Zimmerman from
Hibbing, Minnesota.

Coinciding with the release of *Freewheelin'* he had

walked off the *Ed Sullivan Show* because CBS refused to let him sing his song about the John Birch Society. The oppressive mentality of the Cold War still held sway over the culture, and everyone working to change the status quo, whether through the arts or in politics, was chomping at the bit. To be young and on society's edge in those years made you feel you were standing at the crossroads of something important, energized for what was to come.

When he got up to accept his award, Bob, who was beginning to look like the one giving directions, was dealing with all these things.

During the summer of 1963 a group of young people had gone to Cuba to test the constitutionality of the Kennedy administration's recent ban on travel to Cuba by American citizens. Bob knew a few of the people who had made the trip, as did I (Pete Karman was among them). It was very exciting to listen to these friends talk about their trip to Cuba and recount the plans Castro had for his country, now free from the dictator Batista. A revolution carried out by a ragtag bunch of rebels hiding out in the Sierra Madre mountains was appealing to American kids engaged in the upheavals of the times. Youth culture was on the rise. Young people were angry and dissatisfied with the world as it was.

With all the changes in the world, and everything that had happened to him personally, Bob was in a heady place. And his speech reflected that, not to mention what he'd been imbibing beforehand to calm his nerves.

He got up to the podium and rambled on a bit about looking out on an audience of old people without any hair—

that it was time for them to make way for the young, "who took a long time to get young." To scandalized gasps, he said he saw something of himself in Lee Harvey Oswald before Oswald crossed the line—he, Bob, could never cross such a line. He added that the government should not ban travel to Cuba, because freedom to see for oneself is an American freedom.

He accepted the award in the name of James Forman (of SNCC, the Student Nonviolent Coordinating Committee) and Philip Luce, one of the people who had gone to Cuba. Ironically, Luce was later revealed to be an agent of the FBI, sent on the Cuba trip to get information about those who organized it. Many of the "old people" at the ceremony had fought the good fight in the thirties and forties, and some were still at it. Many of them were highly offended by Bob's words, while others understood his point, disjointed though it was in presentation. Later he sent the ECLC a letter-poem written after the fact that better expressed how he felt about the award, the significance of Tom Paine, and what he had intended by his words at the ceremony.

The people from the old left looked to Dylan as the new spokesperson who would lead the next generation to join the good fight they had so nobly fought. They had struggled long and hard, only to be vilified by their own country, the country they deeply loved and honored, above all. They were not bitter; instead, they continued in the spirit of their belief in the better, more just world that Communism, in the theories of Karl Marx, not Stalin, had outlined.

Bob Dylan had to be the Next One, the Prophet. He fit the bill with the extraordinary songs he was writing, which expressed wisdom beyond his years. The old-left wanted to school him so he would understand well and continue on the road they had paved, the one that Woody Guthrie and Pete Seeger and others had traveled before him. They explained the way of the road and its borders.

Bob listened, absorbed, honored them, and then walked away. An artist can't be made to serve a theory. He headed toward the lights that beckoned at the end of the tunnel. He made for the exit and from there he took the open roads that led him where he chose to go instead. He didn't want to accept the torch they were trying to pass to him.

With Dave Van Ronk in the Village, winter 1963

The scary thing was that many from the so-called New Left of the sixties felt equally betrayed by Dylan. The orthodoxy that had kept the left cemented to Stalinism should not have even remotely been carried forward into the movements of the sixties. But old philosophies and attitudes

tend to linger on and have an influence even after the dec-
laration of their demise.

Though Christmas is supposed to be a festive time of
year, by the holidays in 1963 most people felt off-kilter, still
in a state of shock from the Kennedy assassination. The only
solution was to have a good time.

My mother and Fred invited Carla and Bob and me to
their apartment in Hoboken, New Jersey, on Christmas Eve,
and in turn we asked a friend or two to come along.

Virginia Eggleston, a family friend for many years, was
another guest. An elegant bohemian in her early sixties, she
got along better with young people than with her peers because of her outspoken informality and penchant for smoking pot and knocking back martinis. She had been at the
ECLC fund-raiser the previous week and was one of the few
who staunchly defended Bob. She genuinely liked him and
his music. Apart from my mother's diffidence towards him
and her misgivings about our relationship, and Fred's pro-
fessorial smiles, the evening went well enough.

For Christmas Day my sister and I had decided to throw
a party back in the city at the Avenue B apartment. Albert
Grossman brought some really good wine to help make it a
good one. People came and went as Carla and I worked at
cooking a turkey in the very unreliable oven. We seasoned
the bird the Italian way we had learned from our mother,
with rosemary, garlic, a coating of olive oil, and a bath of
white wine.

As a gift, Bob gave me a handmade, embroidered Romanian sheepskin jacket he had found in one of the East Village stores that catered to the Romanian, Ukrainian, and Polish residents of the neighborhood. It was beautiful and very warm: I loved it. I'm wearing it in a series of pictures that the photographer Jim Marshall took of us that winter.

It was a good party, and the week of carrying on ended with a New Year's Eve party at the Van Ronks'. It had been a complicated year, thick with ups and downs, sad and horrific events, upheavals and changes both very good and very bad. Anticipation was in the air for the New Year.

Not Dark Yet

Geno Foreman came from a distinguished family. Though he was the son of Clark Foreman, the director of the Emergency Civil Liberties Committee, the group that had given Bob the Tom Paine Award, Geno didn't seem to be from any family. It was as if he just flowed loose in the world with an extraterrestrial energy. He was about six feet tall, with very dark, thick hair and a full beard, and he was missing some front teeth. His dark, fiery eyes darted about as fast as his words when he spoke.

In the summer of 1964 we both went to Cuba as part of another group of Americans testing the travel ban. Geno looked like one of the Cuban revolutionaries, Camille Cienfuegos, who had been killed while fighting in the mountains with Fidel Castro and Che Guevara. Cienfuegos's image was on the walls of buildings all over Cuba. Cubans did a double take when they saw Geno walking around with the other Americans.

Geno also managed to speak Spanish like a Cuban within a few days of his arrival. In Italy some years later, when I spoke to him for the last time, he had morphed into an Italian and spoke the language as if he were born speaking it. He was beyond cool and beyond hip—he was an uncontainable force. He knew everyone, was everywhere at once, and was anyone he chose to be.

The Avenue B flat where I had been living since leaving West Fourth Street was always full of people at odd times, especially when Bob was staying there. He had just come back to New York from California, and wherever he went, his expanding entourage would eventually follow.

They all were there the day Geno appeared and bellowed (Geno always bellowed), Hey, Bobby, hey, man, heard about you and Joanie in California being, y'know, together, man. Look, man, she paid for these!

He pointed to his new teeth.

Bob was up like a shot, grabbing Geno and walking him to the other end of the apartment. Even though there was a lot going on around the place there was a sudden shift in mood. Albert Maher, who was an unofficial bodyguard and buddy when Bob was in New York City, came over to sit next to me and started talking in that low, sweet way he had.

I don't remember when I saw Geno again—later that day or weeks afterward—but he had no sense of a gaffe or an of-fense because Geno wouldn't intentionally hurt a fly. He just said what passed through him. Geno. Man. Geno was beautiful, brilliant, and irrepressible. He was the mad prince in the kingdom of the mad ones. He married and fa-thered a child and died in a freak accident in England some five years later.

CODICIL

Sadness so overwhelming it takes the breath away. Numbness affects the ability to move the body, and brain fog hampers vision. The slightest thing can bring on a bout of crying. Constricted throat, burning insides, dull aches. Nothing matters but what went wrong or what can go wrong now that something is beginning to feel wrong. There is a desperate attempt to stifle all doubt. Common sense is a wicked, hideous, backbiting enemy in cahoots with instinct to beat the daylights out of white-hot sentiment. No contest. Everything is obliterated.

BREAKING FAME

He saw right from his side and I saw right from mine, and we wore each other down for it. We talked a lot but told little. We both had overly sensitive personalities with nerve endings exposed. Outside of us were other pressures: He's no good, she's not right. Time to move on but unable to let go.

All those people, the constant crowding—I had the sensation of being in a herd of cattle and being prodded to move, move along with the hustling herd down a crowded road. Pushing, shoving, turning in place, prodding—turn, move, shoving, loud mooing. Go on go on come on come on come this way go that way. We called out over their heads, but the din was constant, and the dust churning up from the road made it hard to see. Soon I saw what looked like a way out far off to the side. I made for it. My fear subsided somewhat. The still and blank quiet of an unknown road. Moo.

That is how it was. Quite a herd goes with fame.

*B*ack in the dark days, during the middle decades of the twentieth century, the personal pronoun used by the media was the masculine one. The titles for most professions ended in "man" unless there was a male and female version: spokesman, newsman, weatherman, steward, or stewardess. There were no spokespersons, firefighters, or flight attendants. The pronoun "he" was used when referring in general to doctors, lawyers, writers, poets, etc. A married woman lost both first and last names and became Mrs. John's Wife, whether she chose to or not.

Most girls took on the life of their boyfriends unquestioningly and made their own lives within those boundaries. Instinctually I chafed at that but did my best until I couldn't breathe. The folk music world was hermetic. It was centered on musicians and their work, the songs they were writing, their ambitions and their camaraderie. It was primarily a boy's club. Girls knew their place if they were girlfriends. Even if they were folksingers working their way up just like the guys, their position was not quite the same. That was my take on it.

$\mathcal{B}$ob was my first significant relationship. I was seventeen when we met and, despite having had to grow up very quickly, I still had more growing up to do. Bob was just twenty, and precocious as he was he still had much to learn about life. During our time together things became very complicated because so much happened to him so fast. We had a good time, but also a hard time, as a young couple in love.

Bob was charismatic; he was a beacon, a lighthouse. He was also a black hole. He required committed backup and protection I was unable to provide consistently, probably because I needed them myself. I loved him, but I was not able to abdicate my life totally for the music world he lived within.

I believed the intention behind his good words to me, but more and more his deeds spoke otherwise. In private he was one thing and in public another. Together we had created a private world, a private way of being that he protected. No intruders: West Fourth Street was his castle, and he held the key. He handpicked those allowed to enter. I could accept that; I was a child of my times, after all, but only up to a point.

As his fame grew, I came to understand the absolute necessity for that privacy. The paranoia and secrecy that were part of his personality early on were essential for his survival later on. He was becoming prey. Either people wanted to devour him or they offered themselves up for him to consume.

With this new recognition and expanded fame came adoration. Heady stuff. It gave him power, but it put him in an awkward position. People wanted to be his friend at all costs. Everyone craved his presence, his wisdom, and his judgment. After *The Freewheelin' Bob Dylan* had been out awhile, at parties I noticed that people would approach him with reverence and tell him involved stories about their lives and then wait for him to speak. They wanted him to suggest solutions for them, to enlighten them in some way.

It made him uneasy. He wanted to make music, not address a congregation. And it made me uneasy because, being close to their object of desire, I was someone they either wanted to befriend or be rid of.

As time went by, those of us who were close to Bob were subjected to trickle-down fame. We would close ranks protectively around ourselves and around him. Some people who knew Bobby only slightly would trade off his growing notoriety. Many resented him and pretended nothing unusual had happened, since recognizing any change would force them to acknowledge loss of the control or power they thought they had over him. Old friends wanted to hold him to where he was before all this clamorous attention—to keep him grounded. They acknowledged his fame but did not defer to it. They held him to himself, yet they let him expand. That was good.

I watched, learning how fame altered his life. He was given permission to do or say whatever he wanted. Restrictions were a thing of the past—of prefame time. The hard part now was to recognize the borders and boundaries that did exist, but which were very different from the limitations of the recent past.

Suddenly Bob had advisers and *consiglieri* in his corner, smiling and shuffling about, proffering "shoulds" and "why don't yous" by the briefcase full. Media people begged for his attention. I would shy away and try to avoid them, but Bob would search me out and pull me near him. He sensed my mood and wanted to reassure me that we were together, that I was important to him.

I attempted to carry on with my life and do whatever work I was doing, and I never talked about Bob except with close friends. But I became more and more reticent even with them and adopted Bob's paranoia. I had a hard time trusting anyone. People crowded around wanting to be my new best friend or claiming to be my oldest best friend, and couldn't we all go hang out with Dylan?

I couldn't handle being "one step closer to God." I was being pecked at because of my proximity to the end of the rainbow. Expected to focus entirely on his needs, I was invisible—downgraded from chick and guitar string, no less. Where was I in all this? I felt lost, confused, and betrayed. We both needed protection from the outside world, but in the end I needed it more. Bob intuited what was happening to me and tried to prevent it, but I was not receptive to his concern.

I no longer knew who I could trust, including or perhaps especially my mother and my sister, as well as Bob. The feeling was devastating and eventually resulted in a crack-up. I wanted to get away from all of it and recapture the self I'd found in Italy the year before—to claim my pronoun.

One afternoon I was in a café with a friend and he mentioned someone who had said something complimentary about me. I laughed and told him that people were nice to me only to get close to Dylan.

He looked at me and said, Don't you think someone might genuinely like you because you are you?

I doubt that very much, I replied.

Bob had an aura of darkness and intensity that enveloped me when I was near him. I couldn't stay in that cold, dark air. It frightened me because I was scared of my own dark.

When I left West Fourth Street, I'd taken my vulnerable sanity with me to Avenue B in the East Village. But Bobby was always there unless he was out of town, and when he was out of town he would telephone. It was like an addiction— he needed to know I would be there for him and I would be, in spite of my attempts to do otherwise.

We were walking together silently along East Seventh Street one night, heading toward the apartment on Avenue B. He was inside himself. I felt uneasy, trapped; I thought I would suffocate. I looked at him and said I had to go. I felt my life was at stake. With a resigned sadness, he gestured toward me with his hand. It wasn't an offer to take it. I saw it as an acceptance of the inevitable, and I echoed the gesture. It was a sacrificial move so we could both move on and live as we needed to. I turned and walked away without looking back.

> I believe in his genius, he is an extraordinary writer but I don't think of him as an honorable person. He doesn't necessarily do the right thing. But where is it written that this must be so in order to do great work in the world?
> (notebook entry, 1964)

BALLAD

For a long time my mother had made it clear she didn't think much of Bobby. By the time *Freewheelin'* came out, she and Fred had long since moved to New Jersey. It was easier all around to avoid contact. I remember her informing me that the career army man an older cousin was married to had lost out on a promotion that involved security clearance because of my appearance on the cover of Bob's album. I was astounded.

True, the times they were troubled. Protest against the escalating war in Vietnam was on the rise, draft cards were being burned, and colleges were erupting with discontent. Blues, bluegrass, and ballads no longer defined folk music, since so many folksingers were now writing songs that spoke to current events. Bob Dylan was labeled a "protest singer." But the absurdity of my mother, Marxist Mary, trying to make me feel responsible for a military man's losing a security clearance because I was on an album cover with Bob Dylan, a rebel with a cause, left me speechless. And that was all she said to me about the cover or the album in general.

My mother had objected to Bob from the moment she laid eyes on him back in 1961, but the animosity between my sister and Bob developed over time. Both my mother and Carla were running interference on our relationship, and he couldn't help resenting that. I couldn't handle the constant pressure.

The way I saw it, Bobby and Carla had some kind of rivalry for controlling interest in me. She was intent on opening my eyes to his manipulative ways. In the beginning, she championed him wholeheartedly, happy to have him be her pupil, listen to her records, sleep on her couch. But Carla needed to be in charge—be the authority. That was the defensive stance she acquired growing up with our mother. Carla felt that others had to measure up to her standards, and Bob no longer measured up.

He saw how she tried to insert herself, and assert her importance, in people's lives. I knew that was true, but family ties bind and blind, and my sister and I had only had each other to count on during some rough years.

Bob and Carla argued and fought, slinging words back and forth. She had many grievances. He had truths to tell. When he wasn't around, the harangue continued. I was sick from it.

$\mathcal{B}$ob wanted me to stay where I was, to be there when he got back from wherever he went without me, and to be with whomever he pleased while he was there. He'd plead with me to marry him, which made no sense to me the way things were; nor did I believe he was sincere. My sister and others pointed to his hypocrisy and his ability to manipulate everyone and everything to his advantage.

Honesty was what I craved, and the more I needed to hear straight words from him, the more he twisted them like ropes to tie me down. I could not live like that.

Carla and Bobby each felt the other was bad for me. Neither of them was mistaken about that. I loved my tough, smart older sister and looked up to her. And I loved Bobby. But at a certain point I wanted nothing more than to get away from them both so that I could find out where I was.

I tended to look at the whole picture. Dwelling on who done who wrong—he said, she said—never got anyone anywhere, except into an argument without end. I grew up in a bickering, fighting, destructive environment filled with accusations and recriminations on an endless loop. I saw no way to make peace though I lived with the conviction that it was my duty to do so. I had failed. I was undone and the pressures were impossible for me to cope with. I saw no way out.

I found out I was pregnant not long after I moved to Avenue B. Terrified, I didn't know how to handle the situation. Bobby and I were going through a tumultuous time as it was; this was a complication we had not anticipated. I did not want to have a child. I was feeling confined, and a child would be even more of a confinement. On the other hand, maybe I would like to have a child. Bob was just as confused and very upset at the idea of an illegal—read dangerous—abortion. Information about where to get one was underground, and discretion when asking for information was imperative. Secrecy worked both ways. No one wanted to get anybody in trouble.

Botched back-alley abortions that left women maimed or dead were very real. Many women who had the money traveled to Puerto Rico, where abortion was legal. Fortunately there were good doctors who risked everything by secretly performing abortions in their offices or clinics. In the sixties everyone knew about a doctor in Pennsylvania who helped women.

The decision to have an abortion was not easily made, but we made it in the end. Through friends, a good doctor was found right in New York City. Everything went smoothly, the only complication was my uneasy state of mind. I withdrew more into myself and let people think I was feeling physically weak from the procedure. Instead I was depressed and wanted to sleep reality away.

CODA

The passage of time—days, weeks, and months—were all lumped together without a linear marking of them. The intensity of the bad created a weight that flattened the good we had together. One night at Avenue B everything came to a head. Like an overstuffed closet, all the bits and pieces I had shoved away into the dark corners of my brain burst open. I was a mess of whirling, wordless, and no longer containable sounds. There was no going forward for us, that much at long last was settled.

TOMORROW IS
A LONG TIME

Breaking up takes time. After a stretch we reconnected again. It was painful, but then it wasn't so painful. Sometimes we just enjoyed each other's company.

We were in contact by phone at odd and even times. He would call when he was in town. No matter where I was living (Avenue B, East Houston Street, or West Tenth Street), I always seemed to have an apartment on the top floor of a walk-up. When I heard the phone ringing as I turned the key in the door, I'd race to answer it and say, catching my breath, Whew, I just got in.

When it was Bob, he would reply with skepticism, Yeah, yeah, you always say that.

But it was true.

One evening he called and said, I have a car, come for a ride with me. While we drove around the city, he spoke about fame and what it meant to become "a thing." People wanted a piece of him, he said. He was learning how to keep whole.

ADDENDUMS

In June or July 1965, Albert Grossman's wife, Sally, invited me up to their house in Woodstock, New York, for a few days. Sally said that no one else would be around except her father, so we could take it easy by the pool. The plan must have been for me to meet her at the recording session for *Highway 61 Revisited*, after which we'd drive up to the country.

The session was in progress when I arrived. Bob was quiet, intense, and twitchy behind his dark glasses. He was working. The other musicians I knew were Al Kooper and the extraordinary guitarist Mike Bloomfield.

What struck me about Al Kooper the first time I met him was his lust for life. Everyone was young and energetic—it comes with the territory—but Al took it up a notch. If I ran into him on the street, in a record store—anywhere—and he was excited about something, his enthusiasm was catching. Al was tall, wiry, and always full of droll tales and shaggy-dog stories. He was a really funny guy and a very serious musician.

During the session, Al was the liveliest thing in the room, popping up all over the place like a jack-in-the-box. He scooted around doing several things at once. I don't recall many people hanging around; Albert Grossman was probably in the control booth with one of the producers, Tom Wilson or Bob Johnston, depending on the day I was there. In a photograph from the session I'm wearing somebody's jacket around my shoulders, so I assume the studio was cold.

At some point Al called me over to the organ and told me to hold down two notes while he played something else. I'm sure I told Al I couldn't possibly, but he paid me no mind—nor did anyone else. So I did what he asked, though I don't remember the song, and Al doesn't, either. It couldn't have been "Like a Rolling Stone" because on that cut Al Kooper made his leap from the guitar to the organ.

At the Highway 61 sessions
with Mike Bloomfield, Paul Griffin,
Bob, and Al Kooper

Historical moments are usually framed in hindsight but that was instantly memorable.

My recollection is strong—I can see Al putting my hands on the keys—because it was such an unusual thing for a recording session. I was no musician.

Though details of the day elude me, the memory of playing those notes remains unforgettable because I was really nervous and because nobody questioned my presence—which speaks to everyone's trust in Al Kooper, perhaps. More likely, this was a run-through, a work in progress—hence everyone's indifference to my stint at the keyboards.

At the Forest Hills concert in August 1965, Dylan went electric for the second half to a raucous mix of booing and cheering, after opening with an all-acoustic set. I was mesmerized by the performance of "Ballad of a Thin Man." The stage seemed to glow, to vibrate; Bob was taunting and challenging his audience with every syllable, and the band was a force behind him. I kept looking around to see if the audience was truly hearing the song.

When we were together afterwards, he was edgy because he was jumping off into the future, where he wanted to be. Transitions are scary; there are dangers of slipping or tripping or crashing and breaking something when moving on with the rest of your life. I worried for him.

By then the multifaceted Bobby Neuwirth, a painter, musician, and very clever wordsmith, was a fixture in Bob's orbit, as was Victor Maimudes, Bob's silent and creepy buddy-bodyguard. They were so cool, so hip, so cold. Things got strange. Negative. Bob was thin and tight and hostile. He had succumbed to demons. He needed to stop doing what he was doing to himself.

He and Neuwirth held court, mainly at the Kettle of Fish, the bar above the Gaslight, and pronounced sentence and declared truth to whoever approached them. It was depressing to see people bow and scrape to the reigning king and his jester.

Albert Grossman called me one morning and said if I signed a paper he could get my passport, which had been invalidated after my Cuban trip, back in plenty of time for me to join Bob's tour to England in 1965. Obviously Bob wanted me to go—otherwise Albert would not have been calling. But this was another cue for me to sever another tie.

Slowly untying all those entanglements. I said thank you but no. Whatever the situation was, I knew I wouldn't be comfortable. I was sick of the director by then.

As the years went by and I got a better handle on life, I understood Bob's ways. Distance gave me perspective and I had a clearer understanding of what a complicated time it had been. Bob was assaulted by many forces, most of them good, since he was gaining the success he always sought; but some were bad, because there was a new kind of complexity to everything going on around him. It was tough going for someone who underneath all the ambition and drive was very sensitive. I was equally sensitive and so overwhelmed by circumstances that I had trouble seeing how hard he was trying to hold things together.

People close to me felt I was defending his bad behavior, but I saw things in another light, even though I was more than grateful for their loyalty to me. Yeah, he was a lying shit of a guy with women, an adept juggler, really; and when he was on his "telling it like it is" truth mission, he could be cruel. Though I was never on the receiving end of one of his tirades, I did witness a few. The power he was given and the changes it entailed made him lash out unreasonably, but I believe he was trying to find a balance within himself when everything was off-kilter. Some of the songs from that period, such as "Positively 4th Street," give a sense of the backbiting that thrived in a hermetic environment.

Bob was driven—focused on his path. He could see how things were so very clearly that it could be scary to be around him. He was his own person from the beginning. There lies his honesty. Artists we admire aren't necessarily exemplary human beings just because they are exceptional in their chosen fields. Their art is the work offered for public consumption, and nothing else.

We loved each other very much, and when it ended it was mutual heartbreak. His way was to do as he wished and let things sort themselves out without making decisions that might hurt. Yet that hurt more. He avoided responsibility. I didn't make it easy for him, either. My mounting confusion and insecurities made me mistrust everything he said. I was difficult and unreasonable. He tried hard to reach me, but I was too far gone to hear him. I made him crazy.

He would have been fine with a girl in every port, but not many girls would choose such a scenario, if they really knew the play. A fling, a million flings for that matter, made no difference, but being seriously involved with two or more at once was not going to go over well with anybody in the cast.

I could say he took the easy way: let it be, let her do what she wants, and I'll ride with it. We both knew it was over, but he left it to me to make it so. He would accept the action I took, whenever I chose to take it. But then when I did, he ignored it. He made me crazy.

It wasn't easy; even when broken, the bond between lovers tends to hold in unpredictable ways. But I knew I was not suited for his life. I could never be the woman behind the great man: I didn't have the discipline for that kind of sacrifice. Though I wasn't sure where I was going and lacked a sense of mission or ambition, I knew what would not work for me, even if I was uncertain what would. I just knew with all my heart that I could not be a string on his guitar. I could not live in his shadow and I was ill-equipped to be his caretaker.

A
r
t

Is

W
o
r
k

k

Content is a glimpse of something,
An encounter like a flash.
It's very tiny—very tiny, content.

WILLEM DE KOONING

Though we had ostensibly broken up—were no longer living together—when Bob recorded the *Times They Are A-Changin'* album in late 1963, it was full of our times and we saw each other a lot then, anyway.

Another Side of Bob Dylan made for tough listening. Bob sure knew how to maul me with crazy sorrow, but I loved the sound in his voice.

Sylvia Tyson once told me that songwriters write their own story in their songs and include messages they want someone in particular to hear, with some abstraction for art's sake. Hearing Bob sing songs that were close to home was always strange for me. In an intimate setting, where half the audience knew us, it was fun, it was all right—in-jokes, inside-story stuff. But as time and troubles went by, I felt laid bare and sorry for it. We weren't in Gerde's or the Gaslight anymore. People would speculate and make judgments and that became an intrusion. I began to feel that people knew more about my life than I did. Gradually I learned to let go and accept the abstraction of his art.

Some of his writings were so beautiful and heartfelt and full of love, longing, and pain while others were ironic, with doublespeak and double-talk. I could find myself in places and not in others, even though I might have been there. When someone paints your portrait, you don't always recognize yourself and don't always get the message. But I always recognized him.

I listen to Dylan's songs spread over his early albums and I remember how it was; it's like reading a diary. A private smile because no one knows about that, a laugh because that was really funny, or a tear because it was so hard. One thing I know: Bob used controversy to feed his art.

People asked: How did he write? With a pencil or pen, I replied. Tinkering on the piano, strumming his guitar, humming. On a typewriter, in a notebook, on scavenged sheets of paper, and on napkins, just like the poets. I knew those weren't the answers people wanted, but they were the only answers.

Someone once asked Bob to help a folksinger he knew write a song. You do it so well, she said, and he doesn't, so why don't you show him how? That assumes someone who can carry a tune can be taught to sing opera.

People say he is so secretive—why doesn't he reveal more of himself? I never understand what they mean by that. Songs and poems reveal the artist's core. Bob Dylan is his work. There is a fine line between analyzing lyrics and destroying the art. When does parsing words and phrases begin to smudge or erase the magic in them?

Over the years I downplayed or ran away from my role in Dylan's life. I offered superficial information when pressed.

The real story is that I think his songs say it all. The songs are translations of moods and sensations he experienced. They are fictions that allude to those experiences. Bob's songs were for himself and to himself in another person's voice as much as they were in his own.

I don't like to claim any Dylan songs as having been written about me, to do so would violate the art he puts out in the world. The songs are for the listener to relate to, identify with, and interpret through his or her own experience.

Our time together fed his work. I know I influenced him. We marked each other's lives profoundly. He once told me that he couldn't have written certain songs if he hadn't known me. But that doesn't necessarily mean a particular song. It means I served as muse during our time together, and that I don't mind claiming.

Fame came fast and hard for Bob Dylan. He was barely twenty-one when it hit. He has to be lauded for learning how to survive fame with all its pressures and responsibilities, glory and riches aside. He managed it. That took work and work is what he does best. He kept doing what he loved to do—make music. He served that gift and he survived.

"The Bob Dylan Story" has been interpreted and archived to create a unified vision for public consumption. That is the way it must be. What counts is if the work is solid and worth the accolades. Bob Dylan's art—the work he puts out in the world—delivers.

In 1964 the surgeon general had delivered the dictum on the dangers of smoking cigarettes and I decided it was time to quit. In fact, I spent another five or six years quitting before I finally managed it. During the interim I dabbled in several methods, and the very first was the decision not to buy cigarettes anymore.

The Beat poet Gregory Corso was in New York City from San Francisco for a reading or to show a film he had made about death; I don't know for sure. I met him casually through people I worked with building sets for a theater production. He had inserted himself into a group of mutual friends as we walked toward my apartment on Avenue B. We were talking about something or other and at some point Gregory asked me for a cigarette. I told him I had quit—or was trying to—and had decided not to buy any. If I wanted to smoke, I would have to mooch from friends, and that would be awkward after a while, I figured; therefore I would quit by attrition.

Gregory listened attentively to my reasoning and then, for some perverse reason, tried to talk me out of quitting in the first place. He began an animated riff about the pleasures of smoking but somehow covered the history of the world, too. Then he veered off down the street in search of a place to buy a pack. By then we had reached my door and I waved good-bye and went upstairs.

After a few minutes I heard Gregory calling me from the sidewalk. He had bought two packs, he yelled, one for me and one for him, and because he didn't want to climb all those stairs he was going to throw mine up to me. I leaned out as far as I could from the fifth-floor window, but it was impossible to catch it.

He seemed to enjoy the game. The pack took a beating. He left it for me inside the front door, but when I got downstairs—which wasn't right away—it was gone. Off I went to wherever I was going. Pondering the merits of Gregory's richly expressed opinions, I bought a pack of cigarettes on the way.

One night maybe as much as a year later, I went to a party given by the photographer Jerry Schatzberg in his loft near Union Square. A few of us went by car. I think Bobby Neuwirth was driving, but I am not sure. We picked up others on the way, including Edie Sedgwick, who was part of Andy Warhol's Factory and starred in his films. She squeezed in next to me in the front seat and offered me a cigarette. I said, No thanks, maybe later.

At that time I was rolling my own. I was still trying to quit and still thinking up diverse ways to do it. For a while I tried weaning myself from cigarettes by smoking a pipe. My father smoked a pipe, so that was an added allure. I combed stores that sold smoking paraphernalia of all kinds until I finally found a "lady's pipe." It was beautiful, with a fine curve to the stem and a small rounded bowl carved from cherrywood. Sylvia Tyson had given me an antique miniature meerschaum pipe in a leather case lined in gold velvet. It was a gem. When a fire broke out in my Houston Street apartment in late 1965, along with many other treasures, the pipe was lost.

I figured that the more complicated it was for me to have a cigarette, the easier it would be for me not to smoke one—the logic of the procrastinator. I patted myself on the back for refusing Edie's offer of an easy smoke. One less.

I had bought a funny blue metal contraption about the size of a cigarette case that worked like a mini-cigarette-making machine. Loose tobacco was sprinkled in a compartment at one end, a cigarette paper was slid in the other, the case was snapped closed, and out popped a fully formed cigarette. There was more involved in this operation than just ripping open a package of ready-mades, and it was also a bit of fun. I got involved in the pleasures of buying loose tobacco, sampling many flavors and mixes until I settled on a Turkish blend similar to the harsh Nazionali brand I had smoked in Italy.

When we arrived, groups of people from the party were milling about on the sidewalk and I started to roll myself a cigarette. The second after I licked the paper and put the finished product to my lips, I was surrounded by cops who asked me for the contraption and the cigarette. I handed them over.

As one of them smelled the cigarette, I smiled and told him it was filled with tobacco, then showed him my little packet of Turkish blend. Someone found Jerry Schatzberg, who swore up and down to the police that I rolled my own tobacco-only cigarettes. I can vouch for her, Officer, he said. She uses tobacco, nothing else.

Nobody moved or spoke. We waited for the verdict. The situation was tense and the police took their time. OK, said the cop finally, giving me a look that told me I was lucky this time. He handed back the little machine, but not the cigarette.

Andy Warhol dogged Dylan the whole night, hanging on to his every word. Warhol seemed to enjoy being battered by Bob, who was in high hipster mode. In their pitch-black shades, Bob and Neuwirth, who was even sharper than Bob at times, could wipe the floor with anyone who came within their orbit.

Neuwirth had a wry sense of humor. He could turn anything around to mean something else, so being with him required being on your toes. He was guarded and knew how to protect himself; he was a survivor. I liked him, even if he was scary at times. I guess after being with the original scary guy, everything else was everything else.

Dylan, Neuwirth, and Albert Grossman were a very special trio. They were very different people and they weren't really a trio—more like two duos with Dylan in common. What they shared was the ability to silence all conversation or unwanted questions with a blank stare. The look could be interpreted as condescension, a mask to hide behind, or complete indifference, depending on who delivered the look and the situation at hand. Any version from any one of them was guaranteed to unnerve those on the receiving end. With Neuwirth, it was less intimidating only because he wielded less power than Albert or Dylan, but he still could put someone on notice with his display of attitude. He

Albert used his inscrutable expression in business deals or whenever he thought the situation required it. He

was an astute and wise businessman who drove a hard bargain. He didn't talk much, and when he did he could be very
enigmatic. As a result, he was often misinterpreted.

He was a controversial figure in the music world. He
emphasized the word *business* in music business, but he
was the first manager to present his musicians as "artists,"
demanding respect for their work from club owners, record
companies, and music publishers.

Personally I never saw any reason to bad-mouth him—
quite the contrary. And I have no knowledge of what happened between Bob and Albert in later years that led to Bob
breaking his management contract. I will always remember
Albert with affection. He was a good bear of a man.

Sometime around 1964, I believe, Albert bought an apartment on Gramercy Park. He had parties there and it became
another stop-off location, albeit a more upscale one. It was
also a refuge for Bob, who stayed there now and then. I remember the apartment as having beautiful parquet floors
and very little furniture.

One night after some party or other, when Bob and I
were still unable to definitively separate, we ended up back
at Albert's place. Bob wanted me to stay. I refused, and instead of leaving it at that, I continued to talk a lot of shit
while he sat listening on the bed. I don't know what got
into me that night but I couldn't stop myself—I needed to
hurt him.

When I turned to make my dramatic exit, I discovered I
had lost my wallet. I sat down, feeling very foolish. When

the phone rang, it was Ronnie Spector, lead singer of the Ronettes, who had found my wallet at the party. Bob gave me money so I could take a cab and go get it.

Around the time Albert moved to Gramercy Park, he bought a wonderful big old house in Bearsville, outside Woodstock, New York, with fireplaces in every room and a pool on the grounds. After Albert and Sally got married, they lived there. Sally is the elegant woman in a red dress on the cover of *Bringing It All Back Home.* The photo, by Dan Kramer, was taken at the house.

One weekend at the Grossman home in Woodstock we were sitting around the table enjoying ourselves when Albert received a frantic call from the New York management office asking if he happened to know where Dylan was. Bob was scheduled to play a gig in Cambridge or Boston and hadn't shown up. Rumors were flying that he was drunk in a bar somewhere or holed up at someone's apartment. Fans were out scouting for him. Stories that he had been kidnapped or worse were already circulating.

Albert hung up the phone and returned to the table with that look on his face. He explained the call and said with a shrug it must have been a scheduling mistake. Either that or Bob and Albert had simply forgotten. There was nothing to be done, so Bob had to laugh. Cigarettes, not all of them filled with pure tobacco, were lit, and speculation began about the new tales that would be added to the Mysterious Dylan Legend.

Part Three

I've got child eyes, yes,

but an old mans brow

and I'm just scribbling around

to find out which is coming out my mouth

(NOTEBOOK ENTRY, 1964)

Restart

I was in pretty bad shape after the breakdown I had gone through earlier in the year. A friend of my mother's gave her the name of a psychiatrist: it was only a consultation, I was told, but I was feeling so lost and sad that I would have accepted anything anyone suggested.

In the doctor's waiting room I was surprised to see one of the actresses from *Brecht on Brecht.* No doubt I said something flip about life's difficulties because, looking at me closely, she replied: Yes, but life is good.

I was thankful she'd reminded me.

When it was my turn to see the psychiatrist, I was feeling pretty shaky. No matter how I presented myself I assumed he would sense my condition, so I didn't say much. He looked at me with a concerned expression; he was too busy to take on another patient, he said, and then he gave me the name of a colleague.

By the time I went to see the colleague, I was better at masking my broken insides. The colleague was sitting at his big desk in a big dark room with thick drapes on the windows and a rug with a complicated pattern on the floor that held my attention. I sat in the stuffed armchair across from him.

He leaned toward me and said I should consider this a consultation. I should think about it, and when and if I felt ready to talk, I could call his office and make an appointment. It was up to me.

He smiled, and added that I appeared to be doing well. I was surprised he couldn't see past my levelheaded, wise-beyond-my-years exterior to the smashed and broken bits inside. If he were worth his salt, he would have, I concluded. I smiled back, shook his hand, and left.

Halfway to the subway, I realized I had left my bag. When I went back, I joked with the receptionist: I left my bag. What could that mean?

She smiled kindly. I never called.

I hid out in Hoboken with my mother and Fred a while longer, listening to the Beatles, reading and drawing. They pretty much left me alone. Time heals, after all—although the clock that marks that kind of time has no hands.

Letter from Bob, April 1964:

> I made you an easter egg man out of eggs an things. . . . it is fastly done but tied firmly. . . . altho I put it together with you in mind, I was too lonesome t send it. so it sits on my shelf. an keeps me company. (if he talked I'd probably throw him out).
>
> I have ridden the motorcycle thru the roads around here. . . . I have rode alone tho thru the hills on backroads an have discovered all kinds of magic places. an great sweepin views. . . . the only person I've spent any time with is father francis at his church on the mount . . . I wish that we'd of gone up last year when we first heard of him.
>
> yes that was me in life *[Life* magazine]. That was me there with the cigarette. did you get a look at my bodyguards. god damn them screamin

Bearded "bodyguards," Albert Maher and Geno Foreman, travel with Dylan on concert tours to help protect him from the hordes of teen-age admirers. They get their expenses but no salaries.

Life Magazine, 1964

girls. geno nailed two just after the picture was
taken. albert rubbed his beard against a few. . . .
they got immediately infected.

At last I was living alone on Avenue B and feeling much
better for it. I was amazed that no one saw through my mask
and instead complimented me on my "ability to pull
through." It was a little disconcerting, but after a while I believed that I had managed, after all. Life actually was better
without Bob and his entourage.

Once a week I went to the School of Visual Arts to draw
from a model. Mr. Potter, the instructor, was a galvanizing
character, a tall, muscular man who strode into the studio
wearing a form-fitting black T-shirt and black pants and
sporting a shaved head.

I focused on drawing what was in between objects. I
would draw just the outline of something—a person in a
chair—and then draw with obsessive detail the things next
to, in front of, or behind the figure, with everything on the
same plane. As we drew from the model or a still life Mr.
Potter had set up, he encouraged us to see what was in the
negative space. He strode around the room and spoke with
drama and flourish: Don't stop with the model! See the surroundings! See in between the space! Draw that! He ampli-
fied my instinct to work the space between. He was
inspiring; I loved going to his class.

As usual, I was freelancing, and one good job I found
was working for the stage designer Ben Edwards, making a
model of the set he designed for a Broadway production of
Hamlet starring Richard Burton and directed by John Giel-

gud. The play was to be performed in casual dress and the set was austere. I was making the model of the castle of Elsinore and had to cut many bits of board into very small pieces and glue them onto the façade. I liked the peaceful monotony and the close attention to detail that the work required.

For the World's Fair of 1964 in Flushing, Queens, I was hired to make props for a show to be presented at one of the U.S. pavilions. Though most of the props were easy enough to make, one was troublesome. I had to construct a pitcher that could break apart into three pieces and then be easily reassembled. I really wasn't sure how to go about it. I hired my friend Gordon, an artist I'd met at the School of Visual Arts, but we got nowhere and I was very relieved when the show was canceled. For once I didn't get upset that a job had fallen through and I hadn't been reimbursed for the supplies I had bought.

Though the Avenue B apartment was quieter for a time, things picked up again at the end of May. Friends who had been away at college and showed up in the Village only during school vacation were in the city all the time now. The worlds of politics, poetry, music, art, and theater all rolled in and out of the apartment.

Despite the worries we had about the world and what to do about it, we were having a good time. The Beatles had crossed the Atlantic and had been on *The Ed Sullivan Show.* Their music had taken over the airwaves and our lives; folk music wasn't what it used to be.

In February 1963, the State Department instituted a
ban on all travel to Cuba in the wake of the Cuban Missile
Crisis. The following summer a group of students accepted an invitation from the Cuban Federation of University Students to visit post-Batista Cuba. They wanted
to see for themselves what life was like four years after the
revolution, and to challenge the travel ban. The United
States was not a Communist country, after all, where citizens didn't have the right to a passport and free travel.
Freedom of movement was embedded in the American
way of life. Not only was a travel ban un-American, it was
unconstitutional.

Travel bans had been issued and tested before. When
I was in high school and a member of a current events discussion club, we invited a few college students who had
defied the current prohibition on travel to China to come
speak to us. This was in the late 1950s, when only "Reds"
or "Commie sympathizers" would be the sort of people
interested in traveling to or hearing about China. The
school decided it wouldn't be a good idea to let the students come.

The consensus of those in public life and in the media
who questioned the validity of travel bans was that they
made the United States look like East Berlin, with a wall
around itself, which was hypocritical in the eyes of the
free world. Many felt that the excuse for the ban on travel
to Cuba was to prevent American citizens from finding
out for themselves what things were like on the island
since the overthrow of the Batista regime, which the
United States had supported. Those who had taken the

C
u
b
a

trip in the summer of 1963 returned home with enthusiasm about the revolution. The fact that illiteracy on the island had been wiped out in just a few years was an impressive accomplishment. As a result, many more wanted to join up for the following year.

My motivation for making the trip in 1964 had to do with my preoccupation with the censorship of writers and artists in the Soviet-bloc countries and the effect the blacklist had on artists. I would get to see how the Cuban revolution, and its romance with Communism, was dealing with artists and writers. Since I knew Albert Maher, one of the organizers, and was enrolled in an art class, I managed to fudge the "student" requirement and join the trip.

In Communist countries, and in the American Communist Party, an artist showed his or her commitment by making work that promoted the ideals of Communism. Artists were to be educators, propagandists, rallying the masses through their work to make sacrifices now for a better life for the next generation—no introspective or abstract work allowed. Growing up a red-diaper baby, I had accepted this idea though it made me uneasy. I had secret and serious doubts that continued to grow as I did.

There could be severe consequences for those who violated the travel ban. Though they included—in addition to an invalidated passport—the possibility of fines and prison, they didn't really register in my twenty-year-old mind.

If the ban was unconstitutional, the threat of prison didn't seem likely. I was committed to freedom of travel and

I had profound respect for the U.S. Constitution. The only drag was the loss of our passports, but everyone in our group was confident that lawyers would find a way for us to get them back. And eventually—after close to two years—that was exactly what happened.

The process was more complicated for the second trip. Since there were over eighty students signed up, the organizers decided to divide us into two test groups. The majority would travel clandestinely to Cuba via Spain a week earlier than a second group of five, who would openly declare their intention to challenge the ban, without revealing when or how they would do it. They would also disclose that a group of eighty American students had already arrived in Cuba the previous week.

I volunteered to join the second group. Since I was the only female, I was made the leader: who would ever think the youngest, and the girl, would be in charge? I would handle all the money, instructions, and any problems that might arise between our departure from the United States and our arrival in Havana. At each stop I would get further instructions. I felt like an undercover agent.

The plan, once worked out, was simple. At a press conference at Kennedy Airport in New York we announced our intention to fly to Cuba that day but refused to give precise information about our travel plans. We informed the press that only five people would be making the trip; however, we did not say who in the group were the actual travelers—there were more than just the five of us present. After the press conference the others—acting as decoys—lined up for bogus flights to various destinations while we actually took ours. A graduate student from Columbia named Steve Newman and I were booked on a British Airways flight to London, in first class, no less, and the three others—Alan Lowe, Jeffrey Goldstein, and Robert Collier—were together on another carrier, also going to London. The flights would arrive within an hour of each other; we would go through customs and then meet up for the next leg of our circuitous route to Cuba. At the airport I was to buy tickets to Paris for all five of us together. Once in Paris, someone would take me to the Cuban embassy, where I'd pick up our visas for Prague. From there, we'd fly to Cuba on Cubana Airlines.

Each traveler was asked to pay one hundred dollars toward expenses. The Cuban mission to the United Nations paid for the air tickets and travel arrangements outside Cuba. In Cuba, hotels, meals, and other expenses were picked up by ICAP, the Institute for Friendship among the Peoples, the part of the Cuban government in charge of handling invited foreign guests. The money, all of it in cash, was handled by the Student Committee for Travel to Cuba, an offshoot of Progressive Labor, a left-wing organization. As the group leader I carried the money. I put the thick wad of bills in my handbag.

We had been thoroughly instructed by the organizers not to give our passports to anyone, except of course when we went through customs. Under no circumstances were we to get our passports stamped upon entering or leaving Cuba.

I'd never flown transatlantic before—I'd gone to Italy by ship—and here I was flying clandestinely to England in first class. In the past, clandestine travelers stowed away on ships, sharing quarters with rats after they had crossed a mountain range on foot in snowstorms with forged passports sewn into their clothes. Steve and I weren't sure what to make of the grand style, but we had a sense of humor to go with our sense of purpose. We settled in with the champagne the cabin attendant offered, and too wired to sleep, we talked, drank, and ate our way into the night.

Once we landed at Heathrow and were inside the terminal, we saw two gates, one marked for "Aliens," and one for British citizens. We chose a friendly face at the Aliens desk to stamp us into the country. When I handed the official my passport, he consulted a list of names in front of him. My heart raced. He looked at me and handed my passport back. He said he was sorry but he could not stamp me in.

There is someone here from your embassy to speak with you first.

He pointed to a man with a briefcase leaning against the opposite wall.

I looked the customs official in the eye and told him I was a U.S. citizen—one of the five names on his list—traveling to Cuba to test the legality of our government's travel ban to Cuba. The U.S. embassy representative waiting for us was under orders from the FBI, who expected him to be party to their attempt to deny us entry into England.

The man blanched and said, They what?

I smiled. They want to prevent us from entering England, I said. They are interfering with our right to travel and intend to invalidate our passports. What they are attempting to do is illegal. What we are doing is not.

Indignant, he glared at the American official and said in a loud voice, The U.S. government cannot tell the British government what it can and cannot do. They have no jurisdiction here.

Then he grabbed our passports and stamped us in with a loud clunk. One. Two.

There were three more names on the list, I told him, and they'd be arriving soon on another flight. I looked at Steve for confirmation. He looked from me to the U.S. official to the British official, and nodded solemnly.

It was early morning and the representative from the U.S. embassy didn't have a complete grasp of the situation. He looked sleepy and unsure of his mission. When he asked for our passports, I replied that they were our personal property and we had no intention of giving them to him. Steve took over at that point because he was levelheaded and rational, whereas I was all drama and instinct. Steve talked about the U.S. Constitution and the right to travel, while I went off to inquire about the flight the others were taking.

When I found out their flight had been delayed at takeoff for several hours, I got worried. Had something happened? The delay meant that as the day progressed, more information about our plans would be transmitted to the U.S. embassies in London and Paris. They would be better briefed than the sleepy-looking man Steve was educating.

It was a very long wait. When reinforcements arrived, they were the real thing, sporting hats and raincoats and briefcases. After they'd lined up directly behind the British customs agents, Steve and I could no longer go back into the customs area beyond the glass door that served as a partition. I wanted to get word to our fellow travelers before the federal agents got a hold of them.

Finally the flight arrived and we saw Alan, Jeffrey, and Robert walking right toward the U.S. officials. Steve and I signaled frantically through the glass, but they couldn't see or hear us. They went to the first customs agent, who checked their names against the list just as the U.S. officials approached with their paperwork. Our fellow travelers looked worried and confused and unsure what to do. We saw them hesitate and begin to read the papers they'd been handed.

I pushed the glass door open and yelled: You don't have to pay any attention to that shit!

A guard grabbed my arm, trying to pull me back. I regretted the "shit" immediately, but it did get everybody's attention.

Your passport is your personal property, I continued. They have no jurisdiction over you!

The British customs agent who was our ally caught the ball. After he leaned over and said something to his fellow agent, the man immediately stamped in the three of them with an indignant look that said: They were once our colony. How dare they? Foiled, the feds walked away.

We were interviewed for the story that appeared in the British press the next day.

It was time to buy tickets to Paris. I managed to find a flight—only first class was available!—that left within the hour. I was tense, hoping I hadn't been seen buying them by

U.S. officials who would then alert their counterparts in Paris. The five of us separated, just in case.

I heard an announcement for a "Mr. Rotolo" to please come to the information desk. It was repeated in English and French several times. I panicked and went to the restroom, stuffed all the money I had into my bra, and changed my clothes. I was in a cold sweat as we boarded the plane. All went smoothly, though, and we landed in Paris without incident.

The English press takes note

Passport-to-Cuba row

U.S. students go into hiding after bid to stop trip

Express Staff Reporter

FIVE Americans went into hiding in London last night after beating off an American Government attempt to prevent them going to Cuba.

The five, all students, are fighting a State Department ban on "the free travel of free Americans."

Their reward, they said, if their fight succeeds, may be 15 years' jail and a £1,785 fine each when they return to America.

Determined

That risk did not deter them yesterday when an American Embassy official met them at London Airport and asked them to hand over their passports.

First to refuse were 28-year-old Steven Newman, and blonde artist 20-year-old Susan Rotolo, both of New York. They arrived en route to Paris, after finding they could not fly to Cuba from America.

Said Susan : "We were told that if we insisted in going to Cuba our passports would be invalidated. I told the embassy man that my passport was my property and I refused to give it up."

Newman did the same.

Subsidised

Three hours later Robert Collier, aged 27, of Boston; Jeffrey Goldstein, 23, of New York; Alan Lowe, 26, of San Diego, staged a repeat performance.

Said Collier : "The embassy official told us our passports were being invalidated, but we kept hold of them."

Their journey is being subsidised by the Cuban Federation of University Students.

It was late when we arrived and the stress had worn us down. The hotel was a nondescript place on a quiet side street with a winding staircase to our rooms on the upper floors. The man at the desk asked for our passports. In Europe this was standard procedure, but the others would have none of it. Our indoctrination had been never to surrender our passports. Steve had also been to Europe before, and we managed to convince them to part with their documents overnight.

The four wanted to see something of Paris, but I declined. I was worn out and I still had to telephone New York to let Albert Maher, as one of the organizers, know where we were. When I called down to the desk from my room to place an international call, the man who had checked us in said he'd call me back.

After a bit I heard a knock on my door. It was the deskman, smiling. In my limited high school French, I repeated my request to call New York. He smiled again and offered to show me around the room.

Thank you, I smiled back, but I must—*très important*—place a call to New York. Once he finally left my room, the call was made, and I was ready for some sleep. But soon he was back at my door again, asking if everything was all right. Short but built like a wrestler, he pushed his way into the room. What ensued was a chase around the bed. The whole day had felt like a suspense movie, and it was ending like a farce with scary overtones.

With impeccable timing, Steve knocked on the door, wanting to know if I had managed to get through to New York. The little hotel man made obsequious *pardon, pardon* noises and retreated from the room. After locking the door and sliding a chair under the knob, I fell into bed, exhausted.

The incident with the officials at London airport had unnerved us and we weren't sure what to expect in Paris the next day. I had to go to the Cuban embassy to pick up our visas and tickets for Prague, the next stop on our roundabout journey. A young Frenchman came to drive me there, while the others waited in a café. After what seemed like a long drive in heavy traffic, the young man dropped me at the embassy building in the middle of a lovely park. A friendly woman at the desk asked me to wait. There was no one else around, and the wait seemed interminable. She offered coffee but no explanation.

Finally an official handed me a manila envelope with visas and five tickets to Prague for the next morning. After another long wait and more polite smiles, the same young man arrived to drive me back to the café.

Driving once again in slow traffic, I was very antsy because I knew how agitated my fellow travelers would be after waiting so long with their imaginations running. Suddenly, the car in front of us stopped short, and when the Frenchman slammed on his brakes, my knees hit the dashboard forcefully enough to make them bleed. Though it was a mess, I saw humor in the situation. White-faced and tense, Steve and the others were shocked to see me exiting the car with bloody knees. They weren't sure if Commies or capitalists had been my torturers.

We spent the rest of the day and the evening absorbing a bit of Paris, trying not to worry about anything. I was relieved to see a woman on duty at the hotel.

Everything went smoothly until we landed in Prague and were told we didn't have the right visas. After much conversation in a language none of us understood, the problem was sorted out and we got on the bus that took us from the airport to the city. Paris had been sunny; Prague was rainy and cool, and the long ride into town through a dreary landscape was depressing. I looked out the window and saw an immense sculpture of a hammer and sickle looming in the middle of a field and tried not to think stereotypical thoughts about Communist countries. As a red-diaper baby, I should know better. Welcome to the other side of the Iron Curtain.

The city of Prague, however, was beautiful. We stayed in the same hotel as the Cuban rowing team, who we would fly with to Havana on Cubana Airlines in a few days' time. We went to a jazz club where everyone smoked, drank, and looked inscrutable and hip—no different from a Greenwich Village club. The musicians may have been Czech, but they were good.

The next day a middle-aged man who spoke English offered to show us around. He said he was a teacher and his demeanor was intense and a little odd. Thinking of Kafka, I slipped into paranoia as we followed him up and down the narrow cobblestone streets. He took jerky drags off his cigarette and looked around furtively as he hurried us on.

Alan noticed me hesitate.

You got us through London and Paris, he said. We trusted you. Now you have to trust me. This guy is OK—don't worry.

I believed him and relaxed.

When we arrived at the man's home—a room cluttered with books and papers—he was noticeably calmer than he had been on the street. Smiling sadly, he told us life was difficult and repressive for intellectuals. He wanted us to understand and think about what he said.

This was anti-Communist talk. The irony was apparent; I thought of the humongous hammer and sickle statue.

Since Cubana Airlines was delayed, we ended up spending five really good days in Prague. I made friends with Manuel from the Cuban rowing team and met a Czech girl my age who was studying English and was engaged to one of the Cubans on the team. She told me she couldn't get a passport to go to Cuba with him.

A real travel ban. I had more doubts and tried to ignore them.

I concentrated on Cuba and what Manuel told me about how much better life was with Fidel. It is a young revolution and so are we, he said. This country is part of the old, stodgy Communism created by Stalin in the Soviet Union. Cuba will be different. We have hope.

By the time we landed in Havana, we were feeling very relaxed and happy. Together with the exuberant rowing team, the five of us were greeted with songs and members of the

Cuban Greets U.S. Students

Cuban secret police officer (left) welcomes five American students on their arrival by plane in Havana from Prague. Shaking hands with Cuban is Alan F. Lowe. Others who flew to Prague to obtain Cuban visas are (l. to r.) Steve Newman, Susan Rotolo, Robert Collier and Jeffrey Goldstein. (UPI Radiofoto)

international press who asked questions and took pictures. When we met up with the Americans who had arrived before us, there was much to discuss.

As North Americans, during the two months we spent on the island, we got a lot of attention. Though many students and businesspeople from all over the world were there as well, it was especially exciting for Cubans to have U.S. citizens visiting their country.

We toured factories and schools all over the island. We learned about sugar cane and visited a nickel mine. We ate rice and beans and deliciously creamy-tasting avocados, and those who wished to smoke Cuban cigars did. We learned Cuban songs and slogans. We went into stores that had hardly anything on the shelves. We traveled around the island by bus and stayed in little and big hotels. Already the

Suze Rotolo

shortage of parts for their American cars was a problem, but the Cubans were very resourceful. No matter the shortages, the Cubans improvised. They had energy and spirit and will.

We met Fidel's brother, Raúl, and Che Guevara. It was exhilarating to sit in a room with the leaders of the Cuban revolution and ask them questions. Che more than lived up to his image. Though he smiled easily and his eyes twinkled, there was no doubt that he was a serious revolutionary. Smoking a good cigar, he leaned back in his chair and explained everything we wanted to know about the hopes, dreams, and concrete plans of the Cuban revolution.

Jerry Rubin, later of the Yippies, was on the trip with us, and at every factory, school, or organization we were taken to he asked very detailed questions. This quiet and intense young man was constantly writing in his notebook in tiny, tight handwriting. Some of us would groan when Jerry got up to ask a question, because we knew it would be long and convoluted, requiring a long and convoluted translation, followed by the reverse for the answer.

He never seemed to enjoy himself; he was all work—a fact gatherer. After his return to the United States, something or someone cut him loose. After taking LSD, he broke out from his constrictions and was ready for Abbie Hoffman and the birth of the Yippie Party.

We listened to Che and the head of agricultural planning explain why they decided to continue growing white rice, even though they knew refined rice was less healthy. White flour, white rice, white bread were signs of affluence, and it was psychologically the wrong time to introduce the unrefined flours and grains associated with poverty. It had been a difficult decision, they said. And we heard about the struggle to duplicate Coca-Cola, which Cubans really missed.

Fidel loved American baseball and we went to a game between Cubans and a team of international players. On an especially hot day, a few of us sat on benches on the edge of the field. Someone had given me a straw hat with a

A Cuban press photo inscribed by Manuel

In Havana with Manuel

wide brim and I looked down, not out, at the game. Daydreaming, I suddenly noticed a circle of feet around me.

When I looked up, a crowd of people, players, and press surrounded me and Fidel Castro was sitting next to me, smiling. I was overwhelmed by his presence. The air around him seemed to pulsate. He had a magnetism that easily explained his mythic status. When he asked me something— probably my name and where was I from—I stammered a reply as everyone laughed and the photographers clicked away. As quickly as he appeared, he was gone. I remained frozen in place. Manuel, who replaced Fidel on the bench next to me, found my shocked demeanor, while understandable, hysterically funny.

The trip home was easy. We flew to Spain and then to New York. When we arrived at JFK Airport, wall-to-wall agents met us, but nothing happened that we hadn't expected when we violated the ban on travel to Cuba by U.S. citizens: our passports were stamped "Invalid."

While I was in Cuba for two months, my friend Sue Zuckerman sublet the Avenue B apartment. Once I returned I had it to myself again, but there were people in and out all the time. Members of the Cuba contingent now joined the old regulars. Albert Maher was the magnet for them, because he had been one of the organizers of both Cuba trips.

We discussed everything going on in the world, in addition to music, movies, and books, and what was happening in our lives. The Civil Rights Act had finally been passed in June, and many university students had gone down South that summer to work with the voter registration drive. In Mississippi three young workers—James Chaney, Andrew Goodman, and Michael Schwerner—were missing and had most likely been murdered. In August, Congress had passed

A sketch I made of Albert Maher

the Tonkin Gulf Resolution, resulting in an all-out escalation of the Vietnam War; and of course, we talked of Cuba. We were concerned and affected by all of it.

[Mixed messages, Avenue B, 1964]

With a Vietnam War protest coming up, we debated the dress code at demonstrations—whether we should dress as we usually did or consider jackets and ties for the guys and skirts for the girls. I thought we should dress up, believing that if we presented ourselves as upstanding citizens it would be harder to write us off as long-haired beatnik hippies of dubious moral character.

After much back and forth, we left it up to the individual, but we agreed to look presentable. The right-wing take on the burgeoning youth culture was that it was made up of "long-haired degenerate free-love Communist fags" who were easily identifiable by style of dress. A decent young girl never had a hair out of place, and no self-respecting boy had hair growing down his neck. Everyone should be slicked up and locked down. The Beatles appeared clean-cut, but they had long hair. Confusing. Something was in the wind that just might get out of hand.

Not long after my return from Cuba, the FBI began show-ing up at Avenue B. The agents climbed five flights of stairs and knocked on my door in the early morning, asking to speak to me. They pretty much visited everyone who'd gone to Cuba, on the off chance that someone would unwit-tingly—or possibly willingly—divulge information. For the FBI it was important to begin a conversation and develop a relationship any way they could. They did their job well; their tenacity was impressive. One agent would act friendly while the other remained expressionless with a cold-eyed stare—good cop, bad cop.

Dealing with children of Communists wasn't easy, how-ever. Many of us had lived through early-morning FBI visits to our homes when we were children. We had all been schooled about the FBI—their tactics and our rights—at a very young age. We knew we weren't obligated to respond in any way. And who else would knock on my door at 7:00 a.m.? I just ignored them and after a while they didn't bother me anymore.

Some years later when I was living in Italy they knocked on my sister's door looking for me. This was right after Mar-tin Luther King's assassination. Her reaction to their in-quiry was that it was no wonder they were so inept at finding the killers of civil rights leaders if they still had no idea where her sister might be living.

One lazy evening while I was sitting around listening to music and talking with a mix of friends, the phone rang. My friend Sue picked it up and when the caller asked for me, she said, Yes, speaking, given that we have the same name.

The man was from England, so she handed me the phone to speak to someone who said his name was George Harrison. He was holed up in the Delmonico Hotel with his band mates and Bobby Dylan, he told me. He suggested I bring some girls and come up: He'd leave my name with the people at the desk.

Though I didn't think anyone could get through the mob of fans surrounding the hotel, I figured it was worth a try.

I wasn't sure how to handle the crowd at the apartment, though. Everyone wanted to come with me—even the politicos. I figured I'd play the whole thing by ear once I got there.

The Delmonico Hotel was impenetrable. I finally managed to convince a guard to at least go to the desk and check for my name. The crowd pressed close, hungry and eager. The guard returned shaking his head. Oh well, nice try—if he even bothered to check.

Albert had an idea. From a pay phone he called the hotel and, feigning an Irish brogue, conned the operator with a story about a very ill wife in a hospital or some such desperate tale. When he finally got through and asked for Dylan, he talked to him a bit, then handed the phone to me. Bob was annoyed that I had brought other people with me. We both got testy, and I told him: Oh, never mind. Or maybe he was the one who said it. Either way, the implication was clear. We weren't ready to deal with each other easily quite yet. Beatles be damned: I hung up the phone and went home.

Everyone was obsessed with the presidential election in 1964. I was, too, but with my twenty-first birthday more than two weeks after election day, I couldn't lie about my age to the Board of Elections. In 1964, there was a definite difference between the two candidates. Arizona Senator Barry Goldwater was a conservative Republican and Lyndon Johnson, who had taken over the reins after the assassination of John Kennedy, was a traditional Democrat. Lines were drawn in the sand; the stakes were high.

With the country still traumatized by the assassination and the turmoil over civil rights and with the dangers of the Cold War turning hot, not to mention the war in Vietnam, the choice between the two candidates was a crucial one. People from both Cuba trips dropped by Avenue B even more to hang out and talk politics with Albert Maher, who was around quite a bit.

Albert was a tall, blond, lanky Texan from a wealthy family who had been a student at Harvard when Timothy Leary and Richard Alpert were professors there conducting experiments with LSD. Albert became more interested in politics than in following the expanding psychedelic drug culture, and he evolved into an East Coast radical who spoke with a slow Texas drawl.

In those days there were many friendships that intertwined and overlapped in the connected worlds of the arts and politics; Albert was another who lived in both. It is possible that Bob and I first met him at a party in Cambridge, Massachusetts, but I really got to know him in

New York City in 1963 when he began showing up at Avenue B. As Dylan's fame grew, and larger and larger crowds surged around him after performances, he needed protection. Since Albert was already a buddy, it made sense to use him as a bodyguard too.

Albert was always interested in what I was reading and what I was doing. He read the Beat writers and poets, and by the time he gave me the *Love Poems of Kenneth Patchen* our friendship had changed course. When Albert decided to move back to Cambridge in the late fall of 1964, he asked me to go with him. A move to Cambridge was a way to leave the Village, where I felt I would forever be linked to Bob Dylan and harassed by those who wanted to know what he was really like.

Whenever I had extra money I would take a course in a subject that interested me at the New School for Social Research, an open-enrollment university in the Village that offered inexpensive classes without college credit. When Albert told me about the Harvard Extension School in Cambridge, I registered for a course in theater history and production and an Italian language class.

The Harvard Extension School was founded in the early 1900s by the president of the university. The enrollment fee was adjusted yearly to the price of the harvest, making it possible for the general population of Boston to have access to Harvard, minus the hefty fees and entry requirements, with classes scheduled at the end of the workday. The school was a precursor to adult education programs.

Once I had moved to Albert's Somerville apartment, just outside Cambridge, I bought a secondhand bike to ride to the campus. To anyone who didn't know better, I could have passed for a real Harvard student.

The apartment was roomy and had big bay windows facing the street with window seats that I loved to curl up in with a book or an art pad. We painted the apartment and moved around the furniture already in it, filling up the shelves with record albums and books, slowly settling ourselves in. Albert's brother John lived nearby, and friends from the city came and stayed with us every so often. I was cooking pots of food and baking bread and trying to feel good about life, but I don't think I really succeeded.

Some months before my move to Massachusetts, while still in New York City, I had found out about the macrobiotic diet and its philosophy of balance from the musician Johnny Hammond (son of the producer); and had begun experimenting with it. In Italy, an Argentine friend who was studying Buddhism had given me a book about Zen philosophy. When I returned to New York, I read more. As articulated by the Japanese philosopher George Ohsawa, the macrobiotic approach espousing the necessity for balance in all things, beginning with food, appealed to me.

The diet required ten days of eating nothing but organically grown short-grain brown rice. Cigarettes kept me from feeling hunger pangs. I was so health and balance conscious I really should have quit smoking, but I was still working on that.

After the ten-day initiation ordeal, the allowable foods on the diet included vegetables, nuts, tofu, fish, delicious grainy breads, and crunchy seasonings based on sesame seeds either ground into pastes or whole, toasted, and mixed with salt. Since I liked to cook, I enjoyed making the breads, soups, and stews. When I went to a macrobiotic center somewhere on the East Side, probably with John, they told me I was addicted to dairy products. They could tell from my complexion. I was to compensate for my cravings by eating more sesame paste.

I got a job as a waitress at a macrobiotic restaurant on Second Avenue called the Paradox, an easy walk from Avenue B. The owner was very strict about following the rules of the diet, not at all like the man who ran the anything-but-kosher kosher luncheonette where I used to work. I was required to hand over my tips every night; then I'd be paid for the hours I worked that day. I thought that was odd since I was the only employee. But a job is a job, so I complied.

I took to wearing a dress with two deep pockets in the front where I could surreptitiously drop the major part of my tips. Back then credit cards were not common; everyone paid cash. After each customer left, I handed over a portion of my tips to the owner, and at the end of the night he would count out my wages. Gingerly, I'd walk out the door, trying to keep the coins in my pockets from making noise.

The owner grew suspicious and began keeping a very close eye on me. Even after I was fired, I stayed on the diet.

Cambridge had a big macrobiotic center where Danny, a friend from New York, was staying. Danny took the philosophy and diet very strictly and refused to eat anything but brown rice, even after the start-up phase. He became so very thin, very peaceful and philosophical. All his friends were extremely worried about him. I brought him bread but he wouldn't touch it.

The people who ran the center were also concerned and did what they could to get Danny to eat. Nourish the body, nourish the soul, they said. But no matter what anyone tried, he would not eat any more than one small portion of brown rice a day. Slowly he starved to death. He was beatific in the end, which was very disturbing. Danny was seduced by his visions. Probably it was Albert who said that starving to death was one of the kinder ways to die, because the person goes into a trancelike state and no longer feels pain of any kind. It made me think about some of the stories of the Catholic saints.

One of the hardest things to do when I moved back to New York was to go with Danny's girlfriend to visit his parents outside the city. And one of the easiest was to get off the macrobiotic diet.

Albert and I were invited to a concert Bob was giving at a venue somewhere in Cambridge. Though we went, we left after intermission. Some of the songs Bob sang were too close to the bone; I felt exposed. Later that night when we ended up at the same party, Bob demanded to know why I hadn't come back for the second half. He was pissed. And he didn't appreciate Albert, of all people, trying to cool him down. Others at the party did their best not to notice the commotion. Several girls were hanging on to Bob. Afraid I would forever be pulled his way, I kept silent, feeling a pain I thought had passed.

Though I avoided the music scene in Cambridge as much as possible, I was happy to see friends I had gotten to know with Bob. Some friendships transcended the mess that accompanies love stories, so I wasn't shy about seeing Betsy and Bob Siggins; he was one of the musicians in the Charles River Valley Boys. I was definitely looking forward to reconnecting with Jim Kweskin, who was back in Cambridge after living in New York City and traveling around the country with his jug band, which sometimes included Maria Muldaur, still Maria D'Amato back then, another friend from the Village. Geoff Muldaur, the man Maria later married, had a unique voice I truly loved; it was high and honey-toned with a vibrato that sounded like the voices on jazz recordings from the 1920s that Dave Van Ronk played.

I was living a relatively quiet existence—almost too much of contrast to my life in New York.

Albert decided it was time I learned to drive and began giving me lessons in an open parking lot in his beautiful Porsche. On a reckless night, with too many people crowded into the small sports car, Albert decreed I was ready to drive for real and off we headed toward Storrow Drive. I was in a daring and confident mood that masked my underlying terror. Following Albert's right-turn, left-turn directions, I stopped and started easily enough with little harm to the clutch or any grinding of the gearshift. Suddenly Albert gave me a direction to turn without enough advance warning; I took the turn way too fast and came to a dead stop in front of a very big tree on the wrong side of the road. I fell apart completely as Albert calmly explained that he'd been testing my reactions.

That was it for Albert and me. He was way too composed and even-keeled in the face of doom. I could hear and smell the accident and was quaking in my boots. After Albert took the wheel, we headed back to where we'd come from.

During my time with Albert in Cambridge, I enthusiastically agreed with his idea of spreading the news about what our group saw in Cuba and demonstrating why the travel ban was un-American. At a party we met a very nice student from one of the colleges that might have been somewhere around Boston, but I no longer remember. I talked to him about my trip the previous summer and my belief that the arts would survive and flourish under Castro—that his government wouldn't stifle or censor artists as had happened in the Soviet Union under Communism. While in Cuba, a few of us had traveled around the island with a theater troupe to places so remote that no one there had ever seen a play performed before. These novice audiences would get so entirely caught up in the play that they would join in—break the fourth wall—and call out or jump onto the stage to help a character in distress.

I described how we visited the newly constructed Cubanacán, the Cuban National School of the Arts for music, dance, and visual art. The building was low and sprawling, with a Mediterranean feeling. Built entirely of bricks, it had arched entrances and domed studios at the end of wide corridors. The atmosphere was exuberant and hopeful about all the changes taking place and the worlds opening up to the students despite the scarcity of supplies. We also toured the previously wealthy area of Havana, where officials of the Batista regime had lived in stately houses on palm tree–lined streets. These houses were being converted into residencies for writers and poets. Impressed by my passion for all that I'd seen, the young man invited me to speak at his university, together with others who had traveled to Cuba that summer. Off he went to discuss the details with Albert.

By the time the Cuba talk was scheduled in early 1965, I had already moved back to New York City. Albert and I did much better as friends.

The organizers of the event paid my expenses so I headed up to the college, where about four others were scheduled to speak before me. I had been so upbeat about Cuba informally at the party in Cambridge just a few short months previously that my talk was meant to close the evening on a rousing note. The others were more experienced speakers since they had been traveling around college campuses giving talks.

As I listened to each one of them, I realized that I had nothing to add to what they were saying. The auditorium was full of interested listeners, but I was in a gloomy frame of mind that evening. In general, I had lost a good deal of my enthusiasm for politics.

After my trip to Cuba, I worked with people who were active in organizing antiwar marches and also did a stint as art editor for a short-lived political arts magazine called *Streets*, which appealed to me more than political discussions. Though Lyndon Johnson had won the presidential election, I didn't think for one minute there was nothing more to be worried about. But I lacked revolutionary zeal.

Most of the people who went to Cuba were politically knowledgeable and dedicated souls, but others were regimented in their thinking. Some even believed it was antirevolutionary to pay attention to popular culture.

I remember telling them that the number one song on the radio was "Eve of Destruction," a genuine protest song. While I didn't claim the song was great art, it was worth noting that it was on the top of the charts. Maybe they should start paying attention to what was going on outside their castle windows.

What really alienated me was the constant use of the terms *the proletariat, blue-collar workers,* and *the working class.* In another outburst of antirevolutionary ire, I told them that I was the only one among them who came from a genuine blue-collar, working-class family and that my father, who had worked in a factory, never referred to himself as "a proletariat."

None of this went over well. Not only was I antirevolutionary in my thinking, I was a great disappointment to "the cause," to boot. It was clear that it was time for me to give so-called revolutionary politics the boot. It wasn't Cuba I was disillusioned with but rather the harangue of political correctness—the old party line.

To say the least, I didn't give a rousing closing speech at the Cuba talk at the university. I spoke credibly but without conviction. Embarrassed, I felt very bad for the student who had expected so much from me. That was the end of my efforts at public political discourse.

When I moved back to New York, Sylvia Tyson helped me find a place near her apartment on Stanton Street, a few blocks below Houston on the Lower East Side. Though it was a dingy-looking building, the apartment, on the top floor of a walk-up on East Houston just off Clinton Street, wasn't so bad. Peter Stampfel, of the Holy Modal Rounders and the Fugs, lived on the first floor with what looked like an awful lot of people given the size of the apartment. Ian and Sylvia were touring, so unfortunately we didn't see each other much.

My new place had a tub in the bathroom, the only room with a door, a minuscule bedroom, a living room with a little alcove-sized room just off it, facing the back of the building, and a kitchen. There was a window in every room.

I was making small clay sculptures of female figures I painted in a variety of colors and placed in boxes with other objects, like little environments or stage sets; a friend commented that I was making altars. I scrounged the streets for wooden milk crates to make freestanding cases for the "altars," and to hold my books and records. Today these are made of plastic and are also for sale, but back then they were left on the street in front of supermarkets and delis. No one was supposed to take them but everyone did. They were made of hardwood, with hand cutouts on the sides, which made lifting easier. I painted the more banged-up crates in bright colors and stacked them along the living room wall, where they made a real nice unit.

Viewing the whole apartment as an empty canvas, I

painted decorative borders on the moldings and win-
dowsills. I painted the kitchen yellow ochre and with black
paint doodled abstract designs and patterns as the mood
struck me. There was no closet in the small bedroom, so
with help from Jon, a friend who built theater sets with me,
I put up a bar across the narrow room for my clothes. At Bon
Bazaar, a store on Waverly Place that sold dyed burlap by the
yard, I bought some in rich colors and made curtains for the
closet and the windows. The price was right and the colors
were wonderful—they made me think of Indian food and
spices like red lentils and curries. Another choice spot was
a Japanese import store on Eighth Street that sold, among
other unusual things for that era, intricately printed lightweight cotton bedspreads from India perfect for making
into skirts and dresses.

I was wound up with all-natural creative energy—no
drugs. At night I was working at some theater or other, and
during the day I took freelance jobs making sets or props for
the theater or for industrial shows. On and off, I helped
friends silkscreen posters and album cover designs at their
storefront studio on East Ninth Street. They listened to
Stockhausen and other modern composers who were new
to me.

Quinton Raines had written a short theater piece and,
with his brother Charles and another playwright, fashioned
a play titled *Like I'm Talking to You Now,* which linked the
scenes together like a novella. I had a role in a two-
character scene by Quinton with the actor Tom Aldredge.

We were part of the Loft Workshop theater group and the play was performed at a few small theaters and at the Café Au Go Go.

One of the producers of the Workshop wrote a note telling me I gave the best performance in the best scene in the play and I should seriously consider an acting career. I felt good about that.

When actor friends from the production suggested I go along with them to auditions, I did; but when I got a call back, inevitably I failed to show up. Hyper and unguarded in that period, I used the I Ching obsessively and listened to the Beatles and strange experimental music. I bought a pair of rose-colored glasses and wore them all the time, telling everyone that the world looked so much better through them. Then they disappeared. When I bought another pair, they broke. I didn't buy a third pair; I got the message.

In the 1960s we were open to experimentation in all things, from natural to unnatural to supernatural. I believed that knowledge acquired from instinct and observation was as valid as an academic search for factual verity. Parsing everything was not a path to discovery—it was a deterrent. It wasn't that I was against study and excavating for information, but I believed that overanalyzing was harmful and interfered with the ability to see. I was wary of entering a tunnel of thought that ignored the surrounding terrain and the weather above it.

One of the people on the Cuba trip was, like me, more interested in the arts and the mysteries than in the politics of revolution. He was into a lot of stuff, as we used to say, experimenting with being open to everything—no ego and no boundaries—using a lot of LSD to get there. Though I wouldn't take the drugs, I was interested in our meandering talks, which covered different subjects triggered by the trip to Cuba, including the survival of artists, eccentrics, and outsiders in general within a Communist society—or any society, for that matter. We mulled over the ideas of the French Surrealists and Antonin Artaud, the mad genius and founder of the French Theater of Cruelty, responsible for the concept of theater in the round and the belief that theater was about the communion between spectator and actor. I had read Artaud's book *The Theater and Its Double* while in Cambridge.

Although I wasn't using any drugs or drinking anything stronger than wine, I was highly sensitive—a receptacle. I had trouble sorting what I was receiving. Quieting my overactive mind was exhausting at times.

Occasionally I would smoke some marijuana, but usually it made me overly sensitized to what was going on around me. I didn't need it; I was already there. It was painful to see too well and too much. Everything resonated. I became high-strung and paranoid. I found that if I sat around while others smoked I would have a good time. The only things I was using were cigarettes and the coins I tossed to access the wisdom of the I Ching.

One night at the Kettle of Fish, Bob and I had an intense conversation. I sensed something about him that kept me from saying much; mainly I listened. He talked about drugs, fame, faith, mysticism, women. There were only a few women he respected, he said, and I was one of them. Only Sara, whom he married, and I knew what was up. It was as if he were going down a list and checking people off.

Allen Ginsberg was not to be discarded, he said.

He was giving me advice: Know you cannot need anyone or anything and don't believe. All is meaningless.

The bleakness of his words made me anxious because they reinforced my general sense of apprehension. I rarely knew what to make of the feelings of foreboding that came over me—they came and went without warning. At times they coincided with bad things, like the car accident I'd been in some years earlier. Maybe, I thought, this meeting with Bobby was the reason I had been feeling uneasy that day. How painful it was to know him.

At some point I lost my sense of place and began to float. At a theater I met an actor who was a bit of an eccentric, which wasn't unusual for that place in those times. He was older, probably in his midthirties, and he reminded me of Antonin Artaud. Though not quite in the same manner as Artaud, this guy turned out to be an eccentric who was genuinely scary.

One afternoon he announced at the theater, where I was working on scenery, that he needed a place to stay. My first thought was to hand over my keys. Why not be spontaneous and generous? My political and mystical beliefs would coincide. The generosity of spirit that was prevalent among the Cubans I'd met and in my reading of Rimbaud, Krishnamurti, and Zen texts seemed to point that way. I mistakenly saw in this actor a quiet spontaneity—a kindred spirit—yet he was anything but that. He had madness to mix with his mysticism and that was what I failed to see in his flat dark eyes and seemingly peaceful manner.

I did not hand over the keys right away, at least. I continued doing whatever I was doing and later we talked some. I saw him several times and then stupidly, casually offered him a set of keys. It would have been better to be more rational and analytic, after all. Some part of me had to know I was overriding the basics tenets of big-city survival smarts.

At a rehearsal for Quinton's play, when he read the scene I was in with me, he changed the whole tenor by making it hip and offbeat. He told the director he knew the real truth, one that the play was unable to deal with.

A friend who had worked with him tried to warn me about this man, but it was a strange time and I was in a strange place. I wish I had been able to heed her good advice and that of the wiser people around me, but at that point, I was acting out, loose and free. If I'd been doing drugs, the whole scene would have been that much worse.

In an old dusty loft on the Bowery, he played a vinyl LP album called the *Nirvana Symphony*, which he insisted I needed to hear. I didn't note the name of the composer or the performers. Later I learned that the piece was by the Japanese composer Toshiro Mayuzumi and that an artist with a great-looking name, Yoko Ono, had done the album cover.

Listening to the music put me into a trancelike state that stalled into complete stillness while the record was being turned over, yet once side two began playing, the visions I'd been having resumed. At the end of the record, shaken by what I had gone through, even though everything returned to normal, I felt a sense of foreboding as well as anticipation. I tried to write and draw what I had experienced, but it wasn't easy. I had gone through the looking glass.

Over a period of a month I listened to the album a few more times. Although the experience was unsettling, I was not frightened. I wanted to understand it somehow and in some way, and see if the event would repeat itself. At the second session, the reverie ended with a vision of burning and fire accompanied by a feeling of great sadness and a foreboding sensation that was even more pronounced. The third time was more like the first and ended with me feeling shaken yet calm and reconciled. Sometime later I read *The Psychedelic Experience: A Manual Based on the Tibetan Book of the Dead*, by Timothy Leary and Richard Alpert. Though I'd taken no drugs, this was the closest I could come to an explanation of the experience I'd had.

One night in October I came home from the theater to find my apartment destroyed by fire. The Fire Department had managed to contain the fire where it had started and there was no damage to any of the other apartments in the building. Fortunately neighbors had rescued my two cats, Harley and Ofelia. The cause of the fire was thought to be faulty electrical wiring, a common problem in old buildings. But I suspected that the eccentric actor had started it. After my experiences listening to the *Nirvana Symphony* he thought I had special powers. I was frightened by him and didn't want to go in his direction anymore. After the fire, he disappeared.

It was a terrifying sight to see my home all burnt and soggy and smelly. I have a lasting image of one of my boots lying half charred on the gunk-filled floor of the small bedroom, and a sweater with its sleeves partially eaten by fire hanging on a hook at the entrance. They looked like dismembered body parts. It was horrible. With a jolt I recalled the vision I had experienced a few weeks before.

Bob's old Gibson guitar was nowhere to be found. The green coat that I had bought in Italy and was wearing on the *Freewheelin'* album cover was somewhere in the pile of black, stinking clothing in the bedroom.

Most of my books and records survived the fire because the wall unit I had made from the stacked milk crates did not burn, although everything in them held the smell of fire for a very long time. A dark pattern of fire licks decorated the edges of the covers and backs of the books and record albums. All my "altars" and other artwork had burned to ash. A few mementos and other irreplaceable items vulnerable to flames survived because they were in the alcove off the living room that the fire, in its blind fury, had bypassed.

That night and for a short time afterwards I stayed in the storefront on East Ninth Street that my friends used as a studio. Other friends gave me clothes, and Bob gave me some money; so did my mother and Fred. I was very distraught and haunted by the fire, and my feelings were augmented by what I realized too late was a premonition or warning vision. Yet at the same time I felt oddly liberated by this "cleansing by fire." I could not bring myself to tell anyone about what had happened when I listened to that mysterious album. It was too incredible on its own, and I didn't relish the thought of being cast as a psychedelic, spaced-out hippie freak.

A short time later my friend Janet took me in, with my two cats, to live with her in her one-bedroom flat on West Twelfth Street. It wasn't very roomy but it had a working fireplace and was on the third floor of a nice elevator building. Janet had been living in France for the past few years, and when she came back to New York she had stayed with me on Houston Street. We were used to living together in small places. After Johnny Herald and Janet had broken up, we were no longer a foursome, but Janet and I remained a twosome. We were always in and out of each other's lives in some way, no matter where we were living. She had come to stay with me in Italy in 1962, and some years later when both of us were living in different countries in Europe we visited back and forth.

We named the apartment Melody Lounge to counter-balance the glum state of mind in which we found ourselves. We read from the wisdom of the Indian seer and philosopher Krishnamurti and deliberated over the I Ching as we played medieval music and drank wine from deep-red-colored glasses. We played the Beatles at top volume and made sure we had as much fun as Harley and Ofelia, who were especially adept at bouncing off the walls and running relay races at all hours of the day and night. We credit each other for saving one another's life at a shaky time.

Through someone I knew, I found waitress jobs for both Janet and me at a place called the Donut Wagon on Thirteenth Street and Third Avenue. At the end of the day we brought home the unsold corn muffins for our breakfast the following morning. I felt as vulnerable as the puffy baked goods easily breaking into a yellow pile of soft crumbs on my plate.

After one of the producers of Quinton's play kept encouraging me to take acting seriously, I finally followed her suggestion and in November 1965 signed on for an acting workshop somewhere in the West Seventies.

The first exercise was about trust. We worked in pairs and took turns. One partner would sit behind the other and at a signal from the teacher the front sitter would drop back, trusting that the partner sitting behind would catch his or her head before it hit the floor. In the middle of this interesting exercise, all the lights in the room went out. The half-light of evening lit the room from the windows facing the street, but it took a few minutes for our eyes to adjust. All heads were safely cradled in a partner's hands.

We waited a few beats, still holding heads. We waited some more, but the room stayed dark. From the windows we could see that there were no streetlights and that the traffic lights were out. Cars were honking and swerving and moving with caution across the intersections. Though nobody knew what was going on, we speculated that a huge fuse had blown somewhere where it counted. We were nonplussed and a little freaked out.

The pay phone on the street didn't work, either. Since I was wary about the long hike downtown, I decided to walk a few blocks over to the Ehrenbergs' apartment on West End Avenue. Inexplicably, their telephone worked, and from the shortwave radio we learned that the blackout extended as far as Canada. There was no electricity anywhere and no information from authorities about when it would be restored. I stayed with the Ehrenbergs until I found a ride downtown with someone on a motorcycle.

The moon was full and cast an eerie light over a blacked-out cityscape. We rode through streets where volunteers with flashlights assisted traffic cops at intersections and directed the cautious drivers into an orderly flow. Candles flickered in windows high above, and stores sold candles and batteries on the sidewalks in front of their unwelcoming dark interiors. It was controlled chaos. New Yorkers accustomed to living under those conditions every day come together as a community when the chaos is no longer controllable.

When I got back home safely to Melody Lounge, Janet was in a state. She had filled the bathtub with water and was waiting for the invasion—of what, or who, she couldn't say for sure, but she was very worried all the same. In truth, our nerves were on edge because the guy who probably had started the fire in my apartment had begun stalking us and had left a cracked mirror in front of the building's entrance the day before.

Barely a month had passed since the trauma of the fire; I was still struggling to recover—and now a total blackout. Janet had a point—everything seemed eerie and mutable. But I did not want to be worried. I looked at the cats sleeping peacefully. They showed no sign that they sensed impending danger. Fuck it. I poured us some wine.

A few weeks later a reporter from the *East Village Other,* a new local biweekly claiming to be hipper than the *Village Voice,* asked me to be part of a feature the paper was starting up called "Slum Goddess," inspired by a song by the Fugs, "Slum Goddess of the Lower East Side." The feature would be the counterculture's answer to the Miss America aesthetic of overly made-up and girdled women with beehive hairdos. I thought it was a fine idea and said yes. I was to be the Slum Goddess for December 1965.

The reporter asked me three questions: what I did, why I lived on the Lower East Side, and what I wanted from a man. Walter Bredel was the photographer and we walked around the East Village one afternoon while he took pictures. I wrote that I lived in the East Village because I liked the view—I was being sarcastic, since the neighborhood was really grungy. But when the paper came out, the quote was transformed to I liked the "new":

> If a man can learn to develop all his inherent and latent powers there is nothing that he will not be able to apprehend. For the knowledge is in man the same way it is in God. Only a heavy veil of darkness hides it from view and prevents his seeing these things and understanding them.
>
> Arthur Rimbaud said that, and that's all I have to say. Because if you look at it close enough it answers the three questions: How come the Lower East Side? Men in general? What I do?

SLUM GODDESS

Walter Bredel Photo

SLUM GODDESS FOR DECEMBER

Suze Rotolo, age 22: "If a man can learn to develop all his inherent and latent powers there is nothing that he will not be able to apprehend. For the knowledge of everything is in man in the same way it is in God. Only a heavy veil of darkness hides it from view and prevents his seeing these things and understanding them.

"Arthur Rimbaud said that, and that's all I want to say. Because if you look at it close enough it answers the three questions: How come the Lower East Side? Men in general? What I do?

"I live on the Lower East Side because I like the new. I want my man to have a toothpick in his ear and a purple boot on his right foot. I do artist and earn money when I do."

like the new. I want my man to have a toothpick in his ear and a purple boot on his right

> I live on the Lower East Side because I like
> the new. I want my man to have a toothpick in his
> ear and a purple boot on his right foot. I do artist
> and earn money when I do.

The feature gradually became very popular and got coverage in the mainstream press. An article in an April 1966 issue of the *Herald Tribune* titled "Miss America, Move Over" reported: "They are all fully dressed. They all have undone hair, most of it long, and little make-up. And when they say 'beautiful,' they don't mean anything to do with cosmetics or external fixing up. It's living or soul they are talking about."

Feeling a little more stable around the time of my twenty-second birthday, in November 1965, I began looking for an apartment; and it didn't take too long to find one with an affordable rent. I moved into another fifth-floor walk-up, this time on West Tenth Street between Bleecker and West Fourth streets. By the time I was an *East Village Other* Slum Goddess in print, I no longer qualified in real life, since I had moved back into *Village Voice* territory.

The West Village felt healthier than the grungy tenements of the Lower East Side and the East Village. My interim stay with Janet at Melody Lounge had made a difference. The apartment on West Tenth was a nice sunny studio with a separate kitchen. Using gels from one of the theaters where I was working, I made "stained glass" windows. I bought black window shades and cut out shapes and inserted the gels. I made a chandelier of sorts out of large tin cans that I punched holes in, attaching a tin funnel to the top, and with a light bulb inside, the pattern was reflected on the walls. People were generous with furniture and dishes and stamina, helping me haul heavy things up the five flights of stairs. Once Harley and Ofelia had tested the bounce of the walls, they adjusted to their new home. It had taken time, but once more I was back on my feet.

Not long after I moved to West Tenth Street, I got a call from the stage designer Peter Harvey, who was doing the scenery and costumes for a show at the New Theater on East Fifty-fourth Street. The theater had more seating than the Off- and Off-Off-Broadway theaters downtown so the regulations required a mix of union and nonunion workers. Based on *Mad* magazine, the play was a musical revue called *The Mad Show,* with a book by Larry Siegel and Stan Hart and music by Mary Rodgers. I was happy to join the crew—no more interim waitressing jobs.

Leonard Bernstein walked into the theater one afternoon while a few of us were painting a piece of scenery and the cast was rehearsing. He stayed for a bit watching, listening, and talking with everyone. His love for every phase of putting together a theatrical production was evident in his camaraderie.

At some point I was offered the job of running the sound for the theatrical run. Live musicians accompanied all the musical numbers, but there were skits that required prerecorded voice-overs and sound effects. The last few years of working in downtown theaters doing everything for a production—including technical work—paid off because I knew how to run a soundboard. Admittedly, this was back in the precomputer era, and the *Mad Show* soundboard consisted of two reel-to-reel tape recorders with a tape-splicing gizmo, a control panel with a few buttons and switches, and a headset with a microphone. I could handle that.

A small crew, we were stashed away in an above-the-balcony long, narrow perch about a few inches from the ceiling. Up there with me was the lighting technician from the union and the people who worked the lights and the follow spots—as in, spotlights that follow the actors around on stage. Joy, not quite five feet tall and a singer in real life, worked one follow spot and Bill, in real life an artist and who towered over Joy, worked another. The three of us were nonunion. Joy lived in the Village and we traveled together on the subway until New Year's Day 1966—the day John Lindsay was inaugurated as mayor of New York—when a subway strike brought the city to a standstill. Joy and I hitched and walked the nearly three-mile trip twice a day until the strike ended two weeks later. We slogged through a lot of wintry weather, but once again New Yorkers came together to help one another. We got rides easily, rarely having to pay for taxis.

The *Mad Show* cast was terrific: Linda Lavin, JoAnne Worley, MacIntyre Dixon, Dick Libertini, Paul Sand, and for a short stint David Steinberg. A few of the actors had passed through the improvisational theater group Second City, either in Chicago, where it originated, or in New York.

Joe Raposo, who went on to compose music and lyrics for *Sesame Street*, among many other credits, was the musical director, and Danny Epstein played percussion. When I left the show after several months Joe gave me a book of poetry, and Bill, the artist, did a poster-sized cartoon of me at the soundboard with a machine gun and a sign saying PLEASE DON'T ANNOY THE ITALIAN, inscribed by all the *Mad Show* participants.

The technical rehearsals were complicated. The follow lights had to be quick and fast to illuminate the actors, and

tiny Joy was a whiz at shifting the focus of the heavy spot from one end of the stage to the other. I had many complicated setups and there was always a danger of the tape breaking,

with all the fast-forwards and rewinds at each performance. I became very adept at making a quick repair splice.

Everything worked smoothly at the dress rehearsal—which of course meant that opening night was marked for some mishap or other. Cast and crew were ready for it. The lighting technician checked all wiring, and I checked and double-checked that I had correctly cued up the prerecorded tape. The stage manager gave me the cues from backstage, but I also had the visual of stage and actor, albeit far below, to add to my accuracy in timing.

The first few sound snippets worked fine until a skit where the recorded narration was crucial to the story: when I hit the button, nothing happened. It had jammed. I hit it again and heard a whirring sound blast from the speakers. I tried to keep panic at bay and fast-forwarded the tape as I saw Paul Sand look up from the distant stage in the general direction of my perch with what appeared to be a beseeching expression, but given the distance I couldn't be sure. The next sound from the speakers was similar to singing chipmunks. I heard the stage manager choke out a Shut It Off into my earphones as the very professional Sand improvised appropriate narration. For the rest of the night, the play button worked perfectly, and the only explanation anyone could come up with was that the machine had had an attack of opening-night nerves.

The Mad Show got really good reviews and was set for a long run. As time went by, there were some cast changes as actors moved on, but the backstage crew remained mostly the same throughout the months I stayed with the show. Mishaps came and went, but I never again had any button malfunctions.

My private life interfered one time only. My Siamese cat Ofelia had a habit of jumping from the outside window ledge in the main room of my apartment to the outside ledge of the kitchen window. The studio apartment wasn't an L shape, but there was enough of an angle to the building to make the jump possible. I thought she was terribly clever and didn't worry once I'd seen her do it a few times.

But one day she missed and plummeted to the cement courtyard five stories below. When I realized what had happened I flew down the stairs, believing she had ended up like her namesake. Instead I found her alive, crouched low on all fours, her head bobbing like those toys with the heads attached by a string that nod slowly and continuously. I was due at the theater for a matinee of *The Mad Show* in less than an hour. I telephoned the stage manager in a state, frantically explaining what had happened and promising I would be there as soon as I could. Not to worry, he kindly sympathized. Take care of your cat. I wrapped Ofelia in a towel and took a taxi to the ASPCA, far uptown, where I called the theater again to say my cat seemed OK. The curtain was literally going up when I slid into my spot behind the soundboard.

The ASPCA kept Ofelia overnight and said it was most unusual that she survived unscathed. She wasn't quite the same, though. Every now and then she would stop in her tracks, crouch low, and bob her head for a few minutes before she could continue on her way. She never attempted the jump again. Fortunately my other cat, Harley, named after the motorcycle because she purred most of the time, would never even think of doing fancy jumps like that in the first place.

Summer

My mother and Fred were spending half the year at the little house they had bought in Sardinia and the other half in Hoboken, New Jersey, where Fred was a semiretired professor. Both were looking forward to living in Italy full-time in a few years. Feeling magnanimous, they invited Carla and me to visit them that summer to see Sardinia. We decided to combine our vacation with a trip to Perugia and London. I wrote to Enzo, someone I had met in Perugia in 1962. He was still there and said he would be happy to meet us; coincidentally, he was going to London, too.

We booked passage on the *Maria Costa*, a cargo freighter that took passengers. Though Genoa was the ship's final destination, it would be making stops in various ports to unload the cargo. We disembarked in Naples, where Enzo met us, and went to Perugia for a week before going to Sardinia.

Back then, freighters were the cheapest way to travel to Europe. I paid for the trip with money that had finally come my way the previous year from the car accident. The money seemed like manna from heaven, after all that time.

Traveling by freighter was not at all the same as crossing the Atlantic Ocean on a passenger ship; there were no amenities like movies or swimming pools or live music. The ship wasn't very big, and there were few passengers. I read books to pass the time.

The crossing was tranquil and the passengers were an interesting group of primarily middle-aged people; my sister and I were the youngest. One traveler was a very thoughtful retired judge from Brooklyn, another an Italian portrait painter who painted my portrait, which was purchased by a young man from Switzerland. In addition to spending some time with the young Swiss man, I read the poet-naturalist Loren Eisley's *Immense Journey*, contemplating the sea and remembering that as a child I wanted more than anything to be a sailor when I grew up.

It felt odd to be in Perugia again. The many months I had spent there in 1962 had been like time in a magic place, a new world within the old world. But at the same time I had been harboring an inner pain that left me melancholy and detached. Visiting now was different; that painful past was not forgotten but it was gone. Enzo and I hit it off right away and made plans to meet in London.

Sardinia was beautiful beyond words. This outermost island, an overnight or all-day boat ride from mainland Italy, occupied over time by as many civilizations as Sicily, has developed a language and a culture all its own. The huge rocks that line the island have been sculpted into immense undulating and cloudlike forms by centuries of winds constantly whipping at them.

The island is arid and whatever vegetation there is grows low and thick to the ground, sucking out the available moisture. Growing wild and dense in front of my mother and Fred's house were rosemary and oregano bushes and stunted bay laurel and lemon trees. When I brushed my hand along them, their perfume filled the air.

People came from all over the world to scuba dive in Sardinia. The bottom of the salty and crystal-clear Mediterranean Sea was visible no matter how far out you went. And we discovered what it meant to eat fish that was truly fresh.

But in our short skirts, my sister and I were like bait. We

were hooted at and wooed continuously. Cries of *Mini gonne, dove andate?* (Miniskirts, where are you going?) followed us everywhere. Divine as it was, Sardinia was the outback. Foreign women wearing the clothing of the times were a very unusual and enticing sight.

When Carla and I got off the train in Victoria Station in London after a few weeks in clamorous Italy, we were suddenly aware of how loudly we were speaking compared with the hushed hum of the crowds moving through the station. Self-consciously, we lowered our voices to a whisper. In England, even when we spoke in a normal New York tone of voice, we still seemed to be shouting.

London was swinging, and as two miniskirted young women we blended in easily, though being very tanned in cool, overcast London marked us once again. But the voices of the young men who took notice of us were always muted and terribly polite.

We sailed to New York on the newly renovated *Queen Elizabeth* ocean liner. Tickets were a bargain because of the growing competition these old ships, modernized or not, were encountering from the jet planes that crossed the Atlantic in less than half a day rather than a week. Our five-day voyage turned out to be one of the great liner's last transatlantic crossings before it and the *Queen Mary* were retired forever and replaced by the newly built *QE2*, which in turn lost out to airplane travel in a very short time.

The basement of 1 Sheridan Square, the building where I lived for a few months in 1961 while Bob camped out with other folkies in an apartment a few floors below, had once been the legendary Café Society, the club where Billie Holiday's career was made. When Barney Josephson opened the club in 1939, he made it the first downtown spot that openly allowed an integrated bandstand and audience. John Hammond did the bookings.

That same basement became a theater and performance space in the early 1960s, and a few years later it was made over into a disco called the Downtown.

While Janet and I were living at her West Twelfth Street apartment, and after I moved to West Tenth Street and she to Jones Street, we went to the Downtown often. Live bands played on a raised stage in front of a big open dance floor encircled by tables and chairs. Hanging above the floor was a rotating ball made of little mirrors that reflected the colored lighting effects on the dancers as they boogied about below. The Chambers Brothers, who were electric in every way, opened at the Downtown and were hands down the best group that played there.

I loved to dance—fling-my-hair-around dance. Dancing is a haven for shy people, or at least it was for me. Even as an insecure young girl, I never held back when it came to dancing. In the predawn of rock and roll, there was great music to dance to: Johnny Ace and his "Pledging My Love," "Earth Angel" by the Penguins, Bill Haley and His Comets' "Rock Around the Clock," followed by Buddy Holly and the Crickets, to cite a very small sampling.

When Bob and I were together, we both loved, and

listened to, music not necessarily filed under the category "folk." And although we were of prime dancing age, we didn't do any dancing in public—an unfortunate side effect of folk music's reign. There was no place to boogie until somebody plugged in and got the party started.

Janet and I were making jewelry from found objects and papier-mâché, still calling them Suja-baubles, and as we peddled our goods around town, trying to focus our lives, we hoped our vulnerability didn't show.

We had some success selling our handmade jewelry—we even got a write-up with pictures in the *New York Post*—yet our earnings were meager. A big store would buy Suja-baubles outright, but the little stores worked on consignment only and took forever to pay us when anything sold. Our real joy was in making wearable miniature artworks, some figurative and others abstract. Many were hippie-style colorful and others were Franz Kline–graphic black and white. Still others were hand-drawn takeoffs on elaborately designed or carved art objects we admired. Our taste in decorative art was greatly influenced by Art Deco and Art Nouveau and the late-nineteenth-century artists Beardsley and Mucha. I loved drawing stylized Art Nouveau heads of women with flowing hair outlining the oval or round shape of the pin. Some styles we'd glue into Mason jar lids to create a faux-brass frame.

The Downtown was a good place to let off steam dancing and enjoying ourselves among friends. The times had evolved way past Allan Block sandals, and now Janet and I

THE WORLD OF WOMEN

Teen Talk

SUSAN SZEKELY

Jewelry Without Jewels

One of the little revolutions taking place nowadays has to do with the materials things are made of. Clothes used to be made of cloth, furniture of wood and sculpture of marble. Now clothes can be made of paper or metal, furniture of cardboard and sculpture of junk. Jewelery, which used to be made of jewels, can now respectably be made of anything. It isn't that plastic masquerades as gold or glass looks like diamonds. Plastic is plastic, paper is paper, paint is paint and it's all OK.

Two young New York girls, Suze Rotolo and Janet Kerr, who are willing to share their inspiration and secrets with readers of this column, have been creating a unique line of jewelry from tin, poster board, cork, papier mache and paint. The end products, called Suja-Baubles from the girls' first names, are being sold in department stores like Stern's, Martins, B. Altman and boutiques like Cleopatra and Elaine Starkman's.

The two girls met several years ago when both were part of folk music circles here. Suze went to high school in New York, studied art in Italy at the Academy of Fine Arts in Perugia and has worked making scenery and props for off-Broadway theater productions. Janet majored in art at the University of Washington, worked in the publications department of the Metropolitan Museum of Art, folk-sang in London, assisted a microbiologist in Paris and studied textile design at the New School for Social Research.

Each started making jewelry on her own, and when the two discovered that their minds and talents were mov-

Clockwise from upper left: Pin made of instant papier-mache cut out with a cookie cutter is painted black and white and adorned with a fake green jewel. Design carved in piece of linoleum painted black and white is mounted on poster board rectangle painted red. Tin backing is cut in irregular circular shape, then another irregular shape is cut from poster board, painted and glued to backing. Cork is carved and painted to be worn as a pin.

ing in the same direction decided to collaborate. The result was sophisticated, artistic jewelry made simply from simple materials.

The girls make four basic pins. In each ...

wore knee-high boots with a Suja-bauble clipped to the sides, the fake stones glued onto the jewelry catching the light as we danced. We wore miniskirts and little tops and had a penchant for purple because it was the color of creativity, mysticism, and spiritual unity. Janet loved purple fishnet stockings, and I added a ring with a purple stone to the several rings I always wore.

We also hung out at the Riviera on Sheridan Square, across Seventh Avenue, where it still is today. The Riv, as it was known, was a restaurant and bar with a great jukebox. What really made the place special were the short music films shown on a television screen as the song played on the jukebox, like prehistoric music videos. Ike and Tina Turner were the big draw, making rock and roll out of the traditional song "Mockingbird" in grainy black and white.

Despite the good times there was an underlying atmosphere that felt bleak, false, and malevolent. The times had definitely changed, and we knew something was happening here that warranted attention.

Melody Lounge had a working fireplace and while Janet and I lived there we'd walk west along Twelfth Street toward the river scrounging for things to burn in it. We'd split and roll old phone books into logs and burn them with pieces of wood we'd found. On cold winter nights the two of us would sit before the fire with all the lights out except for the one from a deep blue glass globe liberated from the subway by an artist friend, Jim. The blue ball bathed the room in a soft pink glow as we plotted our escape listening to Mozart, Bach, the Beatles, and music from the Middle Ages.

Janet and I talked about leaving New York City and moving to Europe. It was a seedling of an idea at first, but we kept watering it until it took root. We deliberated for months as we continued living our precarious lives, and as we went around town peddling Suja-baubles, we discussed the details.

Janet wanted to go back to France, while I was set on returning to Italy. We both felt stalked by the darkness of bad times past and bad times coming. The idea of returning to Europe symbolized sanity and a better quality of life. We searched for freighters going to the right destinations on dates that would be feasible.

New York City was getting grittier and more dangerous. The streets late at night were menacing and people were acting crazier. Paul Clayton and Phil Ochs were erratic and broken, and friends I cared about were doing drugs.

The counterculture was imploding; chaos lurked along the edges. Long before the violence at the rock concert in Altamont, I felt that darkness coming.

The country was mired in Vietnam. There seemed to be no end in sight to that appalling war. The U.S. government's continuous distortions and lies prevailed, and more death and destruction and demoralization were the results. Politics and political discourse were overwhelmingly depressing. Dogma and drugs seemed to be the choices and I wanted neither. I anguished over what was going to happen to America, so torn apart by the war that people actually called for the use of nuclear weapons in Vietnam—praise the Lord and pass the ammunition.

Everything going on around me seemed predictable or inevitable. I began to see myself circling the edge of a whirlpool of repetitious events and scenarios that led nowhere. Crossing Sheridan Square on my way home one day I ran into a friend who said, Hey, there's a new theater production starting soon, and I gave the set designer your name. Normally that would have had me smiling and hopeful; instead I was indifferent to the prospect of another theater job. It was time to move on. To take a risk as I approached the age of twenty-three—a leap into the unknown—felt right.

News of the terrible flood in Florence in November 1966 added to my sense of unease about the world. Janet had found a Norwegian freighter headed for France after the New Year. My Sicilian grandfather had died and left a few hundred dollars to each of his grandchildren. That was all I needed to make the final decision. I booked passage on a freighter scheduled to leave in early January for Genoa, Italy.

Another journey was about to begin. Although it felt like a lifetime away, it hadn't been so long ago that I got on the subway in Queens and got off in Greenwich Village, without looking back.

Sex, drugs, and rock and roll became the sound bite for the 1960s. It characterized the times—decade of this, decade of that—but it was not really about anything that superficial. Those years were about a way of thinking, seeing, and believing—a way to live. We had depth; we were not superficial. We honestly believed we could change the world, and we did, for the better. What made the 1960s special was the way the culture changed. The civil rights movement and the antiwar movement led to a new outlook and new laws. The draft was abolished in 1973, and in 1971 the Twenty-sixth Amendment lowered the voting age from twenty-one to eighteen. The legal drinking age in New York was eventually raised to twenty-one, completing the reversal of what was deemed permissible in the 1960s and what is acceptable today.

The unique qualities of a time or an era are discovered after it has passed. What puts a place on the map is connected to what happened there that was special. Greenwich Village became a destination because of its bohemian history, which encompassed rebellious politics as well as revolutionary art, music, poetry, and prose. It was a community of people and ideas that soldered and welded itself together into odd structures pointing every which way yet maintaining a solid base with common beliefs in the validity of the voices of the outsider and the underdog.

Some denizens went on to fame in their time and beyond, like Edna St. Vincent Millay, e. e. cummings, Willem de Kooning, Allen Ginsberg, and Bob Dylan, who changed music the way Jackson Pollock had changed painting.

With his creation of the Folklore Center, Izzy Young was a cornerstone of the expansive folk culture of the 1960s. Sam Hood ran the Gaslight despite hassles with the mob and a precarious basement locale. Mike Porco, from a dive, made Gerde's Folk City a music mecca. Art D'Lugoff sired the Village Gate, and Joe Cino created a venue in a café on Cornelia Street where he, along with the Living Theater and others like them, reinterpreted theater.

They and numerous others had the tenacity and foresight to internalize the old ways and forge new ones. Soon an influx of tourists made it possible for the clubs, experimental galleries, and theaters to survive and thrive; yet the commercialization made it harder for younger artists to experiment and to develop their skills or to find a following the way the first arrivals had. Everyone started coming to the Village to audition, to play, to paint, and to write, hoping for exposure, fame, and fortune. It got crowded and more competitive. The hustle was out of the closet big-time.

Record company reps went to the clubs and concerts scouting for the next Bob Dylan, resulting in a glut of pale imitators who wrote even paler songs. The surplus of singer-songwriters suffocated folk music, which was slowly dying of ennui. The population of acoustic folkies performing traditional music gradually thinned out, and those who kept at it found a way to survive with dignity, even with fewer and fewer well-paying gigs in the Village and around the country.

Greenwich Village—with its bohemian tradition overtaken by the hep cats of jazz and the Beats and subsequently the hip folk crowd, which evolved into the hippie culture with a psychedelic soundtrack—had become the place to be. But I was gone by then.

Greenwich Village bohemia exists no more. It was the public square of the twentieth century for the outsiders, the mad ones, and the misfits. Today all that remains are the posters, fliers, and signs preserved on the walls as a reminder of that bygone era when rents were cheap and New York replaced Paris as the destination for the creative crowd.

Those who feel they are not part of the mainstream are always somewhere, however. Greenwich Village is a calling. Though it is a concept now priced out of its physical space, as a state of mind, it will never be out of bounds. In the end, like finds like: it doesn't matter whether there is an actual physical neighborhood or not. A compelling and necessary idea will always find a place to plant itself. The creative spirit finds a way.

Endnote

In retrospect, what preoccupies me in this backward look at my life is the way things presented on these pages might differ from how they were at the time. The truth lies in the recalled emotion, the perception of events. My aim was to capture the emotional truth that defined the experience rather than to present "just the facts."

So many places and faces flit by as my memory fiddled with the surrounding scenery. Like a dragonfly I settled on someplace or someone, pondered awhile, and then went on to another.

There were so many talents in those days who hung their work on gallery walls, who got onstage to sing, to perform, or to deliver stand-up commentary that was part, and way ahead, of the times. Nights started early and ended early in the morning. We were full of truths and enthusiasms, non sequiturs, stories, insights, pronouncements, resentments, and of course poetry, prose, and song. In addition to the stories I tell and the people I include in this book, there were many more who looked, listened, discussed, and made things happen away from the proscenium. History is accumulated one day at a time and there were many of us who moved it along. I'm proud to have been in the mix. I am glad I took the subway and got off at the right stop.

My intention overall was to respect our youth because at the distance I write from now I see no reason to take anyone to task for the foibles of the young. We were a passionate lot, dedicated to whatever it was we were doing. And cool and hip as we might have been, or thought ourselves to be, we truly believed it was worth the effort to shake things up.

It is interesting to note another reversal from then to now, in the words President John F. Kennedy spoke in his inaugural address of January 1961: "Ask not what your country can do for you, ask what you can do for your country."

Today "What's in it for me?" is the question most often asked. To acknowledge that we are in this together, to ask what would be better for the community, or to lend support to someone else's request for improvement or change helps everyone in the long run.

The sixties were an era that spoke a language of inquiry and curiosity and rebelliousness against the stifling and repressive political and social culture of the decade that preceded it. The new generation causing all the fuss was not driven by the market: we had something to say, not something to sell.

ACKNOWLEDGMENTS

Memory, being the thing you forget with, made writing a memoir a daunting proposition. When I was interviewed for the Martin Scorsese film *No Direction Home: Bob Dylan*, the door to the past was opened. That interview laid the groundwork for this book.

If I wore a hat I would doff it to Gerry Howard. He suggested I write a memoir and then trusted I could do it. His thoughtful, measured stance in the face of my worries was as valuable as his risk-taking support. And I was hardly aware of being in the maw of impersonal corporate publishing due to Gerry's genuine manner—also true of Katie Halleron; Terry Karydes, the designer; and everyone else I had contact with at Doubleday Broadway.

I have nothing but admiration for Patricia Mulcahy and her editorial ability to see the forest and the trees simultaneously. Her humor and openness made working together a pleasure.

The knowing advice given at the outset by Sarah Lazin— don't think about the enormous mountain in front of you, just write—worked its magic and led to a mutual confidence in each other's ability to do what was required as agent and author. The natural progression to a friendship was the bonus.

Without the invaluable assistance of fellow travelers I couldn't have managed the details. Special gratitude to Janet Kerr for her recollections, insights, memorabilia, and most of all the friendship we have shared over many years.

This is equally true of Sylvia Tyson, a woman of many worlds and possessor of unique knowledge. From the start she lavished me with pearls of wisdom threaded with humor.

More light to shine into the dark of the past came from George Auerbach, Drew Bailey, John Cohen, Susan (Zuckerman) Green, Pete Karman, Al Kooper, Barry Kornfeld, Charlie Rothschild, Steve Wilson, and the incomparable Israel Young. Life for Izzy is just one long day and it has been an adventure to spend part of that long day with him.

I truly appreciate the generosity of the photographers whose pictures illuminate my memories: Don Hunstein, Jim Marshall, Dave Gahr, Ted Russell, Jerry Schatzberg, Irwin Gooen, Ed Grazda, Paul Klee, and Ann Charters. Thanks go to Terri Thal, who persevered and found a photo at the very last minute. Thanks to Mitch Blank, Don Fleming and the Alan Lomax Archives, and Robert Parks at the Morgan Library, for their generous assistance.

I am grateful to Jim Hoberman, a wise and trusted friend, who offered advice and information from the beginning. Likewise Naomi Fein for her generosity of spirit and ever-present optimism, and Veronica Windholz for her thoughtfulness.

Conversations with Ted Fenton, Lynn Barr, Hilda and Mickey Meltzer, and Paolo and Michele Mazzerioli helped smooth out some tangles.

Without the love, encouragement, and patience of those closest to me, writing this book would have seemed an insurmountable task. It is dedicated to them because above all and everything they made it possible.

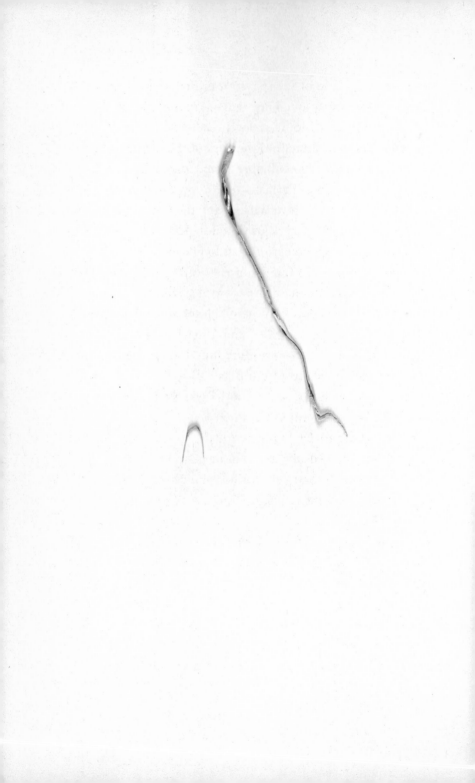

ILLUSTRATION CREDITS

Unless otherwise noted, all artwork and photographs are from the author's personal collection: